How? How? How?

JESUS

Can We
Have Your
Church Fired Up?

So, by us studying the seven churches in the book of
REVELATION, you will find the answer and you will
know how!!!

ARTHUR J. BESLER

ARPress

ILLUMINATING IDEAS.
EMPOWERING VOICES

ARPress
45 Dan Road Suite 5
Canton MA 02021
Hotline: 1(888) 821-0229
Fax: 1(508) 545-7580

Ordering Information:
Quantity sales. Special discounts are available on quantity purchases by corporations, associations, and others. For details, contact the publisher at the address above.

Printed in the United States of America.

ISBN-13:	Softcover	979-8-89330-030-7
	Hardcover	979-8-89330-031-4
	eBook	979-8-89330-032-1

Library of Congress Control Number: 2024900571

How? How? How?

JESUS

Can We
Have Your
Church Fired Up?

THE REFRESHING WIND OF GOD'S REVIVAL

For our Heart's are Stired even now

October 13, 2017   Arthur J. Besler

For   our   Hearts are   Stir - ed   ev -   en   now,   Think   of   His   Own
Good - ness   that   is   His   Love   for   Just   the   Way   we   are,   for
On -   ly   when   we   love   Je -   sus;   when   we're   in   One   Ac -   cord

So   let's   lift   our   voic - es   to -   ward   the   sky   and   be -   yond
Heav - en   is   there, re   turn - ing   to   Je -   sus'   Love   and   just
Let   our   sound   of   Prais - es   ring,   be   fol -   low -   er   of   Christ

When   our   at -   ten -   tion   is   cen -   ter -   ed   on   Christ   Je -   sus
The   Gos -   pel   mes -   sages   will   be   root - ed   more   a -   bout   His
con -   cern   ov -   er   the   lost   sheep   of   the   House   of   Dav -   id

How   can   we   sing   Je -   sus'   beaut - i -   ful   mes -   sage,   but   by
Be   fill - ed   with   com -   pas -   sion   over   the   won -   der -   ful   flock
That   has   I -   deas   where   the   path   leads   and   free - dom   of   love

There   will   be   that   time   when   Je -   sus'   Song   will   come   down   and
Fill   our   hearts to   ov -   er -   flow - ing   as   the   pres - ence,   that
Ho -   ly   Spir - it   of   Pen -   te   cost;   bring - ing   that   Fire   back

As   we   feel   the   Pres - ence,   be -   cause   of   the   Prais - ing   Sound
It   will   and   has   fill - ed   the   air;   so   let's   sing   Je -   sus'
Gos -   pel: which   can   pen -   i -   trate   the   hard - est   of   all   hearts

Then   will   bring   His   Mes -   sages   from   of   old,   though it   is   near
To   our   ears   to -   day   for   He   is   the   same   Yes -   ter -   day
To   day,   the   Bi -   ble;   the   Word,   Je -   sus   in   the   Spir - it,

Je -   sus,   we   can   have   the   Ho -   ly   Spir - it   ov -   er -   flow
But   it   will   on -   ly   come   as   the   Fa -   ther,   Son   and   the
Ho -   ly   Ghost's Love   can   cap -   ti -   vate   our   own   will - ing   heart.

****

I   Do   want   to   Say   Al -   le -   lu -   ia,   Praise Ye   the   Lord
For   as   of   Je -   sus,   Praise Ye   the   Lord,   Praise Ye   the   Lord;
I   Do   Thank   You   God,   Praise Ye   the   Lord,   Priase Ye   the   Lord.

So, Lord Jesus; How Do We Pray for the Church

And therefore, by praying as a Believer to our Lord Jesus Christ; we must first acknowledge the Father in Heaven, of what Jesus said as in [Mt. 6:9-13], **"After this manner therefore pray ye: our Father which art in Heaven, Hallowed be thy name. Thy Kingdom come. Thy will be done in earth, as it is in Heaven. Give us this day our daily bread. And forgive us our debts, as we forgive our debtors. And lead us not into temptation, but deliver us from evil: for thine is the Kingdom, and the Power, and the Glory, for ever. Amen."**

For the Gospel of Salvation will be presented to every human being on the face of the earth, as Jesus walks the whole landscape of our universe; but yet, the old ancient Scrolls, mentions of our calling as to of praying, praying, and praying: for the Holy Spirit, is the Person of the God-head. The Triune God, of being the Father, the Son named Jesus, and the Holy Spirit: that will search every heart through-out the whole world; and convicting them if they are willing, of being mentioned by John the Apostle in [I Jn. 4:13-16,19], "Hereby know we that we (the Believers) dwell in Him (Jesus,) and He (Jesus) in us (the Believers), because He (Jesus) hath given us His (Holy) Spirit. And we (the Apostles) have seen and do testify (as a witness) that the Father sent the Son (Jesus) to be the Saviour of the world. Whosoever shall confess that Jesus is the Son of God (the Father), God (the Father) dwelleth in Him (Jesus), and He (Jesus) in God (the Father). We Love Him (Jesus), because He (Jesus) first Loved z (as all of humanity)."

And so, as we begin to pray, pray, and pray, by entering into God's Presence; of first by spending sometime Worshipping Him, and then of saying. "Jesus, Jesus, Jesus in your name of speaking Blessings on the Church of the Lord Jesus Christ; of which represent, the Body of Believers, and there of with the Father's approval: Jesus of allowing the Holy Spirit, to begin of blowing the wind of your Presence; into every Congregation and also the house fellowship through-out the whole world, as the Holy Spirit allows the Fire to be enlarged. Amen."

The Church's Greatest Challenges and Obligations

For this book address's the most important functions of the Church of Jesus Christ, the Church is dried up as of today; as most Leaders and/or Congregations, have their mindset on thinking: of which, that it is about the rapture, the rapture, the rapture of the saints, of being the believers which will be removed quickly. But how could that be, as what is written in the old ancient Scrolls, of one being as in [Ezekiel 37:1,4,10], **"The hand of the Lord was upon me, and carried me out in the Spirit of the Lord, and set me down in the midst of the valley which was full of bones. Again He said unto me, prophesy upon these bones, and say unto them, oh ye dry bones, hear the word of the Lord. So I prophesied as He commanded me, and the breath came into them, and they lived, and stood up upon their feet, an exceeding great Army."**

For if the Leaders are not concerned by their roll, in preparing the Church of what must be done first; of praying and fasting, as of why God established a gathering of the saints: for it is all of their hearts, of being focused on the Righteous Spirit of the soul that was, and/or is still dead. And because of Adam and Eve, eating the wrong fruit; so now as we are "Born-Again," as wanting the Leaders of preparing the saints: by bringing their whole attentions on the world's focus, on God's greatest Blessings of finding the lost sheep. And as to all of the Church Leaders, of finding them, and there as each members of the Congregations; of being connected to the power of the Holy Spirit's endeavor, of bringing each members to face: a determination of being fit for a victorious battle in Christ Jesus as in [Ephesians 6: 14,16-17], **"Stand therefore, having your loins girt about with Truth, and having on the breastplate of Righteousness; and your feet shod with the preparation of the Gospel of Peace; above all, taking the shield of Faith, wherewith ye shall be able to quench all the fiery darts of the wicked. And take the helmet of Salvation, and the sword of the Spirit, which is the word of God."** For the government cannot fix the problems, the Church must be awakened!

Acknowledgements

And as we consider to the consequences, as to our own beliefs of also, there be a higher intelligence, that exist long before we were born: then let us read what King David said as in [Ps. 141:1-3], **"Lord** (Jesus,) **I cry unto thee: make haste unto me; give ear unto my voice, when I cry unto thee. let my prayer be set forth before thee as incense** (being a sweet fragrance that satisfies;) **and the lifting up of my hands** (of an expression of being satisfied) **as the evening Sacrifice** (your Anointed presence surrounds me.) **Set a watch, oh Lord** (oh Jesus,) **before my mouth** (so I can express truthfully, so Jesus can;) **keep the door of my lips** (of you Jesus, being the door; into the Father's eternal life.

And as for our achievement, as to reaching the world with the Gospel of salvation; of having, one of the "five-fold" ministries, being involved called an evangelist. So, when I was in my (30's) thirties, I had a dream one night; a giant Bible was brought before me, and the pages flipped open to the Old Testament, as to about the prophet [Jeremiah 1:5], "Before I (Jesus) formed thee in the belly, I (Jesus) knew thee; and before thou camest forth out of the womb I (Jesus) sanctified (a believer, which is consecrated to Jesus; that is set apart to sacred duties or uses of ministry) thee, and I (Jesus) ordained thee a prophet unto the nations." There, my life has never been the same.

And as times went on, I realized that the Holy Spirit; must revive Pentecost, for it should have never supposed to stop: for, Jesus is saying that all the Churches world-wide: they must unite, as the "five-fold" ministries are functioning; by what is written in the Scriptures. For this will happen with the apostles, the prophets, the evangelists, the bishops/pastors, and the teachers; or otherwise, the Church's structure are very dysfunctional. And for as to the Holy Spirit, with the "nine-gifts" being demonstrated; among the Congregation, the Body of Christ will by the Holy Spirit: of becoming a powerful entity. For Jesus will find, that (01) of the (99) that needs to be; in Jesus' presence, before that final day.

Table of Contents

Introduction

In Arthur J. Besler's book, readers are taken into a deeper personal relationship with Jesus Christ and the Holy Spirit. When people pick up a book on Spirituality or religion, they're often on a soul-searching quest to find themselves. In the case of Arthur J. Besler's book, How? How? How? JESUS, Can We Have Your Church Fired Up? Readers got more than the answer to their soul-seeking journey; of themselves find an uplifted and illuminated, by a wisdom beyond human knowledge -- an insight that can only come from the fruit of the Holy Spirit.

Author, Arthur J. Besler takes his readers into an intimate journey with Jesus and the Holy Spirit as the book dives into a more in-depth understanding of the Holy Scriptures and what it means to **"watch"** and **"pray"** while waiting for Jesus' return. Arthur pointed out that this **"watch"** and **"pray"** means that Jesus intended for everyone to come with Him on His return to His Father's house in Heaven. The book also talks about the essential function of a Church Body of believers in their role as apostles, prophets, evangelists, bishops, pastors, and even teachers. So as the Church begins to fit and fulfill its proper role, the sooner Churches will expand rapidly throughout the world.

The author's life, in and of itself, represents a life transformation when one chooses to take a journey with Jesus. Arthur's Spiritual awareness began at a very early age. While he was young, Arthur remembered his father reading the Bible almost every morning. After that, the author started experiencing the fulfilling presence of Jesus Christ and the Holy Spirit as he grew into adulthood and began to get involved with different Churches and Ministries.

In his thirties, Arthur had a strange dream one night. In the dream, a giant Bible was brought before him. The pages flipped open to the Old Testament, the book of the prophet Jeremiah, where it reads these life-changing words: "Before I formed thee in the belly I knew thee; and before thou camest forth out of the womb I sanctified thee, and I ordained thee a prophet unto the nations." If you're ready for a life-transforming journey with Jesus and the Holy Spirit, grab a copy.

CHAPTER ONE
THE ESTABLISHING CHURCH

The Message of Jesus to the Church of the Lord Jesus Christ! * * *
THE SIMPLICITY OF THE GOSPEL

Subject #One:

As of **"<u>book</u> <u>number</u> [01 – 27] <u>being</u> <u>Matthew</u> – <u>Revelation</u>,"** it is all about what God is saying and that is (<u>He</u> (Jesus) <u>has</u> <u>set</u> <u>in</u> <u>motion</u>, <u>by</u> <u>establishing</u> <u>the</u> <u>Church</u> <u>of</u> <u>the</u> <u>Lord</u> <u>Jesus</u> <u>Christ</u>; <u>on</u> <u>the</u> <u>first</u> <u>evening</u> <u>of</u> <u>the</u> <u>Feast</u> <u>of</u> <u>Passover</u>: <u>of</u> <u>the</u> <u>Church</u>, <u>being</u> <u>the</u> <u>rock</u> <u>that</u> <u>is</u> <u>unmovable</u>; <u>therefore</u> <u>being</u> <u>the</u> <u>foundation</u>, <u>as</u> <u>the</u> <u>Gospel</u> <u>of</u> <u>salvation</u>, <u>will</u> <u>be</u> <u>presented</u> <u>to</u> <u>every</u> <u>person</u> "<u>Born-Again</u>," <u>into</u> <u>the</u> <u>world</u>.) For as a believer in Jesus Christ, we do have an idea; of what is, our doctrine of Faith, so as time goes on: but yet, we must not lose the genuine effort, as by reminding of the real and most important reasons; being for our goals of persevering as to our eternal blessed life before we leave this earth. And as we are preserving our focus, the Scriptures of the Bible; of which, we need to constantly meditate on. For the journey is not all about our physical works; but also, as of our Spiritual works of Faith in the Lord Jesus Christ: and that is, Faith without works is dead, so as in this writing of the simplicity that is in our walk of Faith; we definitely will endure to the end.

THE BIBLICAL CREDENZA, A QUEST OF OUR FAITH

Our Thinking is Only in the One True God, True God, True God, the
Only Triune God; the Almighty Father the Unseen, the Lord Jesus
Christ the Most Faithful, and the Holy Spirit as Our Comforter.
By the Triune God's Plan, Adam and Eve were God's Creation, but
By the Disobedience; of which, They and all Fell from Perfection,
A Marriage that Began as a Male and a Female, of Populating.
We Believe in the Two Being with the Father, as Jesus, Holy Spirit,
Did Really Come Down from the Heaven; and Jesus Became Truly
Human, an Active Listener, Servant, Teacher, Prophet or More.
Was the True Light, which Gives Light to Every and all Humanity,
All that were Made as by Him were Everything; and with-out by
Him, the I AM, Nothing was Made Unless it was Made by Him.
In the Beginning was the Word, and the Word was and is Our God,
God of all gods, the Triune God; not Made, but He Forever of the
Blood Lineage's Seed of David, Said Before Abraham was I AM.
For Great and Marvelous are His Powerful Works, our Daily Living
Is by His Examples; even Paid His own Taxes, oh what King Jesus
Of being Among the Saints, the True Believers, the Son of God.
We Believe that by Grace, of Jesus Being the Solution, at the Cross
Of being Resurrected and Received Salvation Through Faith; is a
Gift from our Savior Jesus, He is the Rock, we Stand Righteous.
Eternally with a Father from the Beginning, was Incarnate of the
Holy Spirit, Born by a Virgin Mary; of His Father Named Joseph,
The Parents, having Abortion was Never an Option or in Mind.
Repent, as Told by John the Baptist a Prophet; Accept oh Judah,
House of Israel, by our Master the Lord Jesus Christ, we are all
Justified Before God and by His Holy Family of Heaven by Faith.
He is Worshipped and Glorified as King of all Kings, of Who Spoke
Through all the Prophets, and is the Only Fulfilled Messiah to His
Own Chosen people, being a Remnant Saints of the Most-High.

We Believe for our Sake He was Crucified on the Cross, Sacrificially
Suffered Death Under Pontius Pilate, as Gentile; was Buried, and
Was also Being Resurrected to Live, on an Ending of Day Three.
By of the Scripture, Jesus Christ Ascended from Mount Olivet, was
Being Seen by Many, of Taken Up as a Cloud into Heaven; and is,
There He being Seated at the Father's Right Hand in all Power.
Have Acknowledged of the Forgiveness of Sins, by those Willingly,
Being Born-Again, not of Water but of the Spirit; the Baptism, of
Having the Fullness of Power, by Holy Spirit being Poured Out.
Who of being Jesus, Rules and Controls all Circumstances, and He
Will Come Again to the Earth Very Soon; In Glory and Judge all,
For Heaven and Hell of Righteousness, Say John the Revelator.
We Believe in God's Biblical Truths, of Praying and Obeying those
In Authority; Abhorring the Drunkenness, Show Compassion to
Unforgiving, Occultist, Immoral Life-Styles and all of the Likes.
Of Laying Hands by Anointing for Healing, Baptizing in Water, His
Supper of Bread and Wine; Seeking all His Gifts, Like Prophecy,
Also of Adding Spiritual Fruits, Love, Patience, and of the Rest.
All are Expecting Jesus' Return very Soon, so We are Assembling,
Praying, and Watching, of Waiting; Being an Evangelist Like Paul
In our Home, our City, our Land, our World, and those Near us.
Looking for the Resurrection of our Families from the Dead, as for
The Life, Living in the Beautiful World that is to Come; Even so,
Come Soon, by Our Lord Jesus. "Abba, Father," so be it, Amen.

The Message of Jesus to the Church of the Lord Jesus Christ! * * *
THE UNDERSTANDING, AS TO THE LAW

Subject #Two:
For to begin with the Scriptures, the "Law" was established; to
be a governor, as to humanities behavior: as to the Righteous and the

unrighteous expression of the heart, for humanity needed to be accountable to the Father in Heaven. And as times went on, the "Law" did not bring Redemption; for because of Adam and Eve's sin, the "Law" did condemn sins: but it was not the solution, for Jesus as a Redeemer had to step in for humanities solution; as of Jesus facing the Father in Heaven, of the believing humanity having of a Righteous appearance of Godliness. For the Father did prepare a Redeemer, to fulfill the Father's solution; as the prophets of the past, kept speaking of someone coming; and then after Jesus came and died, which was Resurrected day. And as Jesus fulfilled all of the salvation plan of the Father, Jesus' apostle began to preach; the salvation Gospel, which was of telling the world: that Jesus, had fulfilled the "Law," which have puzzled the minds of humanities; even as of today, and therefore Paul was able to clarify the issues once and for all.

But yet earlier, Paul was preparing all the Churches; to be strong, in their Faith in the Lord Jesus Christ: even though, Paul was also facing opposition, from the believing and the unbelieving Jews and Gentiles as to their definition of the "Law" as in [Rom. 8:1-4,6-7], **There is therefore now no condemnation** (to pronounce of being wrong, to declare the guilt of) **to them which are in Christ Jesus** (a believer,) **who walk not after the flesh** (of our mind, being constantly on ourselves,) **but after the (Holy) Spirit** (of our mind's priorities, being on the Lord Jesus Christ.) **For the "Law"** (is God's prescribed and/or prescription's order of victory; that would come in the form of a human flesh: which really means, Jesus is to lay down as a guide, direction, or rule of action, dictate, and ordain; by another, to outlaw or invalidate by prescription. And for the Father in Heaven to fulfill the request; of prescribing a solution, He did send His Son (Jesus) to die on the Cross, between Heaven and earth: and then, Jesus was able to place His Blood, because of His Resurrection, on the Mercy Seat in Heaven; so all, that believe in the Lord Jesus Christ, will be considered Righteous in the Father's eyes) **of the (Holy) Spirit of life in Christ Jesus hath made me free from the "Law" of sin and death. For what "Law" could not do, in that it was weak through the flesh, God** (the Father) **sending His own Son** (Jesus Christ) **in the likeness of sinful flesh, and for sin, condemned sin in the flesh: that the Righteousness of the "Law" might be fulfilled in us, who walk not after the flesh** (of our mind, being constantly on ourselves,) **but after the (Holy) Spirit** (of our mind's priorities, being on Jesus Christ.) **For they** (the carnal

Christians) **that are after the flesh do mind the things of the flesh; but they** (the Spiritual Christians) **that are after the Spirit** (of Christ Jesus) **the things of the** (Holy) **Spirit. For to be carnally minded is death; but to be Spiritually minded is life and peace. Because the carnal mind is enmity against God** (of the triune God:) **for it is not subject to the "Law"** (being any of the Ten Commandments) **of God, neither indeed can be."**

The Message of Jesus to the Church of the Lord Jesus Christ! * * *
THE CROSS, THAT BROKE THE CHAINS OF DEATH

Subject #Three:

For most of humanity, does some-what have a mental concept of what really happened; as Jesus appeared in the flesh, and walked among them on earth: for to them of that time period, He was just another human being. but yet, as time went on; as Jesus hand-picked His disciples, for this was the planned settings: that which, was really ordained and ordered by the Father in Heaven as in [Jn. 1:36,43-45], "And (John the Baptist) looking upon Jesus as He (Jesus) walked, he (John the Baptist) saith (unto Andrew and Peter,) behold the Lamb of God! The day following Jesus would go forth into Galilee, and findeth Philip, and saith unto him, follow me. Now Philip was of Bethsaida, the city of Andrew and Peter (which was of Jesus, finding His first two faithful disciples.) Philip findeth Nathanael, and saith unto him, we have found Him (Jesus,) of whom Moses in the law (wrote the Ten Commandments; and there, preparing our heart's lifestyle; for the Righteous God, that was coming and of Jesus: being the Sacrificial Lamb,) and the (many) prophets, did write (of Jesus' coming,) Jesus of Nazareth, the son of Joseph."

For Jesus was displayed as the real characteristic of the Father; and as Jesus, shared His time by speaking: of what was in the heart of the Father. And there, before Jesus found the twelve disciples; the Father sends, the prophet called John the Baptist: to Anoint Jesus, of the Holy Spirit and then as He received the Anointing; it literally transformed the surrounding as Jesus travelled, which eventually effected the whole world as in [Jn. 5:30 – 14:6-11], "I (Jesus) **can of mine own self do nothing:**

as I (Jesus) **hear, I** (Jesus) **judge: and my judgement is just; because I** (Jesus) **seek not mine own will, but the will of the Father which hath sent me** (Jesus.) **Jesus saith unto him** (Thomas,) **I** (Jesus) **am the Way, the Truth, and the Life: no man** (or woman) **cometh unto the Father, but by me. If ye had known me** (Jesus,) **ye should have known my** (Jesus') **Father also: and from henceforth ye know Him** (the Father,) and have seen Him (the Father.) **Philip saith unto Him** (Jesus,) **Lord** (Jesus,) **shew us the Father, and it sufficeth** (satisfy) **us. Jesus saith unto him** (Philip,) **have I** (Jesus) **been so long time with you** (Philip,) **and yet hast thou** (Philip) **not known me** (Jesus,) **Philip?** He (or she) **that hath seen me** (Jesus) **hath seen the Father: and how sayeth thou** (Philip) **then, shew us the Father? Believest thou not that I** (Jesus) **am in the Father, and the Father in me** (Jesus?) **The words that I** (Jesus) **speak unto you I** (Jesus) **speak not of myself: but the Father that dwelleth in me** (Jesus,) **He** (the Father) **that dwelleth in me, He** (the Father) **doeth the works. Believe me** (Jesus) **that I** (Jesus) **am in the Father, and the Father in me** (Jesus:) **or else believe me** (Jesus) **for the very works' sake."**

For Jesus had it all planned, as Jesus was preparing the disciples; which is, to receive the Holy Spirit, Jesus knew that from the time of their ministries until our time period: they or anyone, will never be able to complete the task, that the Father in Heaven had placed in all their paths; for them to accomplish, unless they or any of us received the powerful Anointing as in [Jn. 14:23,26,20:21-22], **"Jesus answered and said unto him** (one of the disciples,) **if a man** (or a woman) **love me, he** (or she) **will keep my words: and my Father will love him** (or her,) **and we** (Jesus and the Father) **will come unto him** (or her,) **and make our abode** (a continued dwelling place) **with him** (or her.) **But the comforter, which is the Holy Ghost** (Spirit,) **whom the Father will send in my name, He** (the Holy Spirit) **shall teach you all things, and bring all things to your remembrance, whatsoever I** (Jesus) **have said unto you. Then said Jesus** (after His Resurrection) **to them again, peace be unto you: as my Father hath sent me** (Jesus,) **even so send I** (Jesus) **you** (my disciples.) **And when He** (Jesus) **had said this** (just before Jesus, went into Heaven) **He** (Jesus) **breathed on them, and saith unto them, "receive ye the Holy Ghost** (Spirit.)"**

And as the Scripture stated, the Father and the Son named Jesus; did send them the Holy Spirit, as of what we experience today: for Jesus knew, that the Church of the Lord Jesus Christ, will never reach the masses: unless the "five-fold" ministries are in its proper functional order as in [Acts 2:1-4], **"And when the day of Pentecost was fully come, they were all with one accord in one place. And suddenly there came a sound from Heaven as of a rushing mighty wind, and it filled all the house where they were sitting. And there appeared unto them cloven tongues like as of fire, and it sat upon each of them. And they were all filled with the Holy Ghost** (Spirit,) **and began to speak with other tongues, as the** (Holy) **Spirit gave them utterance."** For the Church of the Lord Jesus Christ, must begin to awake; from their slumbering, as the Father is about to shake: the whole universe, for the triune God is saying as the earth quacks.

For all the pastors and the leaders, that are preaching or teacher the Gospel of the Lord Jesus Christ all over the world; must truly understand, that Jesus demands that all follow the Scriptures: for this will be the only way, the Holy Spirit will be able to fulfill the Fathers required accomplishments. And as all are bold, by allowing the Holy Spirit to move freely; and that will only happen, when the "five-fold" ministries are fully developed and the "nine-gifts:" are being fully expressed among the Congregation. For otherwise, it is the time period of the Churches, that are spread through-out the world; of having their view of the formalities, being displeasing to the Father in Heaven: as to the Congregational behavior, for Jesus is aware that most Churches are in the beginning stages of being lukewarm; as the Holy Spirit is being neglected and ignored as in [Rev. 3:15-16], **"I** (Jesus, with the Father acknowledging it) **know thy works, that thou art neither cold nor hot** (as the Holy Spirit is not involved in their ministries:) **I** (Jesus) **would thou wert cold or hot. So then because thou art lukewarm, and neither cold nor hot, I** (Jesus) **will spue** (vomit) **thee out of my mouth."** If a person is being lukewarm toward their focus, it means they have not rejected it; but at the same time, they have by no means accepted it: for in the mind of God, a moderately warm and/or a lukewarm is equal to a negative response.

The Message of Jesus to the Church of the Lord Jesus Christ! * * *
THE UNBELIEVER IN GOD, SO WHO AM I?

Subject #Four:

For it all began, as I (being an unbeliever) was hearing about a man; named Jesus, that was speaking to the crowd, that claimed His Father in Heaven: had sent Him (Jesus) to the earth, of fulfilling a mission; by Redeeming humanities (including mine) of their sins, as I (an unbeliever) heard Jesus tell His disciples as in [Lk. 10:18-20], "And He (Jesus) said unto them (His disciples,) I (Jesus) beheld Satan as lightning fall from Heaven. Behold, I (Jesus) give unto you (my disciples, and those that come after; all of you) power to tread on Serpents and scorpions, and over all the power of the enemy: and nothing shall by any means hurt you. Notwithstanding in this rejoice not, that the spirits are subject unto you, but rather rejoice, because your names are written in Heaven." For those sayings, seems to be the most bizarre ideological ideas; ever fetched, for how could anyone be so out of touch with realities, of thinking that we as humans need a Savior: to rearrange our habitual activities, this to me (an unbeliever,) seems to be of something very abstract as it sounds.

Well, I (being an unbeliever) would say that I (as an unbeliever) is in the middle in spaces of somewhere; somewhere, somewhere, of between and hanging around the robbers or criminals. And so, where do I (as an unbeliever) fits in? For starters, by hearing the many stories in an ancient book; the Old Testament, of what the bold prophets proclaimed as to what was coming as in [Is. 7:14], "Therefore the Lord (Jesus) Himself shall give you a sign; behold, a virgin shall conceive, and bear a Son (named Jesus,) and shall call His (Jesus' original) name Immanuel (of the meaning, "God with us.)" And now, I (being an unbeliever) am standing and seeing it first-hand; of this guy, that was there doing good deeds to many of the people and by telling a few others: what was wrong with their secret lifestyles. He (Jesus) even, had the gall to tell many of the listeners; that He (Jesus Himself) was the "I Am." And in another words, He (Jesus) was bluntly telling them that He (Jesus) was God.

He (Jesus) even had the audacity, by saying to a lot of those that followed Him (Jesus;) including His followers, the hand-picked men (of Jesus' twelve disciples:) that He was the only way to eternal life; of which in other words, the only door into Heaven as in [Jn. 14:5-6], "Thomas saith unto Him, Lord (Jesus,) we know not whither thou goest; and how can we know the Way? Jesus saith unto him (Thomas,) I (Jesus) am the Way, the Truth, and the Life: no man (or woman) cometh unto the Father (in Heaven,) but by me (Jesus.)" For that was to be in the right course, was to take the narrow road; but that the wide, would never get anyone there, Heaven that is.

And with all the loud commotion that was happening near me; around Jerusalem, I heard that Jesus was in Pilate's custody as in [Mk. 15:12-13], "And Pilate answered and said again unto them (the crowd,) what will ye then that I (Pilate) shall do unto Him (Jesus) ye call the King of the Jews? And they cried (expressly) out (loud) again, Crucify Him (Jesus.)" I (an unbeliever) heard that Jesus will be Crucified soon, and that they were considering place all the criminals; would also, being put to death on the same day, for I did not consider myself: that I (an unbeliever) would be picked by the Romans, as one of them. Oh yes, about all the robbers and criminals; that I (an unbeliever,) that was constantly hanging around with them: I (as of an unbeliever) also, got sentenced to death, from the Roman government's criminal department; that gave the orders, for they were very sincere. So, I as (being an unbeliever,) they were taking me (an unbeliever) to the same hill that Jesus would be hung on; you know of being named Golgotha. And of later and today we call that place, the hill of the skull; it really, does look like a dead face.

The Roman government's purposes were intentional; they hand-picked, a couple of the bad guys, then by executing the two robbers or criminals near Him (Jesus:) for they, were able to make a statement to Jesus and His followers, that also included His twelve disciples. Yes, you (Jesus) have robbed and destroyed our hope; of doing what pleases us, before you came along; we could steal, murder, telling off colored jokes and/or the jesting's: and even, covet other's house and/or their wife. And there of myself, I was of not being accountable as to anyone; but for me, it was not of a very refreshing experience: as of what, He (Jesus) said to the religious leaders as in [Mt.23:13], "But woe unto you, scribes and pharisees, hypocrites! For ye shut up the Kingdom of Heaven against men (and women:) for ye neither go in yourselves, neither suffer ye them that are entering to go in." We could be ourselves, and not feeling like we belong to someone or anyone else and of their Biblical rule of conduct. Like myself, maybe of obeying the Ten Commandments: of which, those rules never did seem, to be for us Gentiles.

But as I saw Jesus hanging, on the Cross near me; knowing, that all He (Jesus) did was doing good: I began to think, and think of the possibility that He (Jesus) was right; of which, as of what He (Jesus) had said. And as I thought back to seeing Him before; He could be my only way, to where He is going: so, this is what I said unto Him as in [Lk. 23:42-43], "And he (being me, an un-named person, that was on the Cross; by Jesus, I was considering my future) said unto Jesus (was beginning to believe, being me,) Lord (Jesus,) remember me when thou comest into thy Kingdom. And Jesus said unto him (that is now, me being a believer,) verily I (Jesus) say unto thee (that is now, a believer,) to-day shalt thou be with me in Paradise (Jesus being, one with the Father in Heaven and the Holy Spirit.)" For Jesus is speaking in unison, as a part of the triune God; for there is only one God as in [Eph. 4:9], **"Now that He** (Jesus) **ascended** (where all of them went, into Paradise; except of His three-day journey, being Jesus,) **what is it but that He** (Jesus) **also descended first into the lower parts of the earth** (of Hell, as mentioned by Peter as in [Acts 2:31], "He (David) seeing this before spake of the Resurrection of Christ, that His (Jesus') soul was not left in Hell, neither His (Jesus') flesh did see corruption (of decaying.)"

For He (Jesus) was dragged into the lowest part: which was Hell, and there Lucifer the Devil; tormented Him (Jesus) for three days. And then after three days, the Father in Heaven did enter into Hell, and embracing Him (Jesus;) and there, Jesus faced Lucifer the Devil, and stripped him (Satan) of everything that he (Lucifer) was created with: and now, Satan has no power. For Lucifer the Devil, opened his (Satan's) domain or territory of his activity; and there, Satan can only be roaring as a Lion: but will never be a threat, to the Kingdom of God again. And until Jesus placed His own Blood, on the "Mercy Seat" by the Throne room of Heaven; for from then on, now we all can be in Heaven: being able, of seeing the Father's face, which is all of us and them; for Jesus' Blood has covered all theirs and our sins.)"

And as I (that is now, a believer) remembered; before I (as a new believer) heard, as of what Jesus said to an elderly man named Nicodemus, about the transformation: of the heart as in [Jn. 3:7], "Marvel not that I (Jesus) said unto thee, ye must be Born-Again (by receiving the Gospel of salvation.)"

So, this is what I (as a believer,) was thinking and encountered before I took my last breath.

For the ministers of the Gospel, when you are working in the "nine-gifts," so you must listen. For they also must listen, God does have an agenda for us. And also let our voices and their opinions be said and heard, for we are the "Call Out;" for great leaders, will come out of many assemblies: of those that Jesus will "Call" them "Out," Jesus will tell us who they are. So, as we pray, pray, and pray and ask Jesus; you and I, will walk this through with a goal. And He will send many of His that will come along aside us; that He "Call Out," to confirm our walk, our understanding of the direction that He has Called us.

For Jesus has called us, for a time of unity with the Father. For unity means, as of all hearing of what He is saying through the Word; the Scriptures, so that everyone will have the same thought in mind. For many calls it a "Cell Group," Jesus is calling it a "Call Out" group; their focus is the "Call," a time of prayer as the Holy Spirit gives the "Call:" through them, for as the Holy Spirit Gives the "Call;" it will definitely come to pass. It does not matter, how small or how large the groups are; of being easy or difficult, as it seems to be to you: He will say it again, it will definably come to pass; for His focus, is to find the (1) One of the (99) "Ninety-Nine," that is still wandering.

The Message of Jesus to the Church of the Lord Jesus Christ! * * *
THE BUSINESS TRIP OF MINE, TO JERUSALEM

Subject #Five:

I was born in the territories where they were almost all Jews, and there I was born of being taught the Law of Moses; at very early age, for my parents believe that one day: the Messiah will come to Israel.

I was old enough, of understanding my language; as my parents, talking about our genealogy: there of going back to Adam and Eve, Noah, Abraham, of David; I never heard of those families before.

I was very young of hearing my mom and dad, of saying that the Prophetic utterance of the old written Scrolls; must and will come to pass there soon, for it is being revealed: from beginning of time.

I was later of being a young teenager, of hearing my parents quote those words; there were written in the Scroll by Isaiah: for unto us a child is born, unto us a Son is given, they were just words to me.

I was hearing my father say, of Zacharias a Priest; there prophesied, for He hath visited and Redeemed His people, and hath raised up a horn of Salvation for us of the house of His servant David, soon.

I was traveling now as an older teenager, with my parents toward Jerusalem; there as we stopped near the Jordan River for the night, was seeing and passing the village of Capernaum toward Nazareth.

I was now in a Jewish Synagogue, the Priest is ceremonially doing; of being the Feast of Passover meal; of that evening, there when I heard a lady say softly: "be it unto me according to your Word."

I was telling my parents as we were climbing on our Camel; it seems last night there what I heard was like a dream, it had to be an Angel talking to her: my mind was also busy looking at the surrounding.

I was by then nine months older, of returning to Jerusalem with my parents; to pay his taxes, there I see a couple on a Donkey: I heard Him say to my Father, they were also pay their taxes in Bethlehem.

I was with my parents in the Temple in Jerusalem, as there a couple with a child showed up; I recognized Joseph and Mary, and then the Prophet Simeon: a Prophetess Anna showed up, spoke to the child.

I was told they named Him Jesus, and seeing there as witnesses; for this will be established on earth, He did come in the flesh: as Simeon and Anna both did speak to the child, for as their eyes were on Him.

I was there very near Simeon as he said, for my eyes have seen your Salvation, which you have prepared before face of all people; a light to lighten the Gentiles, and the glory of your people of Israel soon.

I was there hearing Anna say, to the child as others surrounded Him of by speaking; as she gave thanks likewise to the Lord, and spoke to Jesus: as to all them that looked for Redemption in Jerusalem.

I was the next time there older, traveling between Jerusalem and Bethlehem; of when me and my parents saw a caravan of Camels, heading toward Bethlehem, by us all following them to Bethlehem.

I was curious to where they were going, when being close I saw a couple with a young lad; there, was near His parents, they told me that they were Joseph and Mary: and their Son was two years old.

I was staring at the young lad as one said His name is Jesus; and as there the next morning, I noticed some movements: on the streets of Bethlehem, I overheard of one say that Herod's Army had come.

I was looking toward where they were first staying, but it was not what I saw; but of what I heard, there were noises of screaming: as I passed on the streets, one said that they were killing the children.

I was very concerned about the young lad, which was really a young child named Jesus; if He was still alive, and there by the stable of a barn: near were some Shepherds, they were talking to each other.

I was overhearing one saying to another Shepherd, there the couple left sometime last night; but told no one, except they were heading south: of being at midnight, possibly going to the Nation of Egypt.

I was excited to hear, there Jesus was safe and alive; for this will be the story that I must tell all, of this baby or now a lad: but yet He is a child, that will be of growing up; and who knows what He will be.

I was overhearing one Shepherd talking, thinking back of the time when the caravan of Camels showed up; they went to Jerusalem first, asking them there about how they were following King's Star.

I was told by them, that even King Herod heard about the ones; that said as though they had wisdom, there someone will be born: and had to find a King, they had of following the Star that is in the east.

I was baffled as they kept insisting, on finding the location; so, King Herod went to the Chief Priests and the Scribes, they said there it is written by the prophets, that lived hundreds of or more years ago.

I was there as one said the rest, it's written and thou Bethlehem, In the Land of Juda, art not the least among the Princes of Juda: for out of thee shall come a governor, that shall rule my people Israel.

I was questioning the Shepherds, there about the baby; the Angels told them, ye shall find the babe wrapped in swaddling clothes: and found Mary, and Joseph, and the babe lying in a Manger, it was so.

THE TRIP WAS ABOUT ME – PART II

I was years later being much older, deciding to move to the town called Nazareth; there a family with their children had just moved near where we were living: a one yelling out and calling Him Jesus.

I was very much, much older later, when I was by the Jordan River; when someone said to me and those around me, here comes John the Baptist: there he was baptizing Jesus, so I felt God's Presence.

I was now there still feeling God's Presence, heard these words; as the Heavens opened up as we saw the Holy Spirit descending a as Dove upon Jesus: this is my beloved Son, in whom I am well pleased.

I was in Jerusalem, when I see Jesus, walk through the gate; seems like the same person that was walking away, as I heard Him talking: though I did not see anyone, but there He was speaking or praying.

I was hearing someone say that He is fasting, as He was walking into the hills; which there it is like a wilderness, where no one lives there: He just eventually disappeared; that is Jesus, He is always praying.

I was hearing Him several times, expressing of something similar; as He was commanding a decision, there sounds like: He was either talking to His Father or the Devil, as He was commanding a decision.

I was heading into Nazareth, there when I see Jesus entering into the Jewish Synagogue; as I was stepping inside, I heard Him reading from a Scroll: of what was written in prophesies as would happen.

I was somewhat puzzled, as He there reading; I did hear some words, as Jesus said: the Spirit of the Lord is upon me, because He has Anointed me to preach the Gospel to the poor, He did say more.

I was trying to hear more, there seated near me were whispering among themselves; so, I did not hear the rest, for they were already standing and questioning among themselves, of remarks He made.

I was stunned, seeing them grabbing Him by the arm and shoulder; of forcing Jesus out of the Synagogue, and moving toward the hills, there tried to push Him over the cliff; but yet, He just walked away.

I was later sees Him in Capernaum, for evidently Jesus was now of leaving; of there being betrayed, by those that saw His family and Himself: being young and growing up, appearing as God in the flesh.

I was by then seeing Jesus often, either talking to His group of men or speaking, preaching to a crowd; He was always ministering with someone, there they were continually following Him everywhere.

I was even seeing miracles done by Jesus, of healing them; for there were many issues that He was confronting, as He was walking in the power of the Holy Spirit: many different gifts were demonstrated.

I was not understanding, of the different gifts; but Jesus was there performing them, as I watched people's lives being affected by this, as He was walking by them: some knew He is more than a prophet

I was seeing Jesus off and on, as of talking to young men; it was at times of being humorous, for they were always on the boats there fishing, I like fish and like other meat: yet they were by the boats.

I was by of seeing Jesus often, with many of His followers; but yet later there were only twelve of them, that were near and listening to Him as He was talking to them: they were always on the move.

I was noticing there, always listening to Him; as though Jesus was of telling them something important, the stranger that was gazing at them: saying to me, that those were His handed picked disciples.

I was both of living near and far from Jerusalem, there working and establishing business ventures; there as safety of being in a firmly secured territories: of the occupation as of the Roman government.

I was standing, gazing at Galilee's beautiful sunset when I heard noises; it were as of many people, there were such excitements: over food, some were yelling in an expressions of joyful weeping.

I was seeing as thousands of people or more, sitting on the ground and eating something; one said to me, there they were eating fish and bread: as themselves they had enough food from being hungry.

I was thinking of what this, the working of miracles there so openly displayed; that even myself had taken notice, for this also had to be the Holy Spirit that He operated: was definitely from Heaven above.

I was told, they called Him Jesus; He must deliver them from the hands of the oppressors, there were that sense of belongings: to a freedom cause, they were moved within as a happy exuberances.

I was even thinking about myself, I knew there they were thinking about the history of the past; as when they were as a nation they ruled: but now, of being ruled under a very cruel foreign rulership.

I was there just over heard Peter saying to John and James, I think He wants us be with Him now; and as they were returning, I again heard Peter: saying to them, of seeing Moses and Elijah with Jesus.

I was wondering, of what this had to be as Jesus had a face of an expression; of determination, there His challenge was about to face of Him: with demonstration of the Holy Spirit, as of more Miracles.

THE TRIP WAS ABOUT ME – PART III

I was impressed, when being close enough as by looking into Jesus' eyes; they were full of love, there were in the midst of Jesus, His followers, as some disciples surrounded Him while He was talking.

I was hearing Jesus say, that He is the bread from Heaven; therefore said I unto you that no man (or woman) can come unto me, except it were given unto him (or her or any) of my Father, many left Him.

I was then surrounding by some that looked sad, as of losing one of their members of their family; they said his name was Lazarus, there said they are his two sisters: Mary and Martha were also mourning.

I was about ready to leave, when I see Jesus again; He is now being seen with Mary and Martha, as of being escorted toward the tomb: where he was buried, and as I was looking, there comes Lazarus out.

I was mystified by what I saw, of someone coming out of the tomb; where he was buried, still there covering with some rapping in cloth of some sort: of which seems to be of him still looked mummified.

I was there impressed of realizing that this person, which is walking among the people; had to be a prophet or more, like the Son of God in the bodily flesh: for He was exercising the gift of healing to them.

I was realizing Jesus had lot to say, there of the Truth of the Gospel; as to some of the parables, for they heard it: for the Kingdom of Heaven is like unto a man [or to a woman] who is an householder.

I was there of His last saying, is it not lawful for me to do what I will with mine own? Is thine eye evil, because I am good? So the last shall be first, and the first last: for many are called, but few chosen.

I was away for a while and as on my starting back, of being toward Jerusalem; I saw Him again, there was His face, thought of seeing a heart of fiery flint: for His purpose of Jesus facing was established.

I saw Jesus going up to Jerusalem, took the twelve disciples aside; said, the Son of Man shall be betrayed: unto the Chief Priests, and unto the Scribes, and there shall condemn Him to death, as I heard.

I was hearing Him seriously telling there, and they shall deliver Him to the Gentiles to mock, and to scourge, and to Crucify Him; and the third day He shall Rise again, I was thinking of Him being the Lamb?

I was puzzled, realizing that His Father wanted Jesus in of placing His eyes toward Jerusalem; there He had Jesus, now of becoming a Lamb of soon being Sacrificed: was then into holding by His Father.

I was distracted, by Jesus being on the young colt of a Donkey; on the streets by his mother, and there with people shouting: as they, of spreading their garments and the branches in front of His goings.

I was hearing it very loud and clear, Hosanna to the Son of David; Blessed is He that Cometh and, there they looking at Jesus again, saying unto Him: In the Name of the Lord, Hosanna in the Highest.

I was thinking back, by the Old Testament, the Goats or the Sheep of a Lamb; must be found, there ten days before they were to be Sacrificed: of which is, at the time period, when He was on the colt.

I was overwhelmed, as I saw Jesus there entered the Temple of God, as He was casting out all them who sold and bought in the Temple, and overthrew the tables of the moneychanger: of being surprised.

I was there seeing Him walking, them who sold Doves; He said unto them, it is written, my house shall be called the House of Prayer: but ye have made it a den of thieves, but yet He did heal some people.

I was the next morning seeing Jesus, walking up to a fig tree; and realizing there the tree only had leaves, but had no figs on it: for this as resembling Israel, for Israel must be a Nation of producing fruits.

I just saw of what Jesus there did, I heard Him say; let no fruit grow on thee henceforward forever, immediately the fig tree shrunk and dried up: for it even alarmed the disciples as they saw it, I heard Him

I was there seeing Jesus, being close to the city; when it seems like He was there weeping: of saying, Jerusalem, Jerusalem, thou that killest the prophets, and stonest them which are sent unto thee.

I was there hear Him, how often would I have gathered thy children together; even as a hen gathereth her chickens under her wings, and ye would not! Behold, your house is left unto you desolate.

I was also hearing Jesus, with the disciples of admiring the Temple say; see ye not all these things? Verily I say unto you, there shall not be left here one stone upon another, that shall not be thrown down.

I was there listening, he [or she] that endure unto the end; the same shall be saved. And this Gospel of the Kingdom shall be preached in all the world for a witness unto all Nations; then shall the end come.

I was hearing there the last, as Jesus said, for then shall be great Tribulation; such as was not since the beginning of the world to this time: no, nor ever shall be and except those days be shortened.

I was then thinking back of seeing the Miracles that He had done earlier; of one, there of feeding the people, for He was walking in the Power of His Father, so what will the followers of Him also do?

THE TRIP WAS ABOUT ME – PART IV

I was noticing Him then saying, there should no flesh be saved: but for the elect's (the Remnant) sake those days shall be shortened, If any man (or woman) say, lo, here is Christ, or there; believe it not.

I was seeing a woman named Mary, there came unto Jesus; had an Alabaster Box of very precious Ointment, and poured on His head, as He sat at the meal time: for she did it for Jesus' Anointed burial.

I was beginning to head the same direction; so, as I ended up in the City of Jerusalem as they did, there were movements of busyness: in the houses, as it was also the time period of their Holiest Festivity.

I was overhearing Jesus, telling the disciples; to find a room for the Feast of Passover meal, and there He was planning: of eating the disciple's Sacrificial Lamb, that they had of in holding for ten days.

I was amazed, as after the meal; Jesus grabbed a pan and filled it with waters and there, began to wash the disciples feet: of which was by the Holy Spirit; of being clean, time of the Church to be Born.

I was there later, of seeing Him preparing the Bread and of also the Wine; for it was about to happen, of being four days into the Feast of Unleavened Bread: Jesus Himself, will being the Substitute Lamb.

I was much nearer, when some of the disciples; went with Jesus to the Garden of Gethsemane, and there as I myself saw and heard Him saying, stay here and pray: while I go away, I heard Him of praying.

I was soon of seeing Him, standing as of though Jesus was waiting; expecting someone to show up, there that noisy night of the Priest, and of the Elders: grabbed and forced Him with them to the Council.

I was the next morning hearing the Priest and the Elders, discussing among themselves; then the day of the Feast of Passover, for it was also being the Sabbath: there, not much they could do as to Jesus.

I was near of someone saying, that Jesus is being placed on trial; by the High Priest named Caiaphas, there the Scribes and the Elders were assembled: for their plan is of Him, by being put to death soon.

I was surprised, being the next day of going indoor, heard some clamoring; for there were rumors, being that day: Jesus has been turned over to the Militia, which was of facing the Roman's Cavalry.

I was realizing there this was also the beginning, of the seven days of the Feast of Unleavened Bread; the journey of Jesus' mission, by The Father in Heaven: is the fulfillment of the Prophetic utterances.

I was just realizing of that four days, of Jesus as being the Lamb; soon being Sacrificed, and there Pilate as a Governor and also Herod as the King: could not find no fault in the man of God named Jesus.

I was, the same day doing business, of what I heard were crowds yelling out; Crucify Him, there was one with a Bloody face of a great distinction: of then unrecognizable, knowing where I had seen Him?

I was busy, of the earlier part of that day and still on the way back to Jerusalem; of my lodging, there are scenes unheard of being told: If facing death, they did not carry their own Cross, yet this man did.

I was amazed, this man was chained but He was carrying His own Cross; of bearing whose burden, there was of mixture: in groaning's and in cursing's, as that crowd headed toward a very familiar Hill.

I was told, the familiar Hill was called Golgotha; because there are no Redemption nor return for all: there was a mob, as the Romans were definitely being in charge, for they forced Him onto the Cross.

I was taken back, to an encounter on the Hills of Galilee; now this bitter revenge's is that cry, there was a very angry sound: filling The air with hostilities, some as of saying He must and deserves to die.

I was close enough, to hear some that said, He was their Messiah; Jesus is the Savior for our hope, there was still an apprehension by me: as of stepping much closer, for they did nailed Jesus to hang.

I was hearing Him breathing, this had to be His greatest expression of compassion; there He willingly, allowed Himself to hang between Heaven and Earth, so that His connection with humanity will be His.

I was staring at Jesus, when He cried out of to be heard; My God, My God, why hast thou forsaken Me, there is a chill that ran all the way down my spine: as of some of the disciple said, it is Jesus, it is Jesus.

I was by then, standing near the Cross facing His right side; as He open His mouth to speak, there of love was that which came forth: for now Jesus Cried Out again with love saying, Father forgive them.

I was broken by heart, for this man said the Truth about Himself; and was reprimanded of it, there were Bloody bare fleshes where that whipping struck: for His face was bruised, swollen, it was Jesus.

I was of earlier hearing Jesus, saying very loud before those that were standing by Him, there with an expression of what He knew, He was facing Satan: My God, My God, why hast thou forsaken Me.

I was seeing on His face, that notion of His expression; as He was in the place there, of His most challenging position: placing humanity as His most important priorities of Redeeming us back to His Father.

THE TRIP WAS ABOUT ME – PART V

I was not being of any mood to examine Him further, as for Jesus, He should have died much sooner; there as He was hanging with a very large of a written sign: Jesus of Nazareth, the King of the Jews.

I was ready of leaving, then the earth quaked; when the Sun went dark, of the Temple Veil was rent, there again was the Centurion: saying, for Jesus as He Glorified God, truly this was the Son of God.

I was listening to someone near me; talking to a Scribe, and said of the symbolism of the Veil, there of which hid the Holy of Holies; of now Jesus is, for us all to approach Jesus, face to face as our Savior.

I was noticing that the Priests and Elders, were reviewing the Veil of the Temple; next day, there they did not Believe that Jesus was a Lamb of God: has Father in Heaven, then of repairing the large Veil.

I was now finally leaving and looking back; then of my last time, there the Soldiers all sighed, there were this realization: Jesus was dead, and the one grabbed the Sword and forced it into His Side.

I was told, when by asking a bystander much later; where they will bury the Lord Jesus Christ, there was someone named: Joseph of Arimathaea, he placed Him in his very own carved out grave site.

I was almost at the grave site by the door, and there some said; you should not go any closer, there was in front of the grave: a large stone: the Soldiers again, were in process of sealing the entrance.

I was still hesitating, four days later; as I noticed movements, of one that looked like Jesus, and there was of that overwhelming sense to wanting of falling on my knees, of His face seems much brighter.

I was wishing there I would have had a chance to meet Him myself, for many of them did; were speaking to Jesus, as He in return was talking to them: as by then, it was the day of the Feast of First-Fruit.

I was reminded of what it was like, for Jesus to come alive; and then beginning to breath in the flesh again, as there then and forever, He will always be living in His fleshly body, by His Father's Presences.

I was overhearing a conversation, of a lady showing up; someone said, that is Mary Magdalene, and as, there after His Resurrection, told her of not to touch Jesus: had not ascended to the Father yet.

I was grieved, by shedding tears of knowing, I will never see this man again; we all will miss Him, as there were talking near the city gate: hearing as I was leaving, that Jesus was being seen in Galilee!

I was now, planning to take a trip by the Sea of Galilee; on of my way home, of thinking and, there I began of wandering: of probably I might be able to see Him again, for my heart's wants are yearning.

I was by now, standing near the hill by the Sea of Galilee; thinking back to my other encounters, there was Jesus: near the sea for real feeding the disciples, now of with just His true Believing followers.

I was walking toward my Camel, and thought back; thinking of a most unusual Businesses' trip and more, there was a contentment in my searching heart: had an acceptance, of this Jesus truly is Risen.

I was now returning back, outside the walls of the city, of Jesus talking; the disciples were of listing, there of Him saying: do not leave Jerusalem, as we all watching Jesus going up toward Heaven.

I was coming near, of hearing their conversation; they said to me that Jesus wanted of them all, there too Fast and Pray, so as they went and found the upper room: there many people showed up.

I was eager to join them, as they were Praying; of being the Feast of Pentecost, and as it was the beginning: when there the Holy Spirit's Presence came, as us all began to speak in an unknown language.

I was overwhelmed of this feeling by not just sensing in my heart of this inner felt expression; there of the Holy Spirit's Presence, but of truly being Born-Again: by changing my focus on to a real person.

I was then deciding to take up my own Cross, which is the issues of life: there though the journey may be hard, the life Jesus suffered: Is for our Redemption, now it is on us to prove that we do want Him.

I was hearing the disciples, of speaking to each other; this what I heard, there was not about just a regular conversation: was of that sincerity as of what they must do, of what Jesus compelled to them.

I was considering my family, and all my relatives; and as of what I just experienced, I really needed to say and there do, for I had to do: this is the best of anything I have faced, I want them to want it too.

I was thinking about the Church, it has to be like what I experienced as I; was in the assembly, there as they were in agreement: in one accord, by the Holy Spirit's power, the world will never forget God.

I was now climbing on my Camel to leave, looking forward as to going home; and there tell my story, for this Gospel must be told; from Jerusalem and spreading, throughout the whole wide world.

I was pondering on the thought, of what will be the end of this; will His Disciples, that are now called Apostle by Jesus Himself: there be able to themselves, of spreading the Gospel, as a Powerful message.

CHAPTER TWO
THE REPRESENTING FEASTS

The Message of Jesus to the Church of the Lord Jesus Christ! * * *
THE FIRST FEAST, THE FEAST OF PASSOVER

Subject #One:

As of **"book number [01 – 27] being Matthew – Revelation,"** it is all about what God is saying and that is (**He** (Jesus) **has set in mo-tion, by establishing the Truthful Church of the Lord Jesus Christ.**)

And as of being **number [#01], one**, being the first (2,000) "two thousand years" of time of the "New Testament," being the **"Feast of Passover,"** of when the whole Nation was preparing; of doing this once a year. For the Jews devote an entire week to recalling the events of the Exodus; of internalizing these messages and growing in their Faith. One way they do this is, through the ritual Passover meal known as "Seder;" most of us, of which is the heart of the Passover Celebration. And at times, if the Congregation keeps getting larger in population; then it possibly takes a few days or a week just to complete the Passover meals: which exceeded the days normally. And possibly, they did spend the seven days of time; of the "Feast of Unleavened Bread," because of the volume: that came to do the Sacrifices as in part of [I Kin. 8:62-63, 65], **"And the**

King (Solomon,) **and all Israel with him, Offering Sacrifice before the Lord** (Jesus Christ.) **And Solomon offered a Sacrifice of Peace Offering, which he offered unto the Lord, two and twenty thousand oxen, and an hundred and twenty thousand sheep. And at that time Solomon held a feast, before the Lord our God, seven days and seven days, even fourteen days."**

For one day in the future, of Jesus now being the Lamb as was prophesied; by the prophet Isaiah as in [Is. 7:14], **"Therefore the Lord** (Jesus) **Himself shall give you a sign; behold, a virgin** (Mary) **shall conceive, and bear a Son, and shall call His** (Jesus') **name Immanuel** (God with us.)" For at this point of time, now Jesus is openly declared Himself as God; He is walking the earth in the form of human sinews (the nerve, being the substance to connect to the bone: bones, flesh, and skin, for Jesus has the mind; the mental ability to hear and grasp. And as what the Father in the Heavens is saying to Him; for Jesus is now the energy, by the Holy Spirit of what Ezekiel saw as in part of [Ez. 37:1,4-5], **"The hand of the Lord** (Jesus) **was upon me, and carried me out in the Spirit** (the Holy Spirit) **of the Lord** (Jesus) **and set me down in the midst of the valley** (the world scene) **which was full of bones. Prophesy upon these bones, thus saith the Lord** (Jesus) **God** (the Father) **unto these bones; behold, I (Jesus) will cause breath to enter into you** (the saints of God,) **and ye** (saints) **shall live: and I** (Jesus) **will lay sinews upon you** (saints,) **and will bring up flesh upon you** (saints,) **and cover you with skin."**

And there, for [4,000] "four thousand years" Jesus did confront Satan; of everything that he had in mind to do: and was defeated, for Satan's authority is limited; of what he can do on earth. The Father was introducing the only true Lamb that was coming; some (4,000) "four thousand years" later, as a Lamb from a sheep or the goats. But now, Jesus is riding into the City of Jerusalem on a colt; portraying Himself in the flesh, as the Lamb as in part of [Mt. 21:4], **"All this was done, that it might be fulfilled** (as in [Zec. 9:9], "Thy King cometh unto thee, and upon a (unridden) colt the foal (the young) of the (the mother, she is near the colt; being the) ass." And it all started (14) "fourteen days" before Jesus was Crucified; and again, as the Father introduced the Lamb: by having Jesus, the Son of God riding on the colt into Jerusalem as in part of [Mt. 21:5,9], **"And the multitudes that went before, and that followed, cried, saying, Hosanna** (we join in praise, save now we pray) **to the Son of David: Blessed is He**

(Jesus) **that cometh in the name of the Lord** (the triune God;) **Hosanna** (we join in praise, save now we pray) **in the Highest."**

For Jesus is now definitely beginning His plan of implementing the ceremonial Offering of Sacrifice; Jesus had the disciples, retrieve a Lamb: as the Passover time was arriving, for they did eat the meal as in [Mt. 26:19-21], **"And the Disciples did as Jesus had appointed them; and they made ready the Passover. Now when the even was come, he sat down with the twelve, as they did eat** (the Passover Lamb.)" And as they were finishing their Passover meal, of that yearly Offering of Sacrifice; that happens every year, for the sins: if it occurred, which will be their forgiveness; because of the shed Blood of the Lamb.

For as to the Old Testament time period; it was all about the Twelve Tribes of Israel: and now, Jesus is focusing on the twelve disciples of the Israelites. And so, before He was being the Sacrificial Offering, as He first washed their feet: the water, symbolizing of them being clean as in part of [Jn. 13:4-5], **"He** (Jesus) **riseth from supper, and laid aside His** (outer) **garments: and took a towel, and girded Himself. After that He poureth water into a basin, and began to wash the disciples' feet."** And there, Jesus had just Anointed the feet of all twelve disciples; for this, was the birth of the "Church of the Lord Jesus Christ:" and then after, as Jesus had completed the washing of their feet. And this was an expression of the Father's will; for Jesus had Anointed them: by the Holy Spirit, of continuing their ministry that Jesus had just begun. But yet, before Jesus washed their feet; He told one of the twelve as in part of [Mt. 16:18-19], "And **I say also unto thee, that thou art Peter, and upon this rock I will build my Church. And I will give unto thee the keys of the Kingdom of Heaven."**

For now, Jesus was ready to do the Communion Table; with the unleavened crackers and the grape juice: as we call it today, but to them it was very near to the time of the beginning of seven days of the "Feast of Unleavened Bread" and the "Wine." And there as Jesus reached out to them, of them receiving; the "Unleavened Bread" and the "Wine," and then Jesus in that few minutes of the time period: as they all participated, Jesus had portrayed to the twelve disciples as being the "Lamb." And as they ate and drank; this is what Jesus said to them as in [Mt. 26:26-28], **"And as they were eating** (of finish eating the Lamb's meat,) **Jesus took Bread** (the "Unleavened Bread,") **and Blessed it, and brake it, and gave** it to the disciples, and said, take, eat, this is my Body. And He took the cup (the "Wine,") and gave thanks, and gave it to them, saying, drink ye all of it (of Jesus shedding His Blood, after the "Feast of Passover;" of being (04) "four days" later, being on the (14th) "fourteenth day's" journey: since it was the (10th) "tenth days" when He was riding the colt.) For this is my Blood of the New Testament (the old is fulfilled, and this being the New Covenant,) which is shed for many (of those who are willing) for the remission (to cancel and relinquish, by forgiveness) of sins. For in that time period, of it being the (10th) "tenth day; of what happened (10) "ten days" before: when Jesus rode into Jerusalem on a colt, until the day He was Crucified.

For now, Jesus had allowed the Father to place Jesus in holding; as the Jews did with their Lamb: before it was Sacrificed, even though Jesus was having expression of anguish as in [Mt. 26:42], "He went away again the second time, and prayed, saying, oh my Father, if this cup may not pass away from me, except I drink it, thy will be done." And there immediately, the leaders from the Temple in Jerusalem; had the guards laid hands on him and grabbed Jesus, as they would a Lamb. And of not realizing that they were holding on to the "Lamb of God," that will take away the sins of those that are willing to confess; that Jesus is their God as in part of [Mt. 26:47,50], "Lo, Judas, one of the (first) twelve, came, and with him a great multitude with swords and staves, from the (Jerusalem Temple) Chief Priests and Elders of the people. Then came they, and laid hands on Jesus, and took Him."

And as to the continuation of number [#01], one, being the first (2,000) "two thousand years" of time of the "New Testament," of Himself being the "Feast of Passover," from the seed of Abraham (called Jesus;) "a growth of a baby in Mary's womb (called Jesus:" which included the "Feast of Passover." For of the seed of Abraham (called Jesus,) were told to Mary by an Angel; the seed (called Jesus) of being placed: in her reproductive organ, being called "the ovary." And as of this happening, approximately (33) "thirty-three years," and (09) "nine months" earlier; before Jesus was Crucified. For by the Holy Spirit and therefore, the Son being (called Jesus;) Mary having conceived Him (called Jesus) in her womb: being on the evening of the day of the "Feast of Passover." And as all this was happening; with Jesus there, washing the disciples' feet: as Jesus Anointed them, as the "Church of the Lord Jesus Christ;" was in process, of being born or had just been born. And of eating the Unleavened Bread and of drinking of the Wine; as the Lord Jesus Christ, was presenting Himself to them: as the Lamb of God, to be a Sacrificial Offering. For after the "Feast of Passover;" of the (o4) "four days" journey, of the beginning of the "Feast of Unleavened Bread: for the sins of which was being humanity, from Adam to Jesus being on the Cross and His Resurrection.

And again, for Jesus, as a baby was growing in Mary's womb; for the time period had been, the beginning of the (1st) "first day" from the time itself: of then, Jesus eventually taking the form of human being. For of the baby (called Jesus) that happened exactly (33) "thirty-three years" to the day prior; of Mary being pregnant, and then the development of the child (called Jesus) in her womb: for (09) "nine months" later, and then of the child (called Jesus) eventually being born as in [Lk. 1:30-31,38], **"And the Angel said unto her, fear not, Mary. And, behold, thou shalt conceive in thy womb, and bring forth a Son, and shalt call His name Jesus. And Mary said, be it unto me according to thy word."** And then and now, Jesus is the life giver; and He will be the life giver among the "Church of the Lord Jesus Christ:" until the end of time.

The Message of Jesus to the Church of the Lord Jesus Christ! * * *
THE SECOND FEAST, THE FEAST OF UNLEAVENED BREAD

Subject #Two:

And as of being **number [#02], two,** being the first (2,000) "two thousand years" of time of the "New Testament," being the **"Feast of Unleavened Bread,"** for this was the beginning of the Lord Jesus Christ's power on the earth; with the Jewish people, as the Holy Spirit was in the middle of Jesus' affair. And that is, the Father in Heaven was walking His Son through the most difficult time of His life; as Jesus offered Himself as the Lamb before them all as in [Mt. 26:57], "And they that had laid hold on Jesus led Him away to Caiaphas the High Priest, where the scribes and the elders were assembled." For the time had come for Jesus to be reviewed, of the (4) "four days;" before He was Sacrificed, as others did with their Lamb: for this was a Lamb, that had no spot or blemish as in part of [Lk. 23:4,15], "Then said Pilate to the Chief Priest and to the people, I find no fault in this man (Jesus.) No, nor yet Herod: for I sent you (your Jesus) to him; and, lo, nothing worthy of death is done unto him (Jesus.)"

And as Jesus was being sent to His Crucifixion; the Gentiles made fun of Him, calling Jesus the "King of the Jews" as in part of [Mt. 27:27-32], "Then the soldiers of the governor (Pilate) took Jesus, and they stripped Him (as just what they do to a Lamb; as they cut the skin open, and lay everything out to be displayed: before they do the Offering of Sacrifice,) and put on Him a scarlet robe. And when they had platted a crown of thorns upon His head (He will be the Crowning King soon,) and a reed (a mass of plant stems) in His right hand (the reed – does symbolizes of standing in position of power; superior in position, and supreme in power and authority:) and they bowed the knee before Him, and mocked Him, saying, hail, King of the Jews! And they spit upon Him, and took the reed (that was in His hand, be of gathering a mass of plant stems,) and smote Him on the head (while He is bleeding, allot of Blood,) and led Him away to Crucify Him (Jesus.) They found a man of Cyrene, Simon by name: him they compelled (by force) to bear His Cross."

For now, the time had come for them; to kill the true and only "Lamb" of God, by spreading His arms and legs: as they did a Lamb on the Altar of Sacrifice. But yet, as for Jesus being the "Lamb;" was placed on the Cross for all to see His Blood-stained Body as in part of [Mt.27:33,40-41], "And when they were come unto a place called Golgotha, that is to say, a place of a skull, likewise also the Chief Priests mocking Him, with the Scribes and Elders, said, if He be the King of Israel, let Him (Jesus) now come down from the Cross, and we will believe Him."

But before Jesus died, Jesus did the expression of the triune God's feelings; as He was hanging on the Bloody cruel Cross as in part of [Mt. 27:45-46,50-51,58-60], "Now from the sixth hour (12 noon) there was darkness over all the land unto the ninth hour (3 p.m.) And about the ninth hour (of being (3 p.m.), the last day of the "Feast of Unleavened Bread") Jesus cried with a loud voice, saying my God, my God, why hast thou forsaken me? Jesus, when He had cried again with a loud voice, yielded up the ghost He died.) And, behold, the Veil of the Temple was rent in twain from the top to the bottom (now we can speak to Jesus, face to face; instead of the Priests, being the meditator.) He (Joseph of Arimathaea) went to Pilate, and begged the body of Jesus. And when Joseph had taken the body (of Jesus,) he wrapped it (Jesus' Body) in a clean linen cloth. And after His death, they buried Him in a grave as in part of [Mt. 27:60], "And laid it (Jesus' body) in His own new tomb, which he (Joseph) had hewn out in the rock." For there were some that knew, that Jesus is someone very, very special as in [Mt. 27:61], "And there was Mary Magdalene, and the other Mary (the wife of Cleophus, and the sister of Mary; the mother of Jesus,) sitting over against the Sepulchre."

For on the "first day" of the "Feast of Unleavened Bread" of the "Lamb" being placed in holding; but yet, it started with Jesus being on holding by the Temple authorities: the day before, which is the "Feast of Passover." And as of the "seven days," being the center of the "Feast of Unleavened Bread;" that was of its activities, on the "fourth day," and there of Jesus being Crucified. And at the ending of the "Feast of Unleavened Bread;" as being Jesus, from the "fifth day" to the ending of the "seventh day:" of Jesus being sealed up in the grave.

And as to the **continuation of number [#02], two,** being the first (2,000) "two thousand years" of time of the "New Testament," being the **"Feast of Unleavened Bread;"** from the seed of Abraham (called Jesus;) "a growth of a baby in Mary's womb (called Jesus:)" Himself being the "Feast of Unleavened Bread." For of the seed of Deity (called Jesus;) has already being in the Ovary of Mary's womb for (24) "twenty-four hours:" of which is the ending of the "Feast of Passover." For this will take seven more days; as the seed of Deity (called Jesus,) had already been idle for one day prior: for as the seed of Deity (called Jesus,) is now traveling into one of the two Fallopian Tubes. And as the seed of Deity (called Jesus,) reaches one of the two Fallopian Tubes; that which conduct the Oviduct, of allowing it to travel. For the egg of Deity (called Jesus,) will eventually continue from the Ovary to its destination; called the Uterus, and in the ending: of the (07) "seven-day" period of being the "Feast of Unleavened Bread." And for Jesus, as a baby was growing in Mary's womb; for the time period had been, (7) "seven days" to the "Feast of Fruit:" of then totally being (08) "eight days," as Jesus will eventually be taking the form of a human being.

And again, for of the baby (called Jesus) that happened exactly (33) "thirty-three years" prior; of Mary being pregnant, and then the development of the child (called Jesus) in her womb: for (09) "nine months," and then of the child (called Jesus) eventually being born as in part of [Mt. 27:62-

63,66], "Now the next day, that followed the day of the preparation (after the Sabbath, which is the ending of the (3rd) "third day;" of Jesus being in the grave: and also, refers to the "High Sabbath." And of which is the chief day of the ending of the (08) "eight days" of Passover Festival; and also, of which is (07) "seven days" of the "Feast of Unleavened Bread,") the Chief Priests and Pharisees came together unto Pilate. Saying, sir, we remember that that deceiver (Jesus) said, while He (Jesus) was yet alive, after three days I will rise again. Pilate said unto them, ye have a watch: go your way, make it as sure as ye can. So they went, and made the Sepulchre sure, sealing the stone, and setting a watch." For Jesus was Resurrected on the ending of the (3rd) day, of being in the grave.

The Message of Jesus to the Church of the Lord Jesus Christ! * * *
THE THIRD FEAST, THE FEAST OF FIRST-FRUIT

Subject #Three:

And as of being **number [#03], three,** being the first (2,000) "two thousand years" of time of the "New Testament," being the **"Feast of First-Fruits,"** as Jesus being the first and the last; and the first of being Risen from the dead as in part of [Mt. 28:1,5-6], **"In the end of the Sabbath** (and again, after the Sabbath, which is the ending of the (3rd) "third day;" of Jesus being in the grave: and also, refers to the "High Sabbath." And of which is the chief day of the ending of the (08) eight days of Passover Festival; and also, of which is (07) "seven days" of the ending of the "Feast of Unleavened Bread:" and the beginning of the (09th) "ninth day," being of the "Feast of First Fruit;" and at the evening of when the Sun is going down, the ending of the "Feast of Unleavened Bread,") **as it began to dawn** (the evening, of the ending of the "Feast of Unleavened Bread") **toward the first day of the week, came Mary Magdalene and the other Mary to see the Sepulchre. And the Angel answered and said unto the women, fear not ye: for I know that ye seek Jesus, which was Crucified. He (Jesus) is not here: for He (Jesus) is Risen, as He said. Come, see the place where the Lord (Jesus) lay.**

For this has to be greatest good news; that they have ever heard, as Jesus is now connecting with the eleven disciples as in [Mt. 28:7,9], **"And** behold, He (Jesus) **goeth before you into Galilee** (the morning, of the "Feast of First-Fruit;") **there shall ye see Him** (Jesus.) **And as they** (Mary Magdalene and the other Mary**) went to tell His disciples, behold, Jesus met them, and** (there all of the men and women) **Worshipped Him** (Jesus.)" And now, Jesus is not just appearing to His disciples; as he did before His Crucifixion: but as His "Church of the Lord Jesus Christ" as in [Mt. 28:16-17], **"Then the (11) eleven disciples went away into Galilee, into a mountain where Jesus had appointed them. And when they saw him, the Worshipped Him** (before He to them, was just their teacher; but now, Jesus is their God:) **but some doubted** (possibly Thomas.)" But yet, there were more that did not doubt; and therefore, the evidence is an open book, as of the Bible: filled with pages. And of how the "Church of the Lord Jesus Christ;" has survived to our day, and even after today: because of how Jesus proved Himself as in part of [Lk. 24:38-39], **"And He** (Jesus) **said unto them, why are ye trouble? Behold my hands and my feet, that it is I myself: handle me, and see; for a spirit hath not flesh and bones, as ye see me have."**

And as to the **continuation of number [#03], three,** being the first (2,000) "two thousand years" of time of the "New Testament," being the **"Feast of First-Fruits,"** from the seed of Abraham (called Jesus;) "a growth of a baby in Mary's womb (called Jesus:)" Himself being the "Feast of First-Fruits." For Jesus was the baby; being form, by engaging the process of growing: first being a seed (called Jesus,) as it was exiting out from the pair of the Fallopian tubes; at the ending of the "Feast of Unleavened Bread." And the seed (called Jesus) is considered a form of an Embryo; in the ending, of the (07) "seven" day period of the "Feast of Unleavened Bread:" but of the change, the beginning of the "Feast of First-Fruit."

And again, for Jesus, as a baby was growing in Mary's womb; for the time period had been (08) "eight days," after being the "Feast of Unleavened Bread: of then, Jesus taking the form of an Embryo. And again, for of the baby (called Jesus) that happened exactly (33) "thirty-three years" prior; of Mary being pregnant, and then the development of the child (called Jesus) in her womb: for (09) "nine months," and then of the child (called Jesus) eventually being born. For Jesus' plans were, to begin the "Church of the Lord Jesus Christ;"

as a living Spiritual organization (that is, of a group constituting; of carry on the activities of life by the power of the Holy Spirit:) by means, of an organizational deity, yet separate in function. But yet, of mutually dependent; of any-other living being, except of the forces from the Father in Heaven as in [Mt. 28:18-20], **"And Jesus came and spake unto them, saying, all power is given unto me in Heaven and in Earth. Go ye** (the Church) **therefore, and teach all nations, baptizing them in the name of the Father, and of the Son** (Jesus,) **and of the Holy Ghost** (Spirit:) **teaching them to observe all things whatsoever I have Commanded you: and lo, I am with you always, even unto the end of the world. Amen** (so be it.)**"**

The Message of Jesus to the Church of the Lord Jesus Christ! * * *
THE FOURTH FEAST, THE FEAST OF PENTECOST

Subject #Four:

And as of being **number [#04], four,** being the first (2,000) "two thousand years" of time of the "New Testament," being the **"Feast of Pentecost,"** and of Jesus beginning His traveling; that is, of Him meeting with the disciples: for their mindset, has to be focused on the next important thing; Jesus was in the plan of the Father in Heaven as in [Lk. 24:46-48], "And (Jesus) said unto them, thus it is written, and thus it behoved Christ to suffer, and to Rise from the dead the third day: and that repentance and remission of sins should be preached in His (Jesus') name among all Nations, beginning at Jerusalem. And ye are witnesses of these things."

For Jesus is now, beginning by declaring to the disciples and those in the future; that Jesus, is planning on sending them on a mission: and that is, of sending forth men and women with authority to preach; the Gospel, of Jesus Christ as in part of [Acts. 1:2-4], "After that He (Jesus) through the Holy Spirit has given commandments unto the apostles whom He (Jesus) had chosen: to whom also He (Jesus) shewed Himself alive after His (Jesus') passion by many infallible proofs, being seen of them forty days (which was, about (10) ten days before the "Feast of Pentecost,") and speaking of the things pertaining to the Kingdom of God: Commanded them that they should not depart from Jerusalem, but wait for the promise of the Father, which, saith He (Jesus,) ye have heard of me. For John truly

Baptized with water; but ye shall be Baptized with the Holy Ghost (Spirit) not many days (10) ten days) hence (later.)"

And there, the Holy Spirit was ready; as Jesus had spoken to the disciples, of which, by then being called "Apostles:" for the assigned was direct, of them understanding as Jesus spent (40) forty days with them as in [Lk. 24:50-53], "And He (Jesus) led them out as far as Bethany (by Mount of Olives,) and He (Jesus) lifted up His hands, and Blessed them (the apostles.) He (Jesus) was departed from them, and carried up (as they watched Him go) into Heaven. And they Worshipped Him: and were continually in the Temple, praising and blessing God. Amen (so be it.)"

And as they were informed, by Jesus' spending "forty days" with them, they truly understood; that Jesus was preparing them, with energy from the Holy Spirit to complete: the evangelistic Gospel, of the occupation of every country in the world as in [Acts. 2:1-4], "And when the day of (the "Feast of) Pentecost" was fully come, they were all with one accord in one place. And suddenly there came a sound from Heaven as of a rushing mighty wind, and it filled all the house where they were sitting. And there appeared unto them cloven tongues like as of fire, and it sat upon each of them. And they were all filled with the Holy Ghost (Spirit,) and began to speak with other tongues, as the (Holy) Spirit gave them utterance."

For Jesus did tell them, as He prophesied to them of what will happen very soon; of as they received the power of the Holy Spirit as in [Acts. 1:8], "But ye shall receive power, after that the Holy Ghost (Spirit) is come upon you: and ye shall be witnesses unto me (Jesus) both in Jerusalem, and in all Judaea, and in Samaria, and unto the uttermost part of the earth." And then the apostles, had that same mindset; of what Jesus was trying to convey to each of them as in [Acts. 2:42], "And they continued stedfastly in the apostles' doctrine and fellowship, and in breaking of (Unleavened) Bread (and the Wine, by the celebration; of when Jesus revealed to the disciples, that He became the Lamb,) and in prayers." So, now for nearly (2,000) "two thousand years;" being the span of the time period of the "Feast of Pentecost:" the message of the Gospel is still reaching: by one or the masses. For as Jesus is about to finalize the evangelical obligation; of the Church of the Lord Jesus Christ's calling: of this Gospel message happening through-out the world.

And as to the **continuation of number [#04]**, four, being the first (2,000) "two thousand years" of time of the "New Testament," being the **"Feast of**

Pentecost," from the seed of Abraham (called Jesus;) "a growth of a baby in Mary's womb (called Jesus:)" Himself being the "Feast of Pentecost," so as He was coming out of the Ovary to its destination, called the Uterus. And the seed (called Jesus) is considered a form of an Embryo; and now, the seed (called Jesus) is growing in size. And for Jesus, as a baby was growing in Mary's womb; for the time period had been, approximately (40) "forty days:" from the "Feast of First-Fruit." And again, as the time period, from the ending of the "Feast of First-Fruit' to the time period of the beginning of the day of the "Feast of Pentecost." For the seed (called Jesus) being a growing seed (called Jesus) over a time period of approximately (50) "fifty days:" beginning on the day of the "Feast of Passover;" it is now, the seed (called Jesus) has now, of becoming the shape of a man.

And again, for of the baby (called Jesus) that happened exactly (33) "thirty-three years" prior; of Mary being pregnant, and then the development of the child (called Jesus) in her womb: for (09) "nine months," and then of the child (called Jesus) eventually being born. For in its time period, Jesus is calling attention; as to the "Church of the Lord Jesus Christ:" it has the appearance of maturity, the stages of growth will enable it to continue its growth as in part of [Rev. 3:7-8], "These things saith He (Jesus) that is Holy, He (Jesus) that is true, He (Jesus) that hath the key of David, He (Jesus) that openeth, and no man (or woman) shutteth; and shutteth, and no man (or woman) openeth; I (Jesus) know thy works: behold, I (Jesus Christ) have set before thee an open door, and no man (or woman) can shut it: for thou hast a little strength, and hast kept my word, and hast not denied my name." For when the Church is maturing, the Presence of God is felt by most as they walk into the Fellowship's Sanctuary.

The Message of Jesus to the Church of the Lord Jesus Christ! * * *
THE FIFTH FEAST, THE FEAST OF TRUMPETS

Subject #Five:

And as of being **number [#05], five,** being the first (2,000) "two thousand years" of time of the "New Testament," being the **"Feast of Trumpets,"** and also known as "Rosh Hashana;" for the time period, being the rapture (of being removed from the earth:) of the "Church of the Lord Jesus

Christ." And of which has not happened yet; for the Lord Jesus will come one day soon: when the Father in Heaven, gives the Lord Jesus the final call as in [Mt. 24:36], **"But of that day and hour knoweth no man (or woman,) no, not the Angels of Heaven, but my Father only. But as the days of Noe (Noah) were, so shall also the coming of the Son (Jesus) of man be. For as in the days that were before the flood they were eating and drinking, marrying and given in marriage, until the day that Noe** (Noah) **entered into the Ark** (ship,) **and knew not until the flood came, and took them all away** (for they all were drowned;) **so shall also the coming of the Son** (Jesus) **of man be. Then shall two be in the field; the one shall be taken, and the other left. Two women** (or men) **shall be grinding at the mill; the one shall be taken, and the other left. Watch therefore: for ye know not what hour your Lord** (Jesus) **doth come."** And as we also are reviewing this text, the message to the "Church of the Lord Jesus Christ;' is that we, our hearts that has a Holy Spirit's Spiritually developed ear drums: will hear the trumpet sound, all must pray and watch; the last call will only be heard once!

And as to the **continuation of number [#05],** five, being the first (2,000) "two thousand years" of time of the "New Testament," being the **"Feast of Trumpets,'** and also known as "Rosh Hashana," from the seed of Abraham (called Jesus;) "a growth of a baby in Mary's womb (called Jesus:)" Himself being the "Feast of Trumpets." And again, for Jesus, as a baby was growing in Mary's womb; for the time period had been, from the "Feast of Pentecost:" approximately (117) "one hundred and seventeen days" to the "Feast of Trumpet;" of Jesus still taking the form of a human being, but His ear drums are fully developed, to hear clearly. And again, for of the baby (called Jesus,) is that happened exactly (33) "thirty-three years" prior; of Mary being pregnant, and then the development of the child (called Jesus) in her womb: for (09) "nine months," and then of the child (called Jesus) eventually being born.

And as of then, Jesus is now being able to hear; for His ears are totally developed: in Mary's womb, in His form of a human being. For as Jesus grew up, and is walking the earth back then; He is telling them, hoping that they were hearing what He was saying to them: and also, through what the prophets and prophetess's had written; as of what will definitely happen in the last days, as the world begins to focus on everything but God as in part of [Mt. 13:38,41-43], **"The field is the world; the good** seed are the children of the Kingdom; but the tares are the children of the wicked one. The Son (Jesus) of man shall send forth His Angels, and they shall gather out of His Kingdom all things that offend, and them which do iniquity; and shall cast them into a furnace of fire: there shall be wailing and gnashing of teeth. Then shall the Righteous shine forth as the Sun in the Kingdom of their (Heavenly) Father. Who hath ears to hear, let him (or her) hear."

The Message of Jesus to the Church of the Lord Jesus Christ! * * *
THE SIXTH FEAST, THE FEAST OF ATONEMENT

Subject #Six:

And as of being **number [#06], six,** being the first (2,000) "two thousand years" of time of the "New Testament," being the **"Feast of Atonement,"** and also known as "Yom Kippur;" is the "Highest Holy" day. For the High Priests made an Atoning Sacrifice for the sins of the people. The repeated act, of paying the penalty of sin brought reconciliation (a restored relationship;) between the people and God. And after, the Blood Sacrifice was Offered to the Lord; a goat was released into the wilderness: to symbolically, carry away the sins of the people for a year; this "scape-goat," was never to return as in [Lev. 16:10], "But the goat, on which the lot fell to be the scapegoat, shall be presented alive before the Lord, to make an Atonement with him (the goat,) and to let him (the goat) go for a scapegoat into the wilderness (of which, symbolizing of the Father in Heaven; never remembering their sins again.)" For as of Jesus' Sacrificial Offering, as Jesus was bleeding His Blood; as it touched the ground, the Veil of the Temple was torn in two: so now we can truly enter, of Jesus being the door entrance by Faith; into his Holy Presence, face to face by doing it in prayer and supplication.

So as of being the final days, after the trumpet sound; and of the beginning and the ending of the "Feast of Atonement:" humanity which rejected God, cannot distinguish the difference between the true God and Satan; and therefore, they will endorse with Satan's agenda. For the Lord Jesus Christ, at the end of that time period; was facing, of the greatest turmoil ever on earth, for in the history of humanity: and of bringing it to the point of its greatest stability. And there, Jesus steps into the middle of their struggles, the Holy Spirit will bring stability; because of who God is, as the Demons of Hell will be rounded up: and being cast out of our environment as in [Rev. 14:1,5], "And I (John) looked, and, lo, a Lamb (the physical Jesus) stood on the Mount Sion (the Heavenly Zion,) and with Him an hundred and forty and four thousand, having His (Jesus') Father's name written in their foreheads. And in their mouth was found no guile: for they are without fault before the Throne of God (the Father.)"

But yet, in the middle of all this disarray; the Holy Spirit is busy, He is reaching into the soul of the heart: the innermost being of their conscience. And of there, as the Father is searching all for their final commitment; as to who will be their eternal God as in [Rev. 14:6], "And I (John) saw another Angel fly in the midst of Heaven, having the everlasting Gospel to preach unto them that dwell on the earth, and to every nation, and kindred, and tongue, and people."

For this has to be the best, of what Jesus is facing; He knows, that the time for the Redemption of humanity: is about to occur, and when that happens; Jesus will rectify the issue of His people. And as to His people, that are giving themselves to their God; by being faithful to Jesus, which they definitely realize of missing the Rapture of the Church as in [Mt. 25:10], "And while they went to buy (the oil, symbolizing of them praying and watching,) the Bridegroom (with Jesus) came; and they that were ready (praying and watching) went in with Him (Jesus) to the Marriage: and the door was shut." For today is the day as in [Heb. 3:15], "While it is said, today if ye will hear His (Jesus') voice (by the Holy Spirit,) harden not your hearts, as in the provocation (of an expressive call.)" For now, they all must face the consequences of their negligence; of not praying and watching, of when Jesus came to earth: by the twinkling of an eye, the snatching away; the saints from the earth were quickly done.

And so, now of revealing of what happened earlier; is the issue of bringing an end of what Satan and his Demons are doing: to the earth as mentioned as in [Rev. 6:9-11], "And when He (Christ) had opened the fifth seal, I (John) saw under the altar the souls of them that were slain (by the false prophets and the Anti-Christ; which is possessed by Lucifer himself, and his leaders) for the word of God, and for the testimony which they held: and they cried (an open expression) with a loud voice, saying, how long, oh Lord, holy and true, dost thou not judge and avenge our

Blood on them that dwell on the earth? And white robes were given unto every one of them; and it was said unto them, that they should rest yet for a little season, until their fellow-servants also and their brethren (or sisters,) that should be killed as they were, should be fulfilled." For the final called, has already been set in place; by the Father in Heaven, so then let us consider the time period: for Jesus have just destroyed the Armies of the world; of its worst Bloodshed ever as in [Rev. 14:14,16], "And I (John) looked, and behold a white cloud, and upon the cloud one sat like unto the Son of man (Jesus,) having on His head a Golden Crown, and in His hand a sharp sickle. And He (Jesus) that sat on the cloud thrust in His sickle on the earth; and the earth was reaped."

And so now soon, the Lord Jesus Christ is facing the dilemma of Lucifer's world-known leader; of which, being possessed by Lucifer himself: called the Anti-Christ, for his time has come to an end as in [Rev. 20:1-3], "And I (John) saw an Angel come down from Heaven, having the key of the bottomless pit and a great chain in his hand. And he laid hold on the dragon (originally named Lucifer,) that old Serpent (symbolic of a snake,) which is the Devil, and Satan, and bound him a thousand years, and cast him (Lucifer) into the bottomless pit, and shut him up, and set a seal upon him, that he (Lucifer) should deceive the Nations no more, till the thousand years should be fulfilled (and of those billions of people that survived the turmoil on earth; and then, Satan being cast into the bottomless pit: will then, Jesus be the ruler with them for a "thousand years." And as of those that actually survived through the holocaust; they are living through the time period of peace and harmony as Jesus rules and will now be able to prove their heart's loyalty to Jesus; and again, in that "thousand years" of time period as Jesus Himself rules:) and after that he (Lucifer) must be loosed a little season (possibly three to seven years.)" For this has to be the best; of the best, as Jesus now has an environment: that is, a holy space between Heaven and Earth; that is not diluted with any image of humanity's sins.

And as to the **continuation of number [#06],** six, being the first (2,000) "two thousand years" of time of the "New Testament," being the **"Feast of Atonement"** and also known as "Yom Kippur," from the seed of Abraham (called Jesus;) "a growth of a baby in Mary's womb (called Jesus:)" as He Himself being the "Feast of Atonement." And again, for of the small baby (called Jesus) that happened exactly (33) "thirty-three years" prior;

of Mary being pregnant, and then the development of the child (called Jesus) in her womb: for (09) "nine months," and then of the child (called Jesus) eventually being born. And again, for Jesus, as a baby was growing in Mary's womb; from the beginning of the time period of the "Feast of Atonement," had been approximately (09) "nine days" after the "Feast of Trumpet:" of then, Jesus' body is now being able to grow and being healthy.

And also, by producing His own Blood; for He does not need the mother's Blood to be maturing and growing: and also, the power of the Holy Spirit is the one that will direct the focus; for the baby is not being nourished by the mother intravenously. The growth and maturity are such, if there is a miscarriage; the baby will survive, in His form of a human being. For Jesus is now, the only one with the stamina; as the Father has given Jesus the authority of Heaven and of Earth to rule: for Jesus has proved His faithfulness to the Father in Heaven; of His ability to rule in a Righteous lifestyle as in [Rev. 19:1], "And after these things I (John) heard a great voice of much people in Heaven, saying, Alleluia; salvation, and glory, and honour, and power, unto the Lord (Jesus) our God."

The Message of Jesus to the Church of the Lord Jesus Christ! * * *
THE SEVENTH FEAST, THE FEAST OF TABERNACLES

Subject #Seven:

And as of being **number [#07],** seven, being the first (2,000) "two thousand years" of time of the "New Testament," being the **"Feast of Tabernacles,"** and also known as "Sukkot;" for Jesus is near, though many are divided as to what is about to happen: as the Father in Heaven is making the final call. For most, do not understand the symbolism of the "Feast of Tabernacle;" that Satan cannot have anything to say: for Jesus has complete authority over Heaven and Earth as in [Rev. 20:4-6], **"And I (John) saw Thrones, and they sat upon them, and judgement was given unto them: and I saw the souls of them that were beheaded for the witness of Jesus, and for the Word of God, and which had not worshipped the beast, neither his image, neither had received his** (Satan's) **mark upon their foreheads, or in their hands** (for many will not, have the image or a mark, that is in the electronic chip; of which are, signifying to all that they have proclaimed publicly: that Lucifer is their God, to worship and honor;) and they lived and reigned with Christ a thousand years. But the rest of the dead lived not again until the thousand years (of Jesus' ruling) were finished. This is the first Resurrection. Blessed and Holy is he (and/or she) that hath part in the first Resurrection: on such the second death hath no power, but they shall be Priests of God and of Christ, and shall reign with Him (Jesus) a thousand years." For the Lord Jesus Christ in the flesh; is the Tabernacle, and of which symbolizes the "Feast of Tabernacle:" the time being of the Old Testament, as Jesus brings clarity to all that are seeking the Truth; for Jesus definitely will physically come to rule for a "thousand years" on earth.

And as to the **continuation of number [#07],** seven, being the first (2,000) "two thousand years" of time of the "New Testament," being the "**Feast of Tabernacles,**" and also known as "Sukkot," from the seed of Abraham (called Jesus;) "a growth of a baby in Mary's womb (called Jesus:)" Himself being the "Feast of Tabernacles." For of the baby (called Jesus) that happened exactly (33) "thirty-three years" prior; of by Joseph's wife Mary being pregnant, and then the development of the child (called Jesus) in her womb: for (09) "nine months," and then of the child (called Jesus) eventually being born; at the time of the "Feast of Lights." The growth and maturity are such, which symbolizes the "Feast of Tabernacle;" for if there is a miscarriage, the baby will be in a survival mode (manner of doing or being as Jesus were in Mary's womb:) in His form of a human being.

For Jesus is now, the only one with the stamina; as the Father has given Jesus the time to rule in power and authority of Heaven and the authority of earth. For Jesus has proved His faithfulness to the Father in Heaven; of His ability to rule for a (1,000) "one thousand years," in a Righteous lifestyle in the flesh as in [Rev. 19:1], "And after these things I (John) heard a great voice of much people in Heaven, saying, Alleluia (praise ye the Lord;) salvation, and glory, and honour, and power, unto the Lord (Jesus) our God."

For the baby is in a normal survival mode; and again also, if there is a miscarriage: for of the baby, it will survive, in His form of a human being. And of Jesus, as a baby was growing in Mary's womb; for the time period had been, approximately (o8) "eight days" from the "Feast of Atonement:"

of then, Jesus taking the complete maturity and form of a human being as in [Rev. 20:4, "And I saw Thrones, and they sat upon them (the (24) twenty-four Elders,) and judgement was given unto them: and I saw the souls of them that were beheaded for the witness of Jesus, and for the Word of God, and which had not worshipped the beast, neither his (the Anti-Christ's, being possessed by Lucifer himself; of which, being against the Tribulation saints, of not accepting his) image, neither had received his mark upon their foreheads, or in their hands; and lived and reigned with Christ a thousand years." For the time had come, for Jesus to begin His ruling on the earth; in Righteousness, for the time period will last (1,000) "one thousand years:" as Jesus prepares, of those that survived the holocaust of the Tribulation period on earth; to prove themselves of being true followers of the Lord Jesus Christ.

The Message of Jesus to the Church of the Lord Jesus Christ! * * *
THE EIGHTH FEAST, THE FEAST OF LIGHTS

Subject #Eight:

And as of being **number [#08],** eight, being the first (2,000) "two thousand years" of time of the "New Testament;" being the **"Feast of Lights,"** and also known as "Chanukah/Hanukkah:" for Jesus had been the one called the Light, from day one of Creation. For as Jesus being the Light; and also, the symbolism of a Lamb: and as of what they would do with a Lamb, Jesus was born in an animal Manger; which was, possibly a sheep barn as in part of [Lk. 2:9,11, 16], **"And, lo, the Angel of the Lord came unto them. For unto you is born this day in the City** (Bethlehem) **of David a Saviour, which is Christ the Lord. And they came with haste** (hurrying,) **and found Mary, and Joseph, and babe lying in a Manger."** And as of Jesus, He had a goal; of which, eventually Jesus would and did pass the thoughts to His "Remnant:" of what the details would be as in [Rev. 22:16-17], "I Jesus have sent mine Angel to testify unto you these things in the Churches. I (Jesus) am the root and the offspring of David, and the bright and morning Star (of Light.) And the Spirit (the Holy Spirit) and the Bride (of Christ) say, come. And let him (or her) that heareth say, come. And let him (or her) that is athirst come. And whosoever will, let him (or her) take the water of life freely.)"

And as Jesus begins His own trek through life's journey; Jesus being the "Light," is the one that is carrying the heavy burden: for the world, has no idea of who God's Son is. For except to His "Remnant," the faithful followers of Christ; from Adam to the end of time: by what the prophet Isaiah foretold of the new coming Kingdom Age as in [Is. 54:13], "And all thy children (the Remnant) shall be taught (from the Light) of the Lord (as the new Jerusalem, is brought to the earth;) and great shall be the peace of thy children (the Remnant.)"

And as Jesus spoke it out being on earth and forever will speak it out as in [Jn. 6:45], "It is written in the prophets, and they shall be taught (from the Light) of God (the Father.) Every man (and woman) therefore that hath heard, and hath learned (by the Holy Spirit) of the Father, cometh unto me (Jesus is telling the Jews; that if they really knew the Father, they would accept Christ: which is, Jesus Himself.)"

And as Jesus foretells us of the coming new Kingdom Age; as Jesus establishes His Throne as in [Rev. 22:1-5], "And he (possibly an Angel) shewed me (John) a pure river of water of life, clear as crystal, proceeding out of the Throne of God (the Father) and of the Lamb. In the midst of the street of it, and on either side of the river, was there the "Tree of Life," which bare twelve manner of fruits, and yielded her fruit every month: and the leaves of the tree were for the healing of the Nations. And there shall be no more curse: but the Throne of God (the Father) and of the Lamb shall be in it; and His servants (by the Holy Spirit) shall serve Him: and they shall see His face; and His name shall be in their foreheads. And there shall be no night (as of Jesus being the Light) there; and they need no candle, neither Light of the Sun; for the Lord God (being the triune God, the Father, the Son named Jesus, and the Holy Spirit) giveth them Light: and they shall reign for ever and ever."

For Jesus is now given the assignment of being the "Light," which symbolizes the "Feast of Lights," to the Father's Kingdom; which is, of the surrounding that are populated: by people, that have proven to Jesus. And that proof has been, by their daily faithfulness of accepting Jesus as their only God; for the triune God, the Father, the Son named Jesus: and the Holy Spirit, has been an integral part of their way of life as in [II Cor. 4:3-

4,6], **"But if our Gospel be hid, it is hid to them that are lost: in whom the God of this world hath blinded the minds of them which believe not, lest the Light of the glorious Gospel of Christ, who is the image of God, should shine** (the Light) **unto them. For God** (the Father,) **who commanded the Light** (being Jesus) **to shine out of darkness, hath shined in our** (the apostles, and the new converts; that believed in Jesus: and therefore, had an open) **hearts, to** (allow Jesus to) **give** (to all, that confess that Jesus is their God; and there, seeing) **the Light of the knowledge of the glory of God in the face of Jesus Christ."** So now, Jesus had gathered all of His people; for the time period, which is what the prophets of old had conveyed through Scriptural pages of history: that no outsider will ever be able to disrupt or stop the environment of their activity, ever. For the "Church of the Lord Jesus Christ;" which was born, at the time when Jesus washed the disciples' feet: will have its celebration. And as Jesus brings clarity; of who Jesus is as the Holy Spirit covers them with His Presences: and there, the Father in Heaven is filled with exuberance of its final outcome.

And then, Jesus steps to the forefront; to begin His Kingship, as all the saints from the beginning of time are all united as one: as they partake in the "Lord's Supper," which is of the breaking of the Bread and the drinking of the Wine as in [Mt. 26:26-29], "And as they were (completing their Passover meal of) eating, Jesus took (Unleavened) Bread, and blessed it, and brake it, and gave it to the disciples, and said, take, eat; this is my Body. And He (Jesus) took the cup, and gave thanks, and gave it to them, saying, drink ye all of it; for this is my Blood of the New Testament (symbolizing, of the Covenant,) which is shed for many for the remission of sins. But I (Jesus) say unto you, I will not drink henceforth of this fruit of the vine, until that day when I drink (with all of His saints) it new with you in my Father's Kingdom." And there Jesus will have done, of His final obligation; as of the triune God, the Father, the Son named Jesus, and the Holy Spirit: being that bond of unity with the saints of the Church, a symbol of the "Marriage Supper;" to the oneness, that of which cannot be broken.

And as to the **continuation of number [#08]**, eight, being the first (2,000) "two thousand years" of time of the "New Testament," being the **"Feast of Lights,"** also known as "Chanukah/Hanukkah," from the seed of Abraham (called Jesus;) "a growth of a baby in Mary's womb (called

Jesus:)" Himself being the "Feast of Lights." And again, for of the baby (called Jesus) that happened exactly (33) "thirty-three years" and (09) "nine months" prior; of Mary being pregnant, and then the development of the child (called Jesus) in her womb: for of the (09) "nine months" later, and then of the child (being called Jesus) eventually being born. Again, being Jesus, as a baby was of growing steadily in Mary's womb; for the time period had been, approximately (74) "seventy-four days" from and to the beginning of the "Feast of Tabernacle:" of then, Jesus taking the full form of a human being, at the time period of the "Feast of Lights."

And there, at the end of time period; as the baby is ready to be born, or had just been born: on earth, and then growing up, Jesus is watching of what is unfolding on earth as in [Rev. 20:7-8], "And when the thousand years are expired, Satan (Lucifer) shall be loosed out of his prison, and shall go out to deceive the Nations which are in the four quarters of the earth, Gog and Magog, to gather them together to battle: the number of whom is as the sand of the sea." For Jesus has the power, as the triune God agrees; and there, Jesus destroys the battle fields as in [Rev. 20:9-10], "And they (Satan's followers) went up on the breadth of the earth, and compassed the camp of the saints about, and the beloved City (Jerusalem:) and fire came down from God (the Father) out of Heaven, and devoured (destroyed) them. And the Devil (Lucifer) that deceived them (Satan's followers) was cast into the lake of fire and brimstone (hot burning sulfur and,) where the beast and the false prophet are, and shall be tormented day and night for ever and ever."

And as Jesus, being the "Light" forever; Jesus will be everything and more of what we expected from Him: and there, Jesus will unite us with the Father and the Holy Spirit; for because they are one in the bond of love. For Jesus is the only one; that fits the image, that is described in all the Scriptures of ruling; as the new City of Jerusalem is coming down from Heaven, at the end of the (1,000) "one thousand years" of Jesus reigning on the earth: as mentioned in the Bible, He is the one that will come to us face to face as in [Rev. 22:12-13], "And, behold, I come quickly (and to meet all that lived on the earth with Jesus face to face, that saw Him ruling for (1,000) one thousand years;) and my reward is with me, to give every man (and woman) according as his (and her) work shall be. I am Alpha and Omega, the beginning and the end, the first and the last."

For now, Jesus will be the one that will be ruling the Earth; with the approval of the Father and Jerusalem being where His seat of authority will be: the Capital, of where all the saints will gather around Jesus forever and forever as in [Rev. 21:2-3], **"And I John** (the apostle) **saw the Holy City, new Jerusalem, coming down from God** (the Father) **out of Heaven, prepared as a** (lovely) **Bride** (of being His saints) **adorned for her husband** (Jesus.) **And I heard a great voice out of Heaven saying, behold, the "Tabernacle"** (being Jesus) **of God** (the Father) **is with men** (and women,) **and they shall be His** (Jesus') **people, and God** (the Father) Himself shall be with them, and be their God (the triune God as, of what Jesus mentioned as in [Jn. 10:30], "I (Jesus) <u>and my</u> Father (in Heaven) <u>are one</u>.)" And again, all will come to be called; the saints of God, by the triune God: of the Father, of the Son named Jesus, and of the Holy Spirit; of which, they are uniting together, of being the only Righteous force from God. And again, for Jesus, as a baby was growing steadily in Mary's womb; for the time period had been, approximately (74) "seventy-four days," from the beginning of the "Feast of Tabernacle:" of then, Jesus taking the form of a human being. And there, Jesus being in the form of a human being; was born on the first day of the "Feast of Lights:" and as of Him being the Light, Jesus will begin of ruling the Earth on the first day; of the last eight feasts of celebration, being of the "Feast of Lights."

And again, as Jesus being the "Light" forever and forever; Jesus will be everything and more of what we expected from Him: and there, Jesus will unite us with the Father and the Holy Spirit; for because they are one in the bond of love as in [Rev. 19:5,7,9], "<u>And a voice came out of the Throne, saying, praise our God, all ye His</u> (Jesus') <u>servants, and ye that fear Him</u> (Jesus,) <u>both small and great. Let us be glad and rejoice, and give honour to Him</u> (Jesus:) <u>for the Marriage</u> (of symbolizing the Unleavened Bread and the Wine) <u>of the Lamb has come, and His</u> (Jesus') <u>wife</u> (the Bride, which is His saints) <u>hath made herself</u> (the Bride) <u>ready. And he</u> (the Angel) <u>saith unto me</u> (John,) <u>write, blessed are they</u> (the Bride, which is His saints) <u>which are called unto the "Marriage Supper"</u> (the "Lord's Supper") <u>of the Lamb</u> (of Jesus being the Lamb, which was Sacrificed on the Cross.) <u>And he</u> (the Angel) <u>saith unto me</u> (John,) <u>these are the true sayings of God</u> (the Father.)" For the greatest celebration is now being done; as Jesus and all the saints from Adam and Eve to the ending of time: will become one in the Spirit of God. And of which is, of being unified with the Father; with Jesus, and with the Holy Spirit: as of what Jesus said to the disciples as in [Mt. 26:29], "But I (Jesus) say unto you (the disciples,) I (Jesus) will not drink henceforth of this fruit of the vine, until that day when I (Jesus) drink it new with you in my Father's Kingdom." For the "Marriage Supper" of the Lamb of God; called Jesus is celebrated, Jesus is now the one that will bring tranquility and peace: to all of the saints on the new earth, forever and forever.

CHAPTER THREE
THE MINISTERING GIFTS

**The Message of Jesus to the Church of the Lord Jesus Christ! * * *
THE MESSAGE TO THE CHURCH, THE FLAME OF FIRE IS HERE**

Subject #One:

As of **"<u>book</u> <u>number</u> [01 – 27] <u>being</u> <u>Matthew</u> – <u>Revelation</u>,"** it is all about what God is saying and that is (**<u>He</u>** (Jesus) **<u>has</u> <u>set</u> <u>in</u> <u>motion</u>, <u>by</u> <u>establishing</u> <u>the</u> <u>Truthful</u> <u>Church</u> <u>of</u> <u>the</u> <u>Lord</u> <u>Jesus</u> <u>Christ</u>.)**

But yet, we cannot ignore the importance and the function; of the "nine-gifts," from the power of the Holy Spirit, of which being called by the Scriptures: wisdom, knowledge, faith, healing, working of miracles, prophecy, discerning of spirit, divers kinds of tongues, and the interpretation of tongues; which are found as in [I Cor. 12:7-11], "**But the manifestation of the** (gifts of the) **Spirit is given to every man** (and woman) **to profit withal."**

For unless, our standard of Righteousness is by Faith; by His (Jesus') obedience, and there we must first: living a Godly lifestyle. And as to the end result, every of the apostles, the prophets, the evangelists, the pastors, and the teachers; must reconsider of the "nine-gifts" functions, of requiring by the Scriptures, of what will cause the Churches Congregation: to mature in the Lord Jesus Christ, and if they are not freely allowed to function; otherwise, Jesus will consider your Church assembly to be lukewarm. for Jesus had already removed (spued) many of them out from His (Jesus') Presence; as of the time period of today, for the Holy Spirit was not invited to participate: in the activities of the Churches structural system.

For we must not forget what words Ezekiel said about the Revived Church, as he prophesied as in [Ez. 37:4-5], "Again He (Jesus) said unto me, prophesy upon these bones, and say unto them, oh ye dry bones, hear the Word of the Lord. Thus saith the Lord God unto these bones; behold, I (Jesus, by the Holy Spirit) will cause breath to enter into you, and ye shall live."

The Message of Jesus to the Church of the Lord Jesus Christ! * * *
THE FIRST GIFT, THE GIFT OF THE WORD OF WISDOM

Subject #Two:

And as of being **number one [01,]** being the gift called, the **"word of wisdom,"** for to one is given by the (Holy) Spirit the "word of wisdom." The purpose of having the gift of the "word of wisdom;" is to set in motion humanity's hesitation: to finalize an issue at hand and having it solved. For only with "wisdom" can many and/or most decisions; of which will, account for bringing a fair solution. For this gift is possibly directed, to the ones that are of surrounded by the public; or just, with an individual that has an issue, that is unknown to us: or to them being unresolved also. So, by approaching one, with words from the Holy Spirit; and as to those words, it will define what is facing them: with a solution, to acquire the facts, as to bringing a closure to it. And as to King Solomon; he had to deal with a solution quickly: otherwise, the baby would be cut into two pieces as in part of [I Kin. 3:27], "Give her (the real mom) the living child."

And as to this gift, that helps a person; to have the abilities to handle the issues, with "wisdom" being common sense: without the knowledge of dealing with of what they were confronting, which has the achievable plan of making the right decision. For by not knowing anything about the information; and of which, is to the best interest of the once involved: which could be them or others, there facing of making a wise decision as in [I Cor. 1:17-21,24,30;2:4-5,13;3:19;13:2], "**For Christ sent me** (Paul) **not to Baptize** (even though, it was also a part of his calling,) **but to preach the Gospel: not with "wisdom" of words** (we must begin, with what happened; the day of Pentecost, our connection with the Gospel: was when the Holy Spirit as to the gift of wisdom, as of preparing us with the power of the Holy Spirit; as they and as of us, speaking in our own prayer language,) **lest the Cross of Christ** (for because of Jesus' Resurrection, He send us the power; at the time of the outpouring, on the day of Pentecost) **should be made of none effect. For the preaching of the Cross** (of Jesus, shedding His Blood) **is to them that perish foolishness; but unto us which are saved it is the power of God** (for because of Jesus' Resurrection, of being with the Father; for now, the power of the Holy Spirit, for the saints: came because of Pentecost.) **For it is written, I will destroy the "wisdom" of the wise, and will bring to nothing the understanding of the prudent. Where is the wise? Where is the scribe? Where is the disputer** (as of Satan's followers) **of this world? Hath not God made foolish the "wisdom" of this world? For after that in the "wisdom" of God the world by "wisdom" knew not God** (the Father, and because they all did not really know the Lord Jesus Christ,) **it pleased God by the foolishness of preaching** (that Jesus shed His own Blood, on the Cross and is Resurrected) **to save them that believe. But unto them which are called, both Jews and Greeks, Christ** (Jesus) **the power of God** (the Father,) **and the "wisdom" of God. But of Him** (Jesus) **are ye in** (Him) **Christ Jesus, who of God** (the Father) **is made unto us "Wisdom** (facts,)" **and Righteousness, and Sanctification, and Redemption. And my** (Paul's) **speech and my** (Paul's) **preaching was not with enticing words of** (being any of) **man's** (or any of woman's) **"wisdom," but in demonstration of the** (power of the Holy) **Spirit and of power** (being Resurrected and is alive; of Jesus, walking in power:) **that your Faith should not stand in the "wisdom" of men** (or women,) **but in the power of God** (that happened, with the outpouring of Pentecost.) **Which things also we speak, not in the words which man's** (or woman's) **"wisdom" teacheth, but which the Holy Ghost** (Spirit) **teacheth; comparing spiritual things** (of the world) **with Spiritual** (things of

God.) **For the "wisdom" of this world is foolishness with God. For it is written, He** (Jesus) **taketh the wise in their own craftiness. And though I** (myself, being Paul) **have the gift of prophecy, and understand all mysteries, and all knowledge; and though I have all Faith, so that I could remove mountains** (the greatest obstacles or hindrances in our daily carnal life,) **and have not charity, I am nothing** (for Jesus is not, manifesting the Holy Spirit's Presence in us.)**"**

The Message of Jesus to the Church of the Lord Jesus Christ! * * *
THE SECOND GIFT, THE GIFT OF THE WORD OF KNOWLEDGE

Subject #Three:

And as of being **number two [02,]** of being the gift called, the "word of knowledge," to another the **"word of knowledge"** by the same (Holy) Spirit. The purpose of having the gift of the word of knowledge; is to enhance the seeker, as to how a person should conduct as the issues of deciding: for most "knowledge" issues has to do with the mind over matter. For which is of bringing a solution as of its origin; and there, bringing it to its closure. For this gift is possibly directed, to the ones that are surrounded by the public; or just, with a friend or an individual that has an issue in the Church, that is unknown to us: or to them, also being an unresolved issue. And so, as we approach someone, with a word from the Holy Spirit; and as to this word, it will define what is facing them: with a solution, to acquire the facts. And of what Jesus is in the process of doing; as to the healing and/or resolving the issue, that will be in the process of happening: for which is of bringing a solution as of its origin; and there, bringing it to its closure. And as of the prophet Nathan; of him telling King David of his premeditated sin, of killing Bathsheba's husband as in part of [II Sam. 12:9], "Thou hast killed Uriah the Hittite with the sword."

And as to this gift, which brings the duty of knowing; of what is right or what is the wrong information, as to their input: for the "knowledge" of bringing the information to the forefront; as to be acknowledged of being reliable as to its logical solution. For it needs to be, of by being "knowledge;" of which is, the mental ability to understand the information: and again, that information without the effort of doing the research. And as to the information, it is of placing all of its priorities; of placing the questions, to being of importance: for the information is already in motion by the Holy Spirit; to reveal, as though it is being spoken or written, and/or in memory or on paper as in [II Pet. 1:2-9 – 2:19-20 – 3:17-18], **"Grace and peace be multiplied unto you through the "knowledge" of God** (the Father,) **and of Jesus our Lord, according as His** (Jesus') **Divine power hath given unto us all things that pertain unto life and Godliness, through the "knowledge" of Him** (Jesus) **that hath called us to glory and virtue: whereby are given unto us exceeding great and precious promises** (that if we are "Born-Again," we will be with Jesus forever and forever:) **that by these ye might be partakers of the divine nature, having escaped the corruption that is in the world through lust. And beside this, giving all diligence, add to your Faith virtue** (by God; faith, hope, and love; **and to virtue "knowledge;" and to "knowledge" temperance; and to temperance patience; and to patience Godliness; and to Godliness brotherly** (and sisterly) **kindness; and to brotherly** (and sisterly) **kindness charity. For if these things be in you, and abound, they make you that ye shall neither be barren nor unfruitful in the "knowledge" of our Lord Jesus Christ. But he** (or she) **that lacketh these things is blind, and cannot see afar off, and hath forgotten that he** (or she) **was purged from his** (or her) **old** (previous) **sins. While they** (the false teachers) **promise them** (as of the ones, that are listening to them for) **liberty, they themselves are the servants of corruption** (of those, that are in unbelievers and are telling others; that Jesus, is not the Way and the Truth and the Life:) **for of whom a man** (or woman) **is overcome** (of by being convinced of their lies,) **of the same is he** (or she) **brought in bondage. For if after they have escaped the pollutions of the world through the "knowledge" of the Lord Jesus and Saviour Jesus Christ, they are again entangled therein** (of totally, rejecting the Lord Jesus as their only Savior,) **and overcome, the latter end is worse with them than the beginning. Ye therefore, beloved, seeing ye know these things before, beware lest ye also, being led away with the error of the wicked** (which is, by the false teachers will,) **fall from your own stedfastness. But grow in Grace** (by accepting, of Jesus' solution by His Grace; by shedding His Blood on the

Cross,) **and in the "knowledge" of our Lord and Saviour Jesus Christ. To Him** (Jesus) **be glory both now and for ever. Amen."**

The Message of Jesus to the Church of the Lord Jesus Christ! * * *
THE THIRD GIFT, THE GIFT OF FAITH

Subject #Four:

And as of being **number three [03,]** being the gift called, "Faith," to another **"Faith"** by the same (Holy) Spirit. The purpose of having the gift of "Faith;" is to bring a better life into the body, soul, and spirit: for each does have an issue of facing life, of being without "Faith," handicapped as to of health and other needy wishes; which does affect the body movements and consequences of its strength. And as to the prophet Moses, the Scripture says he believed God; and as to the time of his death, this is what was said of him as in part of [Deut. 34:7], "His eyes was not dim, nor his natural force abated."

And as to this gift, that is speaking the oracles of someone's inability to believe by understanding; for the solution, so as someone speaks and/or hears that issue of what they are facing: the Anointing of the Holy Spirit, will inspire to them the "Faith" of facing the solution. For as they, who is facing the issue; as to their unbelief, and as those that surround them that do ministries: of them bringing it by the power of the Holy Spirit, it will no longer be a questionable future. For the question is, as Jesus will come close and/or bring a closure; of fulfilling it to its completeness, the request of desiring that the request of desiring: of which, that the needs are met. For the fulfillment of the heart's desire of meeting the needs; that is, as a large obstacle: and to its unbelief, Jesus will step into the center of that issue.

For the gift of "Faith" will be fulfilled; which is the question, that cause it to have a closure to its solution: as Jesus completely heals and/or fulfills the prayer request as in [Rom. 3:1-8,21-22,30-31], **"What advantage then hath the Jew** (that believe, there is a God?) **or what profit is there of Circumcision** (of those, that does not believe in Jesus; and it is all about by works, which is the cutting of the flesh: or of the believer, which have accepted Jesus as their Savior; are being "Born-Again," the

Circumcision of the heart?) **Much every way: chiefly, because that unto them were committed the oracles** (by making known a Divine purpose) **of God** (the Father.) **For what if some did not believe** (there is a God?) **Shall their unbelief make the "Faith" of God without effect** (of not being accomplished?) **God forbid: yea, let God be true, but every man** (or woman) **a liar; as it is written, that thou mightest be justified in thy sayings** (speaking as though, there is no God,) **and mightest overcome when thou art judged** (of believing, that there are no eternal consequences, to our religious belief without God.) **But if our unrighteousness commend the Righteousness of God, what shall we say** (of feeling convicted and of believing, that maybe there is a God?) **Is God unrighteous who taketh vengeance** (of anyone thinking, as of not having; any consequences for our unbelief?) **I** (Paul) **speak as a man** (a human being) **God forbid: for then how shall God judge the world** (of not upholding the Righteousness, of who God is?) **For if the Truth of God hath more abounded through my** (Paul's) **lie** (of not telling the Truth) **unto His** (Jesus') **glory; why yet am I** (Paul) **also judged as a sinner** (for we are all sinners, and have come short of the glory of God; and is required, to repent for our sins?) **And not rather,** (as we be slanderously reported, and as some affirm that we say,) **let us do evil, that good may come** (which was spoken, by Paul's opponents of?) **Whose damnation is just** (by any of them saying, they are not sinners.) **But now the Righteousness of God without the Law is manifested** (for Jesus, has fulfilled the Law,) **being witnessed by the Law** (of Jesus, being the Law-Giver) **and the prophets** (or the prophetess;) **even the Righteousness of God** (the Father) **which is by "Faith" of Jesus Christ unto all and upon all them that believe: for there is no difference. Seeing it is one God** (the triune God, the Father, the Son named Jesus, and the Holy Spirit,) **which shall justify the Circumcision** (not by the cutting of the flesh; of which is works, but of the cutting by the Holy Spirit: a Spiritual Surgery of the heart, which is) **by "Faith," and uncircumcision** (of believing; that our works, will not bring goodness and Grace: for it is only by allowing the manifestation by the Holy Spirit, of the heart) **through "Faith." Do we then make void the Law** (of by working) **through "Faith?" God forbid: yea, we** (believers in Christ Jesus) **establish** (confirm, by our lifestyle of "Faith;" being the Righteousness of) **the Law."**

The Message of Jesus to the Church of the Lord Jesus Christ! * * *
THE FOURTH GIFT, THE GIFT OF HEALING

Subject #Five:

And as of being **number four [04,]** being the "gift called, healing," to another the **"gifts** (of many different diseases) **of healing"** by the same (Holy) Spirit. The purpose of having the "gifts of healing;" is when the body is feeling the pressure of facing the consequences of its actions, so when the decision is made: they will have to rely on the "gifts of healing," of what will bring as to its future life's events of restoration. And as of the prophet Elisha, sending a message to the King of Syria's Servant Naaman; that had Leprosy and for him to dip himself seven times in the River of Jordan as in [II Kin. 5:14], <u>And his flesh of a little child, and he was clean.</u>"

And as to this "gift of healing," which comes from the power of Holy Spirit, that needs to have the highest respect for it; and if it is not, about the Faith for anyone's restoration: then the focus is distorted. But yet, for of being healed, it is only by its happenings as the Holy Spirit as the driving force. For it is bringing of Jesus' fulfillment, by the needs of that person's desires and/or requests. For at times, the restoration might not come to them; for only the Lord Jesus, can interpretated the right or the wrong motives of their hearts. So as Jesus hears the request, as His will be done on earth; as it is in Heaven, the fulfillment will come as for its blessings to occur as in [Eph. 4:4-15], **"There is one body, and one** (Holy) **Spirit, even as ye are called in one hope of your calling; one Lord** (Jesus,) one (considered being Righteous by) **Faith, one Baptism** (of being filled, with the Holy Spirit,) **one God and Father of all** (as of humanity and His creation,) **who is above all** (in Heaven,) **and through all** (of by judging good and evil,) **and in you all** (of being 'Born-Again.') **But unto every one of us is given Grace** (of Jesus bringing solution, by His Sacrificial Offering; on the Cross and His Resurrection) **according to the message of the gift** (of bringing the believers, for as to Jesus' completeness; and there, being able to communicate in the fulness) **of Christ. wherefore He** (Jesus) **saith** (unto Paul,) **when He ascended up on high** (after His Crucifixion before the Father, and of placing His Blood on the "Mercy Seat;" for the sins of all humanity, of those that repented,) **He led captivity captive** (those that died earlier being in Paradise, having only done animal Sacrifice before;

for those in captivity, had now faced Jesus' Sacrificial Offing on the Cross: the sin debt was paid,) **and gave gifts unto men** (and women, with all the attributes of Christ; of which is, the gifts of being revealing by the Holy Spirit: as to the truth of Satan's decisiveness and as of Jesus' blessings: to strengthen the Church.) **Now that He** (Jesus Christ) **ascended, what is it but that He also descended first into the lower parts of the earth** (and after Jesus' last breath on the Cross; Lucifer the Devil, grabbed Jesus' Spirit and dragged it, of the Father openingly and by allowing Him into the pit of Hell: and then, Satan tormented Him for three days. For the Father, could not look upon Jesus because of humanity's sins; but yet, after three days of being on the beginning: of the day, of the "Feast of First-Fruit;" of then and there, the Father came into Satan's territory. For Satan was the one that opened his domain; to God the Father, which is when the Lord Jesus was reunited with the Father: and there, they embraced each other. And then and there, Jesus faced Lucifer face to face; and there stripped the Devil, of everything that he was created with: and now Satan is just a toothless roaring Lion?) **He** (Jesus) **that descended** (into Hell) **is the same also that ascended up far above all Heavens** (of earth and above the Stars of Heaven,) **that He might fill all things** (Jesus being seated, at the right side of the Father; and there, being the prayer intercessor for the saints.) **And He** (Jesus Christ) **gave some, apostles; and some, prophets; and some, evangelists; and some, pastors and teachers; for the perfecting of the saints, for the work of the ministry, for the edifying of the body of Christ** (as of being reminded as in part of [I Cor. 12:27-31], "Now ye are the Body of Christ, and members in particular. After that miracles, then gifts of healing, (the gifts of) helps, (the gifts of) governments (the Church structural system, and the gifts of) diversities of tongues. Are all workers of miracles? Have all the gifts of healing? Do all speak with tongues? Do all interpret? But covet earnestly the best gifts: and yet shew I (Paul) unto you a more excellent way (by focusing on love first, then Jesus will complete our desired calling:) **till we all come in the unity of the Faith, and the knowledge of the Son of God, unto a perfect man** (or woman,) **unto the measure of the stature of the fulness of Christ** (Jesus**:) that we henceforth be no more children, tossed to and fro, and carried about with every wind of doctrine** (as of the false doctrine, that the spirit called Angel; came down from Heaven, and women were pregnant on earth, of how the giants were born: for all Angels, do not have flesh and bones,) **by the sleight of men** (or women,) **and cunning craftiness, whereby they lie in wait to deceive; but speaking the Truth in love, may grow up into Him** (Jesus) **in all things, which is the head** (being the dominant force,) **even Christ** (Jesus.)"

The Message of Jesus to the Church of the Lord Jesus Christ! * * *
THE FIFTH GIFT, THE GIFT OF THE WORKING OF MIRACLES

Subject #Six:

And as of being **number five [05,]** being the gift called, "working of miracles," to another the **"working of miracles"** (by the Holy Spirit.) The purpose of having the "gift of the working of miracles;" are when many of the persons and/or of the communities of people have needs: as they are facing a problem of having an issue, of that bodily experience of seeking a solution; that will bring a better life of living. And as of what happened to the Son of God; named Jesus, He knew of the crowd had nothing to eat: for the rest of the day, as of how Jesus took a small amount of food and blessed it as in part of [Mt. 14:20], "And they did all eat, and were filled."

And as to this gift, it is of someone that is facing a dilemma; of which is, of bringing a solution in deeds with an active solution. For Jesus will take a situation, that seems impossible to solve; and there, by turning an impossible into an active solution: which is, a positive remedy. For the God, that created this massive earth; will bring the impossible approach: which is, of bringing the situation that can and will be brought to face a solution. And of which will be corrected, by the means with the "working of miracles" from Jesus Himself; as someone on earth, that has the Holy Spirit's Faith: as they are walking on earth with that gift as in [Gal. 3:1-3,5-6,8-14], **"Oh foolish Galatians, who hath bewitched** (being distracted by witchcraft, by the works of the Law) **you, that ye should not obey the Truth, before whose eyes Jesus Christ hath been evidently set forth, Crucified among you. This only would I** (Paul) **learn of you, received ye the** (Holy) **Spirit by the works of the Law, or by the hearing of Faith? Are ye so foolish? Having begun in the** (power of the Holy) **Spirit, are ye now made** (works) **perfect by the** flesh? He (or she) **therefore that ministereth to you the** (Holy) **Spirit, and "worketh miracles" among you** (as mentioned as in part of [I Cor. 12:10,28-29 and Heb. 2:4], "To another (the gift of) the working of miracles. After that (the gift of) miracles, (of Paul asking) are all workers of (the gift of) miracles. God also bearing them witness, both with signs and wonders, and with (gift of) divers miracles, and gifts of the Holy Ghost (Spirit,) according to His (Jesus') own will," **doeth he** (or she, of completing) **it by the works of the Law, or by the hearing of Faith? Even as Abraham believed God, and it was accounted to him for Righteousness. And the Scripture, foreseeing that God would justify the heathen** (Gentiles) **through Faith, preached before the Gospel** (the center of Jesus' image, is the Gospel) **unto Abraham, saying, in thee** (of Abraham being, the Righteous Lineage that came by Faith in Jesus) **shall all nations be blessed. So then they which be of Faith are blessed with faithful Abraham. For as many as are of the works of the Law are under the curse** (as of why, we need Redemption, it only comes through Jesus Christ; by Faith:) **for it is written, cursed is every one that continueth not in all things which are written in the book of the Law to do them. But that no man** (or woman) **is justified by the Law in the sight of God** (for after each person's life ends, being under the Law, is in holding of a place which the Scripture call: its Paradise, until Jesus is Sacrificed with the Blood Offering. And which was said by Jesus, for He had not been to Heaven yet; to place His Blood on the "Mercy Seat" in Heaven as in [Lk. 23:43], "And Jesus said unto him (the one, on the Cross next to Him,) verily I say unto thee, today shalt thou be with me (the triune God) in Paradise (not Heaven.)" And there for everyone's sins, which is where Jesus by the "working of miracles;" went to free them, bringing them into Heaven,) **it is evident: for, the just shall live by Faith. And the Law is not of Faith: but, the man** (or woman) **that doeth them** (by the works of the Law) **shall live in them. Christ hath Redeemed us from the curse of the Law, being made a curse** (of Jesus dying the death, and of suffering the penalty of affliction in Hell for three days) **for us: for it is written, cursed is every one that hangeth on a tree: that the blessing of Abraham might come on the** (Born-Again) **Gentiles** (and also to the "Born-Again" Jews) **through Jesus Christ; that we might receive the promise of the** (Holy) **Spirit** (of the Holy Spirit's power of being "Born-Again") **through Faith."**

The Message of Jesus to the Church of the Lord Jesus Christ! * * *
THE SIXTH GIFT, THE GIFT OF PROPHECY

Subject #Seven:

And as of being **number six [06,]** being the gift called, "prophecy," to another **"prophecy"** (by the Holy Spirit.) The purpose of having the "gift of prophecy," is when someone and/or a group of people; are facing, a various kind of decisions, of bringing into a mental and/or into a Spiritual confrontation: as of what is right or of what is wrong. For the "prophecy," which is heard as it is Anointed; will convict many as to who Jesus is, a real personal God. And as of the prophet Ezekiel; for as he prophesied to Israel, because of sinful lifestyle: before the King of Babylon, captured all of the territories of Israel and Judah, and including all of Jerusalem, as the Holy Spirit revealed to him; and there, as Ezekiel spoke it out as in part of [Ez. 6:2], "Set thy face toward the mountains of Israel, and prophesy against them."

And as to this gift, of someone bringing a message from Heaven; to encourage and edify us, as to our faithful walk of Faith on the earth. For Jesus, He wants us to be able to hear the wishes of our walk of Faith; of which is, our believing by Faith, as Jesus brings us hope: of what we are facing. And as Jesus speaks in "prophecy;" of words to us, Jesus has our account of where we are in our Spiritual walk. And again, for He is taking an account of our next step of Faith; as to fulfilling, the goal of which we wanted to accomplish. And if we do not have a goal in mind; but yet, Jesus will be waiting for us to exercise: the desire, of which we have in mind as in [I Cor. 2:1-2,10-16;3:1-2;12:3], "**And I** (Paul,) **brethren** (and sisters,) **when I** (Paul) **came to you, came not with excellency of speech or of wisdom, declaring unto you the testimony of God** (being the Father.) **For I determined not to know any thing among you, save Jesus Christ, and Him** (Jesus) **Crucified** (for if it was not for Him being Crucified; there would not be a Resurrection, and as of our Jesus walking in power: of which was Pentecost, and then the believers were not; of being able also, to walk in power by the Holy Spirit.) **But God hath revealed them unto us by His** (Jesus' Holy) **Spirit: for the** (Holy) **Spirit searcheth all things, yea, the deep things of God. For what man** (or woman) **knoweth the things of a man** (or woman,) **save the spirit of man** (or woman) **which is in him** (or her?) **Even so the things of God knoweth no man** (or woman,) **but the** (Holy) **Spirit of God. Now we have received, not the spirit of the world, but the Spirit which is of God; that we might know the things that are freely given to us of God. Which things also we speak, not in the words which man's** (or woman's) **wisdom teacheth, but which the Holy Ghost** (Spirit) **teacheth; comparing spiritual things** (as carnal to humanity's wish) **with Spiritual** (things of God.) **But the natural man** (or woman) **receiveth not the things of the** (Holy) **Spirit of God: for they are foolishness unto him** (or her:) **neither can he** (or she) **know them, because they are Spiritually discerned. But he** (or she) **that is Spiritual judgeth all things, yet he** (or she) **himself** (or herself) **is judged of no man** (or woman.) **For who hath known the mind of the Lord** (Jesus,) **that He** (Jesus) **may instruct him** (or her?) **But we have the mind of Christ. And I** (Paul,) **brethren** (and sisters,) **could not speak unto you as unto Spiritual** (things of Christ,) **but as unto carnal, even as unto babes** (new immature believers) **in Christ. I** (Paul) **have fed you with milk** (of introducing the Gospel,) **and not with meat** (the powerful Gospel, with authority:) **for hitherto ye were not able to bear it, neither yet now are ye able** (for they still could not, of totally understanding the Spiritual doctrine of Christ.) **Wherefore I** (Paul) **give you to understand, that no man** (or of any woman) **speaking by the Spirit of God** (of being a true prophet or prophetess, that prophecies as in [Rom. 12:6], "Having then gifts differing according to the Grace that is given to us, whether prophecy, let us prophesy (with boldness) according to the proportion of Faith.)" **Calleth Jesus accursed: and that no man** (or woman, but a believer) **can say that Jesus is the Lord, but by the Holy Ghost** (Spirit.)"

The Message of Jesus to the Church of the Lord Jesus Christ! * * *
THE SEVENTH GIFT, THE GIFT OF DISCERNING OF SPIRITS

Subject #Eight:

And as of **number seven [07,]** being the gift called, "discerning of spirits," to another **"discerning of spirits"** (that of the Demonic or of humanity's spirit, and or of Heavenly's Spirit; by the Holy Spirit.) The purpose of having the gift of "discerning of spirits" or Godly Spirit; is when the issues of us all facing as to a person's behavior: of which, will bring the consequences of bringing someone's decisions and actions; as of revealing to all believers, of having the Righteous environment. For by knowing your environment, the "discerning of spirits;" is essential and/or vital, as of securing our surrounding: as when, it comes to our prayer life. And as of the prophet Elisha, knowing that Elijah was truly a prophet from God; and there he followed Elijah, until Elisha received a double portion of Jesus' Anointing as in part of [II Kin. 2:13], "He took up also the mantle of Elijah that fell from him."

And as to this gift, for Jesus wants us to be free; from any and all Demonic activities, as to the activities that were brought to their attention: by Jesus facing the evil agenda head on. For as Jesus sees the predicament that we are in; by living, by the fleshly impulses: of confronting, of which is really of judging by their heart's desire. For Jesus is ready to bring a Holy Spirit's Revival of Pentecost; that was never supposed to have stopped, of bringing the saints: with the gift of "discerning of spirits," that is surrounding all the prayer groups; which is, the prayer meeting.

And as of where nothing can or will distract the focus on fulfilling; of what the Father has planned to have: the last great move, of fulfilling the outpouring of the Holy Spirit's endeavors as in [Heb. 4:2-3, 10-12;5:11-12,14;6:1,4-6], **"For unto us (the Jews) was the Gospel preached, as well as unto them (the Gentiles:) but the word preached did not profit them (the Gentiles,) not being mixed with Faith in them that heard it. For we which have believed do enter into rest, as He (Jesus) said, as I (Jesus) have sworn in my wrath (to all the unbelievers, that constantly reject the Gospel message,) if they (the unbelievers) shall enter into my (Jesus') rest (which will only happen, if they choose too:) alth0ugh the works were finished (by us believing, within the triune God, that) from the foundation of the world (as when, the creation was formed.) For he (or she) that is entered into his (or her) rest, he (or she) also hath ceased from his (or her) own works, as God (the triune God) did from His. Let us labour therefore to enter into that rest, lest any man (or woman) fall after the same example of unbelief (that as of them being an unbeliever, for they do not have the Holy Spirit; and not of desiring thereof, not being able of "discerning of spirits:" and therefore, are** deceived by any false religion. **For the** (inspirited) **Word of God is quick, and powerful, and sharper than any two-edged sword, piecing even to the dividing asunder of soul and spirit, and of the joints and marrow, and is a discerner of the thoughts and intents of the heart,** (and as what is mentioned as in [I Cor. 2:12-14], "Now we have received, not the spirit of the world, but the Spirit which is of God; that we might know (by "discerning of spirits") the things that are freely given to us of God. Which things also we speak, not in the words which man's (or woman's) wisdom teacheth, but which the Holy Ghost (the Spirit) teacheth; comparing spiritual things (of humanity) with Spiritual (things of God.) But the natural man (or woman) receiveth not the things of the (Holy) Spirit of God: for they are foolishness unto him (or her:) neither can he (or she) know them, because they are Spiritually discerned.)" **of whom we have many things to say, and hard to be uttered (to explain,) seeing ye are dull of hearing. For when for the time ye ought to be teachers** (being the most important ministry, as to the "five-fold" ministries,) **ye have need that one teach you again which be the first principle of the oracles of God** (which is, of the lost receiving salvation; by being Born-Again;) **and are become such as have need of milk** (having a child-like Faith) and not of strong meat (of being able, to understand the Spiritual conflict; as to the walk of Faith.) **But strong belonged to them that are of full age, even those who by reason of use have their senses exercised to "discern" both good and evil. Therefore leaving the principles of the doctrine of Christ, let us go on unto perfection; not laying again the foundation of repentance from dead works, and of Faith toward God** (of being grounded in our Faith in Jesus; and therefore, will lay our life down for the Gospel sake.) **For it is impossible** (so as to safeguard our heart; by refusing, of allowing other religions and/or other cults: of trying, to convincing us that Jesus is not the only way to Heaven, but another) **for those who were once enlightened, and have taste of the Heavenly gift, and were partakers of the Holy Ghost (Spirit,) and have tasted the good word of God, and the powers of the world to come, if they shall fall away, to renew them again unto repentance; seeing they Crucified to themselves the Son** (Jesus) **of God** (the Father) **afresh** (have by the heart, denied that Jesus is their Savior,) **and put Him** (Jesus) **to an open shame."**

The Message of Jesus to the Church of the Lord Jesus Christ! * * *
THE EIGHTH GIFT, THE GIFT OF DIVERS KINDS OF TONGUES

Subject #Nine:

And as of **number eight [08,]** being the gift called, "divers kinds of tongues," to another **"divers kinds of tongues"** (that of different unknown Heavenly language; by the Holy Spirit.) The purpose of having the gift of "divers kinds of tongues;" is of each speaking a language that no one understand, except of God relating to the person: the "divers kinds of tongues" of information, that needs to be heard; which is, only communicated to the person by the Holy Spirit, that is speaking the language. And as of the apostle Paul, of admonishes the Churches; as he is travelling through-out Asia, and Europe, and possibly part of Africa as in [I Cor. 14:13], "Wherefore let him (or her) that speaketh in an unknown tongue pray that he (or she, and/or someone else) may interpret."

And as to this gift, for Jesus' desires for us, is to be able to speak and translate this message; from Heaven, as the Father and the Son named Jesus, with the Holy Spirit: of being in motion, as to first of having someone audibly speaking in tongues as in [I Cor. 14:13-14], "Wherefore let him (or her) that speaketh in an unknown tongue (language vocally) pray that he (or she) may interpret (for as the Anointing comes, you will feel it; and then, the words will fill your mind as you truly begin to speak it out.)" And for the message of that Heavenly language by tongues; to be sent, of that Supernatural message of being translated into humanities' language: known by those living and surrounding them, of which will be interpretated immediately. For the words, of the "divers kind of tongues;" that are coming as someone is speaking that Heavenly language: for Jesus wants everyone in the Church assembly, to hear it clearly and understandably. For many and/or most pastors, elders, or deacons just wants someone to get it over with; and the quicker, is even the better and also yet, there needs to be some discussion, after the message is spoken. Do they realize, that Jesus had just filled their mind among them the message, by the inspiration of the Holy Spirit?

And as many or most bishops/pastors, elders, or deacons does not realize; that to begin, the Spiritual Mandate from Heaven: the phase of their

64

ministries, has to be with all that are present; must hear and understand the inspirited message clearly. For many and/or most bishops/pastors, elders, or deacons will never be able to complete; the Spiritual Application of pursuing, that Jesus' agenda has for that Congregation: for Jesus wants all to take all the gifts seriously. For all the gifts, as of being planned by the Holy Spirit; to achieve of the end result, that is of achieving a Spiritual connection: as Jesus sees the assembly praying and desiring. But yet, many and/or most pastors, elders, or deacons are totaling disconnected to what Jesus' desires are; for because of their own negligence, Jesus is beginning to separate the many or most Congregations: and considered them to be lukewarm, as I (Jesus) considered the Church of Laodicea.

For Jesus wants to send His message, by the Supernatural power of the Holy Spirit with the approval of the Father in Heaven; but as of now, the message will never be conveyed to most of the Churches: throughout the whole world as in [I Cor. 14:2, 4-6,8-14,22], **"For he** (or she) **that speaketh in an unknown "tongue" speaketh not unto men** (or women and/or to anyone else,) **but unto God: for no man** (or woman) **understandeth him** (or her;) **howbeit in the** (Holy) **Spirit he** (or she) **speaketh mysteries. He** (or she) **that speaketh in an unknown "tongue" edifieth himself** (or herself;) **but he** (or she) **that prophesieth edifieth the Church. I** (Paul) **would that ye all spake with "tongues"** (and as concerning of their praying prayer "tongue" that is not audible; but if audibly heard, unless someone interpret: and yet, also being in a Church assembly,) **but rather that ye prophesied: for greater is he** (or she) **that prophesieth than he** (or she) **that speaketh with "tongues," except he** (or she and/or others) **interpret, that the Church may receive edifying. Now, brethren** (and sisters,) **if I** (Paul) **come unto you speaking with "tongues," what shall I** (Paul) **profit you, except I** (Paul) **shall speak to you either by** (the gift of being an apostle of the) **Revelation, or by** (the gift of) **knowledge, or by** (the gift of) **prophesying, or by** (the gift of being teacher of the) **doctrine? For if the trumpet give an uncertain sound** (that the Armed Forces, always has a certain sounding call for War,) **who shall prepare himself** (or herself for the Militia) **to the battle? So likewise ye, except ye** (by the Holy Spirit) **utter by the tongue words easy to be understood, how shall it be known what is spoken** (by the Holy Spirit, with the approval of Jesus and the Father?) **For ye shall speak into the air** (for many and/or most pastor, elders, or deacons; are not taking God's message to the Church assembly seriously: of being heard clearly, so that all can have a heartfelt experience.) **There are, it may be, so many kinds of voices in the world, and none of them is without signification. Therefore if I** (Paul) **know not the meaning of the voice, I** (Paul) **shall be unto him** (or her) **that speaketh a barbarian, and he** (or she) **that speaketh shall be a barbarian unto me. Even so ye, forasmuch as ye are zealous** (having boldness as) **of Spiritual gifts, seek that ye may excel to the edifying of the Church. Wherefore let him** (or her) **that speaketh in an unknown "tongue" pray that he** (or she, or someone else in the Congregation) **may interpret. For if I** (Paul) **pray in an unknown "tongue," my** (as of Paul's) **spirit prayeth, but my understanding is unfruitful** (as to the gift of tongues and the gift of interpretation; which is, of why it needs to be interpreted.) **Wherefore "tongues" are for a sign, not to them that believe, but to them that believe not** (by being convinced, that there is a God:) **but prophesying serveth not for them that believe not, but for them which believe** (of hearing the words, from Jesus Himself.)"

The Message of Jesus to the Church of the Lord Jesus Christ! * * *
THE NINETH GIFT, THE GIFT OF INTERPRETATION OF TONGUES

Subject #Ten:

And as of **number nine [09,]** being the gift called, "interpretation of tongues," to another the **"interpretation of tongues"** (of the language we speak; by the Holy Spirit.) The purpose of having the gift of the "interpretation of tongues;" is when someone hears the language, that is spoken in an unknown language: of not being their own: and there, the "interpretation of tongues" is spoken. For to translate it into the language by the Holy Spirit; of the group, that surrounded them can truly understand; as to the importance as of the issues at hand. And as of the "interpretation of tongues;" that was spoken, needs to be said immediately, after the tongues are spoken: as of what the apostle Paul stated as in [I Cor. 14:27], "If any man (or woman) speak in an unknown tongue, let it be by two, or at the most by three, and that by course; and let one interpret (and also, possibly if only one is available to speak; of the three different tongues)."

And as to this gift, for many and/or most bishops/pastors, elders, or deacons; thinks it is just another message to the assembly, by bringing edification: but yet, how can any message from Heaven receives its greatest acknowledgement, if only a few can hear it very clearly. For Jesus wants to send a message, as of it being from the inspiration from the Holy Spirit; all must respect the words after it is spoken, and also to review those messages: of judging, by making sure that all will understand its content as in [I Cor. 14:16], "Else when thou shalt bless with the (human) spirit, how shall he (or she) that occupieth the room of the unlearned say amen at thy giving of thanks, seeing he (or she) understandeth not what thou sayest?" And so, as someone, that decided to hear all of what were said; and also, of why Jesus wanted it spoken, for many and/or most today's bishops/pastors, elders, and deacons are of just going through the formalities. For the Father in Heaven, and the Son named Jesus; and the Holy Spirit is waiting, for the Holy Spirit is standing outside the borders of the assembly: the triune God is not very pleased, for the Congregation needs to hear and are waiting; for them or someone, to expound on the message that was just spoken.

For too many leaders, the Congregations, are considering it just a place for all to assemble and pray, and sing a few words; and then, again of hearing a fancy titled message from the preacher: which will, be the ending of the Spiritual gathering place called the Church. For this is happening everywhere, in Churches, and on the radio, and on television; and again, the many different fancy titled sermons, they are sounding good and/or pleasingly great. The preaching will have the Congregation's approval; and of not realizing, that there were no Spiritual gifts in operation at their assembly, for to the leaders it was an inspirational gathering. But yet, Jesus is very near and as many and/or most bishops/pastors, elders, or deacons are not aware of the predicament; the world is in, the Holy Spirit, the Father, and the Son named Jesus: of which, is standing outside looking in, as of what Paul faced as in [Heb. 5:11], "Of whom we (the apostles) have many things to say, and hard to be uttered, (possibly of ignoring the value, of having the nine gifts and the five-fold ministries in operation) seeing ye are dull of hearing. But strong meat belongeth to them that are of full age (has a Revelation of Jesus,) even those who by reason of use (of spending time with Jesus) have their senses (of Spiritual values in Christ) exercised to discern both good and evil." For the hearts of the people have waxed (increasingly) cold; for the power of the Holy Spirit, is the only one that will bring back: to the Churches, of those Born-Again experiences.

For as the Congregations obeys, I (Jesus) will come into the midst; into the center of each life: of that assembly, the lives of all that have a heart for the Father. I (Jesus) will walk in among them and blow, there upon the flame of the Holy Spirit's unction; and will definitely, be the only force which will envelope them with the Presence of the Father: directly from the Throne room of Heaven. For the Presence of the Holy Spirit will come and will fill the house; that sweet smell, the frankincense, for all of them that desire to bask in it as in [I Cor. 14:2,4-6,9,12-14,17-18,22-23], **"For he** (or she or others) **that speaketh in an unknown tongue speaketh not unto men** (or women,) **but unto God: for no man** (or woman) **understandeth him** (or her;) **howbeit in the Spirit he** (or she) **speaketh mysteries. He** (or she) **that speaketh in an unknown tongue edifieth himself** (or herself;) **but he** (or she) **that prophesieth edifieth the Church. I** (Paul) **would that ye all spake with tongues, but rather that ye prophesied: for greater is he** (or she) **that prophesieth than he** (or she) **that speaketh with tongues, except he** (or she or others) **"interpret,"** **that the Church may receive edifying. Now, brethren, if I** (Paul) **come unto you speaking with tongues, what shall I** (Paul) **profit you, except I** (Paul) **shall speak to you either by Revelation, or by knowledge, or by prophesying, or by doctrine? So likewise ye, except ye utter by the tongue words easy to be understood, how shall it be known what is spoken? For ye shall speak into the air. even so ye, forasmuch as ye are zealous of Spiritual gifts, seek that ye may excel to the edifying of the Church. Wherefore let him** (or her) **that speaketh in an unknown tongue pray that he** (or she) **may "interpret." For if I** (Paul) **pray in an unknown tongue, my spirit prayeth, but my understanding is unfruitful. For thou verily givest thanks well, but the other is not edified. I** (Paul) **thank my God, I** (Paul) **speak with tongues more than ye all. Wherefore tongues are for a sign, not to them that believe, but to them that believe not: but prophesying serveth not for them that believe not, but for them which believe. If therefore the whole Church be come together into one place, and all speak with tongues, and there come in those that are unlearned, or unbelievers, will they not say that ye are mad** (of being out of your mind?)**"**

The Message of Jesus to the Church of the Lord Jesus Christ! * * *
THE MESSAGE TO THE CHURCH, THE LIGHT MUST BE BRIGHTER

Subject #Eleven:

For the world is getting darker, for how can it be lighter; unless the "Light" show's up, as mentioned by the Scriptures: that are found as in [Gen. 1:3-5], **"And God** (the triune God) **said, let there be "Light"** (of Jesus, being the **"Light;"** for the Sun had not been created yet:) **and there was "Light." And God** (the triune God) **saw the "Light," that it was good: and God** (the triune God) **divided the "Light" from the darkness. And God** (the triune God) **called the "Light" day, and the darkness He** (the triune God) **called night. And the evening and the morning were the first day."**

And as to the Olympic Torch, that are carried to its destination every four years; has the effect, of touching people's heart as it comes into the grandstand of the Stadium. The fiery torch of that flame as it is burning; do represents, the athletes' true spirit of desiring. But only, when the flame moves itself to becoming the fire; on the "Lamp Stand," there the proof of their achievement: that it, will removes all darkness and despair: as the competition begins, setting the stage as to the rewarding; of those that have placed their life beyond the normal.

For it is either, a special blessing of just being able to participate; and/or even, if there are no recognitions of being rewarded: for the acknowledgement of achieving the goal; of which, was the apostle Paul ministry endeavor, but he and all will receive as in [Phil. 3:14], **"I** (Paul) **press toward the mark** (by the power of the Holy Spirit) **for the prize of the high calling of God** (the Father) **in Christ Jesus."** The jest of the main emphasizes would have been the same, of by being involved in Jesus' endeavor of expressing from the searching heart; of fulfilling the run of Faith, of fulfilling the ultimate goal: by having Jesus permanently in the heart, for the prize will be acknowledged by the Father in Heaven.

CHAPTER FOUR
THE FOCUSING CHURCH

The Message of Jesus to the Church of the Lord Jesus Christ! * * *
THE MESSAGE TO THE CHURCH, OH, DRY BONES YOU ARE
ALIVE

Subject #One:

As of "<u>**book number**</u> [01 – 27] <u>**being Matthew – Revelation,**</u>" it is all about what God is saying and that is (<u>**He**</u> (Jesus) <u>**has set in motion, by establishing the Truthful Church of the Lord Jesus Christ.**</u>)

And so, what is this all about? For I (Jesus) am asking you; yes, the Lord Jesus Christ, for Jesus is asking? For is it the end or the climax of all that is the Father's way; the Godly Biblical way, will it or should it be: or is it the humanity's ways, so what are your questions? For the religious, they have multitudes of ways to enter into the now; the experiences of this moment, the good life and also the afterlife: that is of the religious communities. For because of the religiosity's mind set, and they are beginning to engulf the world with their false doctrines; which is definitely not the Biblical mandated. And as a great Army, Jesus will have His faithful workers as in [Mt. 5:19], "**Whosoever therefore shall break** (disobey as to any**) one of these least Commandments, and shall teach men** (or women) **so** (of

70

disobeying the Truth,) **he** (or she) **shall be called the least** (lowest) **in the Kingdom of Heaven: but whosoever shall do** (obeying) **and teach them** (the Truth,) **the same shall be called great** (the highest) **in the Kingdom of Heaven."**

Their conclusion as of the final objective, be of what the world considers; by saying or constantly thinking, is as their normality of their ways: of the natural, and of the physical confrontation; for with Jesus, this is a powerful Supernatural Issues. But I (Jesus,) the Lord Jesus will and is definitely in charge; for the time has come, for all to face the saving knowledge of me (Jesus:) the Spiritual way, a Godly Spiritual experience. For as the Holy Spirit begins, with the approval of the Father in Heaven; that all will, yes all will face this incredible move of the Spirit: that all and again I (Jesus) say all, will face this Spiritual Revival that is the Truth; the Truth of the Gospel, in its fullness of which is definitely coming on the earth. And as a great Army, of believers as in [Mt. 5:41], **"and whosoever shall compel thee to go a mile, go with him** (or her) **twain** (twice as far.)"

For the men, and the women, the boys, and the girls, those at the age of accountability; with a recognition, that they all will make their final stand. And as to the decision, of what is acceptable in the eyes of God; our Father in Heaven, to each of them it will be a starling blunt reality: of the time to accept or the time to reject the Truth, the simplicity of the Gospel. For that is, of what is right or what is wrong; of what is good or what is evil, of what is the Righteousness of our God or what is the unrighteous: as to the ways of Satan's endeavor to deceive. And so, let the earth hear it loudly and clearly; that our Father which is in Heaven is ready, with a distinct gentle proclamation: is saying, to the once dry bones as were and are still in the valley of dry bones; you are alive, you have your flesh on, the sinus on and the skin is there on them. You are standing, standing as if motionless; of waiting, but He (Jesus) is saying of the waiting: the prophetic utterances of the past, wait no longer. And as a great large Army, of believers in Christ as in [Mt. 10:14], **"And whosoever shall not receive you** (of being a believer,) **nor hear your words** (of the Gospel of Jesus,) **when ye depart out of that house or city, shake off the dust of your feet** (let them be accountable, for their actions.)"

For the time has come oh you bones, that once were dried up; lacking the Spirit of God, lacking life, be alert: for this is what I (Jesus) am saying, the Almighty. But now, oh you once dry bones; the "I Am," that has been here forever: yes, forever and forever, from its beginning. For I (Jesus,) the Lord Jesus Christ is saying; to the Body of the Church, the true, the real and genuinely True Church: I (Jesus,) the Lord Jesus is speaking life and vigor into the depth of their being. And as the body, the soul and the spirit that is coming alive will live; I (Jesus,) say live. For as I (Jesus,) the Lord Jesus Christ speaks and fills their being with the infilling of the Holy Spirit; they all will begin to step forward with great authority, because they are no longer alone: but with vitality, being vibrant and full of energy, God given energy. And as a great large Army, of believers in Christ as in [Mt. 10:32], **"Whosoever therefore shall confess me before men** (or women,) **him** (or her) will I (Jesus) **confess also before my Father which is in Heaven."**

So, oh you dry bones, all dry bones that have been dry; I (Jesus,) say look alive, for the time has come to take an account. And of why to take an account of what may be asked? That the dryness has come to an end, for the Spirit; the Holy Spirit is beginning a new and a powerful move. That will go beyond the imagination of anything, that humanity have ever experienced before. Let this mark the new experience for the human race. Therefore, this is what I (Jesus,) the Lord Jesus Christ will be saying, as of the shout of declaration; bones, you bones that now has its flesh on, its sinus on and its skin on: that are standing and are you ready? So, the call is being announced; to march, to march, the march of letting this movement be the signal to the world! And that the Church of the Lord Jesus Christ is on the move; moving, moving forward, toward Redemption: for God is Redeeming the world of that which is hostile. And as a great Army, of believers in Christ as in [Mt. 10:42], **"And whosoever shall give to drink unto one of these little ones a cup of cold water** (for someone, that has no water for a time, it is a big deal) **only in the name of a disciple** (of ministry,) **verily I** (Jesus) **say unto you, he** (or she) **shall in no wise lose his** (or her) **reward."**

For all that has a heart of flesh and not of stone; will begin to take a stand, standing the stand of Faith: but those of stone, the heart of stone, will definitely not. And also, God the Father in Heaven is agreeing; and I (Jesus) am saying, heart of flesh open your mouth oh flesh and begin to shout for joy: for the joy of the Lord is your strength. For I (Jesus,) the Lord Jesus Christ is also saying; it is time to be on the move, beginning by moving forward, all you bones. This is what the Lord Jesus Christ is focusing on; let this echo, from the shouts of my (Jesus') mouth: of the intensity and being filled with power; for as the sound is voiced, then the move is on. For as God, the Father, the Son named Jesus, and the Holy Spirit; of which is to, aligns with those bones to allow the fulfillment of their calling. For the profile of Godliness, and as there is a great movement on the earth; for a powerful awakening is about to occur: with the (01) one of the (99) "ninety-nine." And as of a great large Army, of believers in Christ as in [Mt. 12:32], "**And whosoever speaketh a word against the Son** (Jesus) **of man, it shall be forgiven him** (or her:) **but whosoever speaketh against the Holy Ghost** (Spirit) **it shall not be forgiven him** (or her,) **neither in this world, neither in the world to come** (so if your heart is stirred, then just say; Jesus, Holy Spirit, I by my own permission: I am willingly to give my heart to you, Father in Heaven, Amen.)"

And that is, I (Jesus) will bring all those that have been wandered away; those that have not yet come to the Truth: the Truth of the Gospel, the Truth that will set them and all free from the wiles of the Devil; of which, is the hordes of Demons. And so, hear me you dry bones, I (Jesus,) the "I Am," pronounces judgment; by calling, for the great awakening, by turning their hearts to the only true God: the God of all other gods, of those that have intentionally turned their faces and their ears; from hearing the call, of the Truth. Therefore, they will stumble and fall into deception; so be glad and be overjoyed that your names are written in the Father's Lamb's book of Life! Oh, glory to the Most Highest, our eternal God, the only God of all creation. And as a great large Army, of believers as in [Mt. 12:50], "**For whosoever shall do the will of the Father which is in Heaven, the same is my brother, and sister, and mother** (of one family.)"

So, bones I (Jesus) say, come alive and be moving in a great force; for the time has come to show forth the strength in God: of the Father's call, is to rehabilitate those once dead bones, for life is in them now! And again, as God the Father in Heaven, the Son named Jesus, and the Holy Spirit is saying; let this be the year, the month, the week, the day, the hour, the minute, and the second: that the bones which have everything on them. For to have the tools, the gifts that is; as by stretching out, those arms and receives into their hands all the "nine-gifts:" yes, all the "nine-gifts" of the Spirit as the Scripture reads as in [I Cor. 7-11], "But the manifestation of the Spirit is given to every man (or woman) to profit withal. For to one is given <u>by</u> <u>the</u> <u>Spirit</u> <u>the</u> <u>word</u> <u>of</u> <u>wisdom</u>; <u>to</u> <u>another</u> <u>the</u> <u>word</u> <u>of</u> <u>knowledge</u> <u>by</u> <u>the</u> <u>same</u> <u>Spirit</u>; <u>to</u> <u>another</u> <u>Faith</u> <u>by</u> <u>the</u> <u>same</u> <u>Spirit</u>; <u>to</u> <u>another</u> <u>the</u> <u>gifts</u> <u>of</u> <u>healing</u> <u>by</u> <u>the</u> <u>same</u> <u>Spirit</u>; <u>to</u> <u>another</u> <u>the</u> <u>working</u> <u>of</u> <u>miracles</u>; <u>to</u> <u>another</u> <u>prophecy</u> (a message); <u>to</u> <u>another</u> <u>discerning</u> <u>of</u> <u>spirits</u> (false or true Spirit); <u>to</u> <u>another</u> <u>divers</u> <u>kinds</u> <u>of</u> <u>tongues</u>; <u>to</u> <u>another</u> <u>the</u> <u>interpretation</u> of <u>tongues</u>: <u>but</u> <u>all</u> these <u>worketh</u> that <u>one</u> <u>and</u> <u>the</u> <u>selfsame</u> Spirit, <u>dividing</u> <u>to</u> <u>every</u> <u>man</u> (or woman) <u>severally</u> (of two or more) as He (Jesus) will (to those Jesus chooses; the best gifts, to minister with)." And as a great large Army, of believers as in [Mt. 13:12], "**For whosoever hath, to him** (and/ or her) **shall be given, and he** (and/or she) **shall have more abundance: but whosoever hath not** (of not praying and seeking for more) **from him** (and/or her) **shall be taken away even that he** (and/or she) **hath.**"

And there (Jesus) is saying, by taking your first step; now go and do the work of the ministries, that is laid out before you: being as of though being projected as on a large screen. For of being before your faces, let this pronouncement be the fulfilling of the energy; that they, you, and all desires: and will have, to move and do that which will usher in the Kingdom of God on the earth. And as the Spirit, the Holy Spirit of God bring it to a climax; by the will of the Father, for I (Jesus) say yes, the Lord Jesus Christ does agree! And as a great large Army, of believers in Christ as in [Mt. 16:25], "**For whosoever will save** (by only thinking of themselves, as the life giver; and therefore) **his** (or her) **life shall lose it: and whosoever will lose** (by the attention being placed on) **his** (or her) **life for my** (Jesus') **sake shall find it** (being accepted by Jesus Himself,)"

So, "oh dry bones, you are alive," as I (Jesus) speaks forth the will of the Father's approval in Heaven; and also, as I (Jesus) am speaking forth the powerful Anointing of the Holy Spirit: that will fill and be filled, to overflowing of the once dried bones; and again, by the Presence of the Holy Spirit. As of now, this thing could not be any sooner; so, let this be called into actions, to be dressed in God's Righteousness: being clothed in the Armor of God and being echoed; through-out the whole world, to the four corners of the earth. And for of the dry bones, having now becoming "alive;" as an Army of being in multitudes, the warriors that are being Anointed by the Holy Spirit and are now proclaiming the Gospel: the good news, of the Lord Jesus Christ in its fullness. Amen! "So be it." And as a great large Army, of believers in Christ as in [Lk. 9:5], "**And He** (Jesus) **said unto them, take nothing for your journey, neither staves,** nor scrip, neither bread, neither money; neither have two coats apiece. And whosoever house ye enter into, there abide, and thence depart. And whosoever will not receive you, when ye go out of that city, shake off the very dust from your feet for a testimony against them.”

The Message of Jesus to the Church of the Lord Jesus Christ! * * *
THE MESSAGE TO THE CHURCH, IT IS FLEXING ITS MUSCLES

Subject #Two:

And of a beginning of an exciting journey; of what do you think of this, of your journey being all about: for I (Jesus) will tell you, it will be a walk of Faith? All of you must walk this narrow road; to find eternal life, and on that road: being narrow, not many will be on it. They might talk the talk to you as thou they are coming; no, it is not of their plan, when they are talking the talk to you: for this is because they have set their mind of tricking. And as of deceiving you; to think, that you are going with them on the narrow road: but really their intentions, are to send you down the very wide road toward destruction; so, stand with Faith, the walk of Faith in me (Jesus,) the Lord Jesus Christ. And as a great Army, of believers as in [Mt. 18:4], **“Whosoever therefore shall humble himself** (or herself) **as this little child, the same is greatest in the Kingdom of Heaven.”**

For I (Jesus) will bring comforting peace with an over-helming joy; for the open valley of dry bones, as all of you are a part of the movements: will hear this sounding in the mulberry trees. For the enemy will have no ample warning; but I (Jesus) will have rushed in, I (Jesus) will bring this incredible move of my Holy Spirit: my tender powerful Holy Spirit, for my and your Father will bring that complete connected expression. And it will of being as an echoing sound; but is not an echo, it is a full expression of who my Father is: for I (Jesus) will stand and speak of the Father's words in intercession of prayer, praying as of the Holy Spirit in compassion. For this being flooded, be overflowing as a river of love that is very wide and full; with room for all to come in, and of being completely drenched with the Holy Spirit. And as a great Army, Jesus will have His (Jesus') faithful as in [Mt. 20:27], **“And whosoever will be chief** (as a mature

Spiritual leader; of first being an apostle, the second being a prophet, the third being an evangelist, the fourth being a bishop/pastor, and /or the fifth being a teacher) **among you, let him** (or her) **be your servant** (for Paul, wants them to humble themselves, by Spiritually ministering to the Congregation as a Shepherd of the flock; so each person, will be visited.)"

Oh, that overwhelming embracement; as the Father holds His tightly formed arms: so not one will be lost, yes not one will be plugged out of His hand. For Jesus Christ, the Lord of the Heavens, and the earth will be that deciding factor; of which will, bring humanity head on toward their destiny of choosing, of who their (false gods or true God) will be. For as Abraham, thinking about counting the sand of the sea and the counting of the Stars of the Heavens; so, we and others will begin to sense that awesomeness of that notion as our God begins to unfold: and show that He (Jesus) really does have a plan. And as a great Army, of believers as in [Mt. 21:44], **"And whosoever shall fall on this stone** (being Jesus) **shall be broken: but on whomsoever it** (being Jesus) **shall fall, it will grind** (by destroying) **him** (or her) **to** (a disappearing) powder.)"

For this great plan of taking the masses of people; this confusing world and bringing common sense into their everyday living: and as for our living, as we and the Body of Christ will begin to move: as a great Army with a purpose, by the Word of God, of Jesus' Truth. And yes, He your Jesus is that "Word" that was made flesh, so as of the open valley of dry bones; those that have sinews upon it, and flesh upon them and skin upon them, those once were dry bones: you will see, that those dry bones are not dry anymore; but just waiting for the call as in part of [Ez. 37:4-5], "Oh ye dry bones, hear the word of the Lord, thus saith the Lord God unto these bones; behold, I (Jesus) will cause breath to enter into you, and ye shall live." And as a great Large Army, the "Remnant," of believers in Christ as in [Mt. 23:12], **"And whosoever shall** (by their own desires or own efforts) **exalt** (promote) **himself** (or herself) **shall be abased** (demoted;) **and he** (or she) **that shall humble** (by the Holy Spirit) **himself** (or herself) **shall be exalted** (promoted by Jesus Himself.)"

And as America and all other Countries must listen; this move of the Holy Spirit, originally did not start in other Countries: but in Israel, at the time of the "Feast of Pentecost." For this Revival will be the deciding factor soon, as of the next great shaking; for all Countries will be shaken to its core of their existence: for many will die, of not accepting the Gospel of salvation. And there, coming out of America and the Whole World; will I (Jesus) cause the valley of dry bones to be formulating: into a powerfully great large Army of a meek and a gentle spirit. For by boldly representing me (Jesus,) that will proceed toward a great conquest; of which, as multitudes will be brought into the Kingdom of God.

And as a great Army, of believers as in [Lk. 6:47-49], **"Whosoever cometh to me (Jesus,) and heareth my sayings** (of the Scriptures,) **and doeth** (obey) **them, I (Jesus) will shew you to whom he** (or she) **is like: he** (or she) **is like a man** (or woman) **which built an house** (a heart filled with Righteous thoughts,) **and digged deep** (of the roots; of which, cannot of being persuade to forsake the Gospel,) **and laid the foundation on a rock** (being Jesus:) **and when the flood arose, the stream beat vehemently** (horribly hard) **upon that house, and could not shake it: for it was founded upon the Rock** (being the person Jesus.) **But he** (or she) **that heareth, and doeth not** (by refusing,) **is like a man** (or woman) **that without a foundation built an house upon the earth** (the ground;) **against which the stream did beat vehemently** (horribly hard,) **and immediately it fell; and the ruin of that house was great** (probably was totally demolished.)**"**

And as David killed the wild lion and the wild bear; so, will the prophet's (and/or the prophetess's) prophetic utterances begin to do to the Demonic in the Heavenly: they will be annihilated and what shall we say, we will say, you and I will say, "the Lord (Jesus) lives and rules in Righteousness?" And so when David, after he was Anointed to be the future King; of which, he stood face to face with Goliath: the Giant, saying as in part of [I Sam. 17:26,45], "For who is this uncircumcised (unbeliever in our God of Heaven, a) Philistine, that he (Goliath) should defy (by challenging and also resisting) the Armies of the living God (and David also said to Goliath the Giant?) Thou comest to me with a Sword, and a Spear, and with a Shield, but I (David) come to thee in the name of the Lord of hosts (with many Angels,) the God of the Armies of Israel, whom thou hast defied (challenged and also resisted.)" And as a great Army, Jesus will have His faithful as in [Mt. 5:4], **"Blessed** (joyful) **are they that mourn** (of him seeking salvation, of which Goliath ignored:) **for they shall be comforted."**

So let the world hear; oh Church, the time has come to face the Giant: an image, that seems to overwhelm us and let it be said; thus says the Lord

Jesus Christ, "awake, awake, wake up and open your eyes and listen with your ears." And as the Giant is stalking (the Demonic,) of daring the Church to confront them; but you must listen, of being very careful: and do not be too busy, do you not feel or hear the rumbling of the earth; for our Father which in Heaven is beginning to speak and pointing His finger. And as a great Army, Jesus will have His faithful as in [Mt. 5:5], **"Blessed** (joyful) **are the meek** (humble and patient by watching:) **for they shall inherit the earth."**

CHAPTER FIVE
THE FIVE-FOLD MINISTRIES

The Message of Jesus to the Church of the Lord Jesus Christ! * * *
THE HOW JESUS ESTABLISHED, THE CHURCH'S
BEGINNINGS

Subject #One:

As of **"book number [01 – 27] being Matthew – Revelation,"** it is all about what God is saying and that is (**He** (Jesus) **has set in motion, by establishing the Truthful Church of the Lord Jesus Christ.**)

And as of the **"Church's beginnings,"** as the roles of the "five-fold" positions; there of being intertwined, as to its functions: then will the Holy Spirit bring back the Anointing. For as of what happened on the day of the "Feast of Pentecost;" for that Spiritual awakening was never supposedly to end: for if the "five-fold" ministries were intact, it would still be active as of today. For Jesus is saying to His Church's Body, throughout the world; of being in oneness with the Holy Spirit, the first we must do as of what David did: of protecting each and all the sheep from the lions and the bears. And of the pastors, that have lost their first love for the flock of Jesus' pasture; of being distracted, for because of the leaders ignores of their role: the apostles need to replace the pastor. For this must begin, with someone that will care for the sheep; for as of Satan, he is now scattering the flock in my (Jesus') pasture through-out the whole wide world. For this is what Jesus had to say, as He (Jesus) was still walking on the earth as in [Mt. 11:13], **"For all the prophets and the Law** (being Jesus, He did testify of the Truth) **prophesied** (by revealing the way of Truth, by all the prophets) **until John** (and of now, all of the "five-fold" ministries will complete the task; of spreading Jesus' message of the Gospel.)"

And as all considers the positions, there of being intertwined, as to its functions; then will the Holy Spirit bring back the Anointing. For as of what happened on the day of the "Feast of Pentecost;" for that Spiritual awakening was never supposedly to end: for if the "five-fold" Ministries were intact, it would still be active as of today.

The Message of Jesus to the Church of the Lord Jesus Christ! * * *
THE FIRST FIVE-FOLD POSITION, IS AN APOSTLE

Subject #Two:

And as of **number [01] one, the "apostle;"** of which, do have a pacific role to fulfill: for at the time after the "Feast of Pentecost," of when the disciples were Anointed by the Holy Spirit to become "apostles;" for they, had just an inkling of what was ahead for them as apostles. For the word "missionary," is not mentioned in the Scriptures; and it is because, the apostle would first establish a group of believers: in their own regions or country. And then the evangelist in every Church in the world, they should have been actively involved with each body of believers; in their own regions or country, and definitely would not have to send "missionaries:" to preach, by spreading the Gospel of salvation, to a distant regions or countries. And for as of today, the apostles have not considered it of importance; of allowing themselves, as of facing any challenging risks: when they are speaking out against sin. For many and/or most will not even confront their own population of America or any other countries; of their evil lifestyles, and also of naming each of one of those sinful acts: and even, of having them repenting for it. For only when all live a Godly lifestyle; will the Lord Jesus, come into their hearts and commune with them: otherwise, they will be searching for that peace of mind; but will never ever be able to find it, even as of the Congregation. For this is what Jesus had to say, as in [Mt. 11:18], **For John** (the Baptist) **came neither eating nor drinking, and they say, he** (John) **hath a Devil."**

For as of what Paul stated, which as new believers in Christ; will hardly ever, be able to understand: unless the leaders, by the Holy Spirit reveal that Revelation to them as in [I Cor. 2:11-14], "For what man (or woman) knoweth the things of a man (or a woman,) save the spirit of man (or woman) which is in him (or her?) Even so the things of God knoweth no man (or woman,) but the Spirit of God. Now we have received, not the spirit of the world, but the ("Born-Again") Spirit which is of God; that we might know the things that are freely given to us of God. Which things also we speak, not in the words which man's (or woman's) wisdom teacheth, but which the Holy Ghost (Spirit) teacheth; comparing spiritual things (as of the fleshly issues, that affects our spirit) with Spiritual (as of the fleshly issues; that affects us, after being "Born-Again" within our spirit.) But the natural man (or woman) receiveth not the things of the Spirit of God: for they are foolishness unto him (or her:) neither can he (or she) know them, because they are Spiritually discerned (only being discerned, as the Holy Spirit reveals it to us.) " For this is what Jesus had to say, as in [Mt. 11:30], **"For my yoke is easy, and my burden is light."**

But as of the new believers, that Congregated together to hear the apostles; that had seen Jesus' face to face, of sharing of their experiences: of the Revelation from God, of that person named Jesus; and also, to repent of the sins that they had committed. And as time went on, they had some followers; but yet later, for many were beginning to Congregate: of expecting to hear more about Jesus, and of what God had planned for them; the new believers that is. For they were looking forward, that there will be that Holy Spirit's connection; as to hearing more about what they had in mind: and also, as to their heart felt convictions that were on them, of the doctrines too. And as time went on, the apostles began to assemble; occasionally they would meet and then often, for as they saw the need of gathering: they also, were beginning to have a time of Worshipping Jesus, probably in words and in songs. For the apostles began to, as by the Holy Spirit; of seeing the special need, for an open forum, as Jesus was allowing the Holy Spirit: to set in motion a guiding standard, of how the Church services were to be conducted.

And as the group became larger, Jesus began to reveal to the leaders; that Jesus, had impressed on their hearts of being intimately involved: by counseling, and of establishing (men and/or women) elders and deacons; which would confront the members of the Congregation face to face. For this is what Jesus had to say, as in [Mt. 12:8], **"For the Son** (being Jesus) **of man** (of humanity) **is Lord even of the Sabbath day** (for Jesus wants Himself to be our rest, from the cares of this world.)"

And as they saw the need, to have the bishops/pastors there entrenched; into the middle of the Congregation's daily affairs: for there were many unsolved issues, that has to have a mediator: as of a (bishop/pastor,) of being between the Congregation and the activities. For by hearing the (bishop/pastor,) in their positions of authorities; they were able to deal with the demands: of bringing helps and solutions, of their heart's desires. But as of today, the members of the Congregation; could either be missing for a few weeks and/or of never returning: but yet, the bishops/pastors, are not concerned in doing any following up. For as to their condition, for that is when the sheep of Jesus' pasture has been removed; by their own choosing and never to return, or possibly the lions and/or the bears have destroyed them: or have driven them of the pasture, of where once were filled with Jesus' sheep. For this was, when the apostles began of establishing by the power of the Holy Spirit, of guiding their different guidelines of the many activities; for as to the activities, they were realizing the importance of having the other "four-fold" ministries of being added: of which, as of its beginning was being the apostles' resolutions. And of which began with the apostles; of which, were there of overseeing; by placing, in motion the position of leadership: which would, be effective of the direction as Jesus emphasizes His goings. And of which is to bring that oneness of the Holy Spirit's function; of that salvation experience, of being "Born-Again." For this is what Jesus had to say, as in [Mt. 12:37], **"For by thy words thou shalt be justified, and by thy words thou shalt be condemned."**

And of which it all began, of "first" being under the apostle's ministries; again, of "second" being the prophets, of which were in the role of prophesying: of what is on the Father's heart of the day. And then, the "third" being the evangelists; the preachers, which were bringing members into the Church's assembly: and of them, the evangelists that were spreading the Gospel of Jesus Christ that surrounded their communities and/or territories. For as to the most important, being the Shepherd of the flock; is the "fourth" being also the bishops/pastors, that were designated to be the supervisor: and again, that would be protecting the flock, of whatever were ailing them and/or from any other outside threats. For that means, the bishops/pastors are also being obligated; to be actively involved, by surrounding the Congregation's activities twenty-four hours each day: which is being on call; and again, the elders and the deacons are or should always be, also the ones that are directly involved with the bishops/pastors. For some times, when the ministerial staffs are limited or void of a speaker; the bishops/pastors, can be there to fill that position of the day or longer: but yet, that is not the permanent calling of the bishops/pastors. And last, of the "fifth" being the teachers; that would expound the Word of God to the Congregation. For it was the teacher's position, will be the most important duties; as to the function, of the Congregation's importance: as of the maturing them in the Faith of the Lord Jesus Christ. For this is what Jesus had to say, as in [Mt. 12:40], **"For as Jonas** (Jonah) **was three days and three nights in the whale's belly; so shall the Son** (being Jesus) of man (of humanity) **be three days and three nights in the heart of the earth** (the place of Hell, for Jesus willingly gave His life up; and therefore, Jesus wants those called into the "five-fold" ministries to do the same: of carrying our Cross, for the Gospel.)**"**

And as to the "five-fold" ministries, the apostles are the ones, that were the first to establish; and that is, of setting up a solid foundational ministry and/or ministries: the apostles, are the ones that are called by God, to establish the Congregation. For as the of the Holy Spirit, is by the apostles' side; to pick the prophets, the evangelists, the pastors, and the teachers: and as to those added, which is the other "four-fold" ministries; of setting in place, and of being in its proper position of the varieties of authorities. And as for of its beginnings and of its functions, with all of the "five-fold" ministries in its position of authorities; it will become a powerful, a Holy Spirit's assembly: which will transform the communities that surrounded them. And so, if someone wants to establish a Congregation; they need to fast and pray often, even for one day or more, by asking Jesus to find and/or connect with an apostle: and there, by forming a strong leadership group core of believers. For this is what Jesus had to say, as in [Mt. 12:50], **"For whosoever shall do the will of my Father which is in Heaven, the**

same is my brother, and sister, and mother (for after we pray and fast, the Holy Spirit will reveal; for Jesus wants us to succeed."

And with the approval of the Father in Heaven, Jesus will walk this through with all of us; and the Anointing of the Holy Spirit, will be the inspiration: to completely finalize, as Jesus fills all of our hearts with anticipation. For as of the "five-fold" ministries, as it is in its rightful arranged order; the Holy Spirit's Anointing power will affect the communities, as of its location. And as the pastor humble himself (or herself,) to accept the role of a Shepherd; which is, the hardest and the busiest position: of the "five-fold" ministry, but the reward will be the greatest; as the result of bringing the Father's whole wide world's lost sheep; back into Jesus' sheep pasture and there being eternally safe. For as to an assistant pastor's position, of which is not listed; and therefore, it is an unbiblical position: but yet, the position of the older elders and the younger deacons will definitely bring enhancement to the full ministry of the Anointed pastor's position; of which is, as when the pastor establishes the leadership's positions. For this is what Jesus had to say, as in [Mt. 13:12], **"For whosoever hath, to him** (or her) **shall be given** (of Jesus being acknowledged,) **and he** (or she) **shall have more abundance** (for the Church Body will be able of fulfilling the Congregation's desired accomplishments' goals, of believing:) **but whosoever hath not** (of acknowledging,) **from him** (or her) **shall be taken away even that he** (or she) **hath** (which does means, it was not accomplished.)"

The Message of Jesus to the Church of the Lord Jesus Christ! * * *
THE SECOND FIVE-FOLD POSITION, IS A PROPHET (PHOPHETESS)

Subject #Three:

And as of **number [02] two,** the "prophet" (or "prophetess;") of which, definitely do have a pacific role to fulfill: for as those that consider themselves of being called by Jesus. For the Anointing of being a prophet, he (or she, a prophetess) does have an obligation; as what the prophet Jeremiah faced, for Jesus informed him: that he was truly called to be a prophet, and as of all others; that knows that they were called as in

[Jer. 1:5], "Before I (Jesus) formed thee in the belly, I (Jesus) knew thee; and before thou camest forth out of the womb I (Jesus) ordained thee a prophet (and again, if it is a woman; she is called a prophetess.)" And as of openly hearing the Lord Jesus Christ, by communicating often with the Congregation; and/or of freely expressing as to what is happening around them: and the nation which they live in, by having the Congregation's support. For this is what Jesus had to say, as in [Mt. 13:15], **"For this people's heart is waxed gross, and their ears are dull of hearing, and their eyes they have closed** (by speaking out with boldness;) **lest at any time they should see with their eyes, and hear with their ears, and should understand with their heart, and should be converted, and I** (Jesus) **should heal them."**

But yet, most are walking alone as of what Jeremiah did as in [Jer. 26:12-13], "Then spake Jeremiah unto all the princes (the governors and/or the leaders) and to all the people, saying, the Lord sent me to prophesy against this house (where the leaders lived and ruled from) and against this city all the words that ye have heard. Therefore now (quickly) amend your ways and your doings, and obey the voice of the Lord your God; and the Lord will repent (and removing of) Him (Jesus' proclamation) of the evil that He (Jesus) hath pronounced against you (the Jewish people.)"

And as of today, by being able to hear and taking the warnings seriously; of what the Holy Spirit is saying: and there, of speaking the oracles of God the Father's message; by prophesying directly to mature Churches of the Lord Jesus Christ. For many and/or most bishops/pastors, that controls and supervisee's the Congregation; have very little or no understanding of how much, the impact will be affected: if they would allow the prophetic utterance to be spoken, for the Heavenly atmosphere will come to the earth. For because of the pastor's or the bishop's hesitation; of allowing the "nine-gifts" to operate, Jesus has considered that Church of being displeasing and/or lukewarm to Him. And of which, will definitely affect the observance, as to each individual of that Congregation; of them saying, that the Lord Jesus had or had not visited them. And with His Presence being in the Congregation, as the words were spoken by the inspiration of the Holy Spirit; for their hearts will feel the impact, by the heart's response. For this is what Jesus had to say, as in [Mt. 13:17], **"For verily I** (Jesus) **say unto you,** (for today is the time, to speak it out) **that many prophets** (and prophetesses) **and Righteous men** (and women) **have desired to see those**

things which ye see, and have not seen them; and to hear those things which ye hear and have not heard them."

For Jesus wants the prophets and/or the prophetesses, that are filled with the Holy Spirit; to stir up the "nine-gifts," which are or should be in many and/or most Congregations: for many will, by the Holy Spirit' Presence of spreading the information that is said; as of what the prophetic utterances are prophesying, of reaching beyond the Church's wall. And as to the called-out ones begins to prophecy; this will be a sign, to the nonbelievers and the believers: of which, will convict their hearts, as believers of making thinks right as to their relationship with the Lord Jesus Christ; and of nonbelievers, of confessing their sins and asking forgiveness. And of which, it will bring salvation to their inner spirit; as they are being "Born-Again," of that new inner revived Spirit: of facing eternal life with the Father in Heaven. And so, let us consider the plan of Jesus' message to the Church; throughout the world, that He wants men and women, the boys and girls: to take the Scriptures very, seriously, for the Lord Jesus wants the Church to function as a living Spiritual organism. For as to the Holy Spirit, if it is allowed to function with a Godly liberality; the Holy Spirit's power will Revive and bring the proper influences of the Church Body, of having the Anointing that is from Heaven: to be brought to the earth, which of affecting the very core of the inner heart. For this is what Jesus had to say, as He (Jesus) who was walking with them; that were listening on the earth as in [Mt. 15:4], **"For God commanded, saying, honour thy father and mother: and, he** (or she) **that curseth father or mother, let him** (or her) **die the death** (of then, being under the Mercy of God; of destroying evil and protecting His faithful "Remnant:" but as by Grace, Jesus being our Shepherd, of bringing a solution; by giving His life for the Remnant.)"

The Message of Jesus to the Church of the Lord Jesus Christ! * * *
THE THIRD FIVE-FOLD POSITION, IS AN EVANGELIST

Subject #Four:

And as of **number [03] three**, the "<u>evangelist;</u>" of which, do have a pacific role to fulfill: for the evangelist are being ignored today, as to the local Church's activities. And as of those evangelists of Paul's time period, that had a passion of seeing souls saved; of the lost souls being brought, into the Kingdom of God: of which will, have a greater emotional expression by the evangelists. For as of them, seeing the Gospel of salvation spreading and of filling the Church assembly, as it was with Paul the apostle; which was one of them that was called by Jesus: of doing the work of an evangelist as in [Acts 8:40,21:8], "But Philip was found at Azotus (was previously called Ashdod, by the Mediterranean Sea:) and passing through he (Philip) preached in all the cities, till he came to Caesarea (about sixty-two miles northwest of Jerusalem.) And the next day we that were of Paul's company departed, and came unto Caesarea: and we entered into the house of Philip the evangelist." For this is what the Lord Jesus had to say, as in [Mt. 15:19], **For out of the heart proceed evil thoughts** (for those are the ones, which will hear; because of the evangelists, for they are out among the populations in their community: and preaching the full Gospel of real repentance,) **murders, adulteries, fornications, thefts, false wit-ness, blasphemies."**

And as of then, and of which should be of today; that is, if the "five-fold" ministries were in full unity: as each ministry are Spiritually intertwined, for one cannot fully succeed successfully without the other. And as to the "apostles," the "prophets," the "evangelists," the "pastors," and the "teachers;" for of many do think, that they are a monarch (independently) of having its own leadership. For the Church, of its individualities and/or its characteristics; of being distinguishers, as by recognizing as to the ability of establishing: the knowledge of a Godly lifestyle, of which is as of a Heavenly nature. For when there is a Congregational establishment; a Church that is, of focusing on the thought of others also, being a soul winner for Jesus. For many and/or most pastors, are going through a time period of formality; they have the form of Godliness, but denying the power: which is, the power of that energy, that comes from the Throne room of heaven. And as to the power, the Father's heart is that Righteous power; of which will, of effecting the Congregation and eventually their surrounding communities, with the work of an evangelist. For most churches as of today, are in a stalemate mode; for many and/or most pastors have not even considered any of an evangelist to being an asset: to their Congregation, but only to those of other outer territories, other states or countries. For this is what Jesus had to say, as in [Mt. 16:25-27], **"For whosoever will save his** (or her) **life shall lose it: and whosoever**

will lose his (or her) **life for my** (Jesus') **sake** (of fulfilling Jesus' will) **shall find it. For what is a man** (or woman) **profited, if he** (or she) **shall gain the whole world, and lose his** (or her) **own soul** (by not fulfilling Jesus' will)? **Or what shall a man** (or woman) **give in exchange for his** (or her) **soul? For the Son** (being Jesus) **of man** (of humanity) **shall come in the glory of His Father with His Angels; and then He** (Jesus) **shall reward every man** (or woman) **according to his** (or her) **works."**

For the Lord Jesus Christ, is in the process of removing the Candle Stand in those Churches; for Jesus, by the Holy Spirit has been waiting long enough: and so as of our time period, Jesus has His eyes on others; of bringing the message of His Resurrection power. And as to its closure, the time is quickly running out; of the spaces of time, of reaching that lost sheep: that Jesus has His eyes, focusing on; for it is at the point of its expiration date as of what Paul said as in [II Ti. 4:3-5], "For the time (which is of today) will come when they (the leaders and the Church members) will not endure sound doctrine; but after their own lusts (being in Church and living in their own sins) shall they heap to themselves teachers, having itching ears; and they shall turn away their ears from the Truth (of the Gospel,) and shall be turned unto fables. But watch thou in all things, endure afflictions (of being scoffed at,) do the work of an evangelist (preaching to the unbelievers,) make full proof (that the doctrine, is not in error) of thy ministry." For this is what Jesus had to say, as in [Mt. 18:11], **"For the Son** (being Jesus Christ) **of man** (of humanity) **is come to save that which is lost."**

And as Jesus sends the evangelists out; of also, waiting for those that are sitting in that same Congregation: of where Jesus, is in the process of completely removing the Candle Stand. And again, the word "missionary," is not mentioned in the Scriptures; is because, the apostle would first establish a group of believers: in their own regions or country. And then the evangelist in every Churches in the world; should have been active with each body of believers: in their own regions or country of believers, for they would not have to send "missionaries;" to preach, by spreading the Gospel of salvation, to a distant regions or other countries.

For those that are called to be evangelist, are still seated in that Congregation; and again, they needed to be inspirited by the Holy Spirit: but of how, if the leaders in the Congregations are not aware of what is happening among their own surroundings; of which, as the Father in

Heaven keeps waiting. So, of the Churches, the Lord Jesus is saying; it is time for the slumbering Churches through-out the whole world: the (01) one of the (99) "ninety-nine" is in among the saints and still do not know who Jesus is. And if they are still living in sin; for the pastors and/or the bishops are looking some other way or have compromised as to what a true Righteous lifestyle is: and also, these that are out in the wandering communities near their Congregation.

For they will come, and that is if the leadership's heart is stirred by being willing; of having an evangelist of being busy working in their surroundings and of allowing the Holy Spirit: to complete, the work of revealing to them of who Jesus Christ is. For otherwise, Jesus is saying to many and/or most Congregations; but yet, the leaders are not really listening as, I (Jesus) will be coming soon: when most in the Congregation are not prepared to hear the Trumpet sound. For this is what Jesus had to say, as in [Mt. 18:20], **For where two or three are gathered together in my name, there am I** (Jesus) **in the midst** (literally in the flesh) **of them."**

The Message of Jesus to the Church of the Lord Jesus Christ! * * *
THE FOURTH FIVE-FOLD POSITION, IS A PASTOR

Subject #Five:

And as of **number [04] four, the "pastor;"** of which, do have a pacific role to fulfill: for the time period has already come, as to also the bishops/pastors; that they will have a compassion, as to the sheep of their pasture, of which is their Congregation. And again, as also of many and/or most bishops/pastors; the Lord Jesus Christ, with the approval of the Father in Heaven: with the eyeing of the Holy Spirit, is actively searching the whole world. For the leaders, that truly understand their position; and again, and again also of the role as a bishop/pastor: but yet, for as of many of the leaders: it is a business adventure, an occupation and not a ministry; only in the name, but not by the deeds, which is laid out in the Scriptures.

For as to many and/or most bishops/pastors; they have a routine, of how their activities begin: as they start, of beginning the day of the week. And as the schedules are in place, of facing the office's time-table; there they are reviewing, the financial situation: as to the income of balancing the debit and credit of the finances, of which is the stabilities in their incoming cash flow; so, all or some will be paid for their services. And of which, also has to do with the size of many Congregations; for all must understand, that if the Congregation's members exceed being over (300) "three hundred" people: as for Jesus' proclamation, He will definitely being consider it being an evangelistic outreach and not a Congregational assembly. For this is what Jesus had to say, as in [Mt. 19:12], **For there are some eunuchs, which were so born from their mother's womb: and there are some eunuchs, which are made eunuchs of men** (with their assistance:) **and there be eunuchs, which have made themselves eunuchs for the Kingdom of heaven's sake** (possibly being involved, also as of being the "five-fold" ministries.) **He** (or she) **that is able to receive it, let him** (or her) **receive it."**

And that is of believing, them needing no one else but of being themselves and if they feel this way; it is because Satan has filled their mind with the pride, of valuing themselves over the Lord Jesus' ways: of ruling and/or of governing the Church Body. And of which is the core of the "five-fold" ministries; the Holy Spirit's force, of being the Anointing to build the structural formula, called the Church. And of technically speaking, all those that are involved in the "five-fold" ministries; do have to place themselves into the role of reviewing: by all humbling to the calling, as being the Shepherd over all the flocks, an individually described manner. For every member, that the evangelist brings into the Church Body of Christ; as each, needs an individual attention, to the Father in Heaven's pasture: otherwise, the pastor and/or the bishop, has not fulfilled their duties; as of being the Shepherd of Jesus' flock. And again, they must allow the other "four-fold" ministries; to do the work of the ministries, as of the preaching and the teaching: as the pastor and/or the bishop, by placing their attentions of caring for the wellbeing; to the sheep of the Father's pasture. For this is what Jesus had to say, as in [Mt. 20:1], **"For the Kingdom of Heaven is like unto a man** (or woman) **that is an householder** (of one who occupies the house; but of this time, it is Jesus that had those doing the "five-fold" ministries: and all, will understand of their position of being fully rewarded; for it is, all about the their willingness of protecting and securing the flock in their pasture, and of not being reimbursed,) **which went out early in the morning to hire labourers into the vineyard."**

For if the bishops/pastors, through-out the worlds disagree; has not an understanding, to what their calling is: and again, Jesus wants to send new converts into the Body of Christ; which is, the Church of the Lord Jesus Christ. For only then if they disagree, all must resign from that position; for if we, are unwilling to be paid less and/or of the voluntary obligation: of which is, of our giving by dying for the Gospel's sake as Paul did. And of which means, of us being willing to give everything for Jesus' sake; for judgement will begin in the house of the Lord as in part of [I Pet. 4:17-18,4:10-11], "For the time is come (as of us today) that judgement must begin at the house of God (as to including our Spiritual and moral lifestyle, which does include the Congregation's moral lifestyle; and also, of how the pastors or the bishops fulfill their obligation: as of being the Shepherd of the flock:) and if it first begin at us, what shall the end be of them (of having the pastors or bishops; of ministering, to the Congregation as to what a Righteous lifestyle is all about: and then of them,) that obey not the Gospel of God? And if the Righteous (us believing by Faith) scarcely be saved, where shall the ungodly and the sinner appear (which is the degree, of any and all being punishment in Hell?) As every man (or woman) hath received the gift (and if it is being more than one, being the gift of wisdom; of knowledge, of faith, of healing, of working of miracles, prophecy, decerning of spirit, speaking divers kinds of tongues, and the gift of the interpretation of tongues,) even so minister the same one to another, as good stewards of the manifold Grace (the solution, of Jesus Christ showing favor, by dying on the Cross and His Resurrection) of God (the Father.) If any man (or woman) speak, let him (or her) speak as the oracles (knowledge, of one being a pastor/a bishop, which also includes all the other "four-fold" ministries) of God; if any man (or woman) minister, let him (or her) do it as of the ability which God giveth: that God in all things may be glorified through Jesus Christ."

For this is what Jesus had to say, as in [Mt. 21:32], **For John** (the Baptist) **came unto you** (those that were thinking of being good and Godly; when John approached) **in the way of Righteousness, and ye believed him not** (that needed to hear, of some-one coming; that would Redeem them of their sins:) b**ut the publicans and the harlots believed him** (John, of believing that the Son of God was coming:) **and ye, when ye** (of those that saw John coming) **has seen it** (yet the publicans and the harlots, confessed and believed, but you did not,) **repented not afterward, that ye might believe him** (John and his message of salvation.)"

For anytime the members are being ignored; as to the leader's lack of time to minister to each sheep: and again, by not having the adequate amount of time. For of then, the bishops/pastors or any of the other "four-fold" ministries; they all needed to reevaluate the predicament that they are in and the requirements that they needed: to reset their goals, for before the Lord Jesus, for He is not pleased; so, to rectify of bringing a solution, it must be their priority. For many and/or most of the "five-fold" ministries of leadership; has a misconception, as to the way to correct a procedure of warning the populations of Christians: of the domes and glumes that are coming. And as they mouth out in private or to the public their prophetic prediction on the radio; on television, and/or to their own pulpit in a Congregational setting: for of whatever is being said, should only be addressed to the leaders of the "five-fold" ministries; but yet, the Church leadership expects the government to mend or repair it, of bringing the solutions. For this is what Jesus had to say, as in [Mt. 22:14], **For many are called, but few are chosen** (for as Church leaders, this cannot be an occupational job; but a compassionate position, of focusing on a direct link: of the Holy Spirit's endeavor as to spreading the Gospel, as to transforming the population of the whole wide world; into a mindset, of having an experience with the God that created them.)"

For Jesus, really wants them to understand; because they have not properly focused their ministries on its proper order: and that is, of why there are calamities on the earth. And as of the new leaders, of beginning to fulfill their calling; they will be able to prepare the Congregations all over the whole world: in their time of many as to fasting and praying, of what they are about to face ahead. For their solution of its resolution, will only come about when the Holy Spirit is involved, of which will bring repentance and of being "Born-Again;" and there, salvation will be the requirement by the Father in heaven: of healing the population of what ailed them.

For the Lord Jesus' understandings, of the going condition; for even the Holy Spirit is being neglected to its function, by having one or all the "nine-gifts" functioning: as it comes to the required amount of time to process as to the Congregation's wellbeing; of which, is as when it comes to the encouragements and the healings that needs to happen.

And as for all the Church leaders that are facing, of their "first dilemma;" of establishing a new Congregation, for as of today's procedures and the assignments: the bishop/pastor usually are the one, that has the key to the door of the Church's building; so as of having a Biblically functional required ministry. For usually in the beginning, the apostle is the one; of which, actually has the first assigned requirement as to the Church and/or the Churches of being establishment, of including the "five-fold" ministries: of securing an adequate Church staff.

And that also is, by facing, of the "second dilemma;" of first having an Anointed apostle, to oversees the overall Church's communities' ministries: some are over many Churches assembly. For this is what Jesus had to say, as in [Mt. 22:30], **"For in the Resurrection they neither marry** (for in many/most of the Church's function, allot of emphasis is placed on having a friendly family environment; of which is, really proper and good,) **nor are given in marriage** (and as of now, there are so many marriages; and very many divorces,) **but are as the Angels of God in Heaven** (for more attention, needs to place on the heart condition; first of all, as to their relation with Jesus: then on someone finding a mate."

And as they are facing, of the "third dilemma;" of establishing an environment, of the pastor being the ones giving the shots: of normally ignoring the idea of having the need of a prophet? For usually in the beginning, the Anointed prophet was next, paid or unpaid; they will be speaking the oracles: of which is, the messages from Heaven as to setting in motion Jesus' desire of seeing and bringing the ministries; into is properly establishments, as of the Congregation hearing directly from Heaven.

And as they are facing, of the "fourth dilemma;" as of establishing, of to how they can bring and fill the Congregation's sanctuary: of normally ignoring the idea of having the need of an Anointed evangelist? For usually in the beginning, the evangelist was next as to its importance; paid or unpaid, that is constantly preaching the Gospel, beyond the walls of the Churches assembly: so that the Church's building will be filled, as of reaching the lost sheep of the whole world.

And as they are facing, of the "fifth dilemma;" of placing as to how, they can have an Anointed teacher, of teaching the true doctrines of Christ: of the message being presented to the Congregation more clearly, especially to the new believers in Christ; of normally ignoring the idea of having the need of a qualified teacher? For usually in the beginning, the teacher was next; paid or the unpaid, which has the very most important position of any and every Church's functional activity ministry: of its important position, of making known how to implement the knowledge of the Scriptures into its practical uses. For as of now, the bishops/pastors are the central figure; as to the other "four-fold" ministries, for as of Paul's time, being a supportive ministry to the bishops/pastors: the "four-fold" ministries should be actively preaching the sermons or many sermons, and of inspiring the Congregation; in becoming actively, of doing the work in the ministries. And again, of the "four-fold" ministries that surrounds the bishop/pastor; and again also, of being a great supporter of the bishop/ pastor: as the bishop/pastor is focusing on the wellbeing of their sheep. For again, as of young David protecting his Father's flock; by killing a lion and a bear, by removing the sheep from the jaws of the predators: for David's heart was of them being fed with food from the father's own grazing pasture. But yet, of the most important assignment which his father request's; was as of the sheep being protected. For many and/or most pastors have heard, about how the Congregation's population are dwindling; and yet, it is not an alarming warning to the pastors; for Jesus is saying to the pastors, and again, I (Jesus) did not call you to preach or to teach the Congregation. For this is what Jesus had to say, as in [Mt. 23:4], **For they** (that sits in the seat of authorities) **bind heavy burdens** (obligation) **and grievous** (painful) **to be borne** (placed on the Church staff,) **and lay them on men's** (or women's) **shoulders; but they themselves will not move them with one of their fingers."**

For if David, setting his voice volume up; by yelling and shouting to his sheep: they all, would have scattered themselves among the hills and the valleys; far from where, as David originally was. And when it comes to the bishop/pastor themselves, of allowing the volume of their worship time with words and with songs; to be so loud that the Congregation themselves, cannot project their own voices of being heard: it is a literal sham, it is God's Sanctuary of Worship; for as to Jesus' view of where are their common sense? For as to the modern bishops/pastors, that having allowed the worldly/secular mindset of the entertainers; to dominate, the religious arena must wake up: for they would have been better off, to have gotten a job in the secular field.

For the mind of the bishop's/pastor's heart must display of what Jesus faced; for Jesus' proclamation, was to allow all a way to express their Worship: to Jesus, with the normal sounds and at times in silence. For the noisy wilds of the world have come in the door; to distract the

Congregations, of those special times of Worship: so how can the bishops/pastors protect and to give his (or her) life for the sheep; and there, Jesus is not pleased, and neither is His Father in Heaven? For David was there, of his father's commission; to herd the sheep, and there to protect them from the foes: which are the ones, that are trying to distract the sheep of being near David; he was near as the sheep found food to nourish their body. For this is what Jesus had to say, as in [Mt. 23:39], **"For** (of then and of now and even after, the Rapture of the Church's believers) **I** (Jesus) **say unto yo**u (of this happening, after Jesus wept over Jerusalem, and as of now; Jesus is weeping over the Church's dilemma: for the predicament, they have allowed themselves; to be distracted, of bringing the Gospel to the world,) **ye shall not see me henceforth, till ye shall** (of even after realizing our shortcoming and error; we will) **say, blessed** (of the time of facing judgement, for our behavior) **is He** (Jesus) **that cometh in the name of the Lord** (Jesus.)"

And Jesus is saying again, I (Jesus) did not call bishops/pastors to preach or to teach; even though at times, someone has to be there, to cover the vacancy as to someone ministering: which is, if there is no one available to minister. For a pastor, is not called to focus their attention on information; of which, as when it comes to being a preacher or a teacher: but yet, they are turning their attention; to of yelling and shouting it out, into other people's ears. And again, by forgetting that I (Jesus) had called them to protect; the flock from the false preachers and the false teachers. For of many, it is much too late; the lions and the bears have devoured many: actually, they have distracted multitudes, of His "Remnants."

For now, as of the modern bishops/pastors, of ignoring the warning signs; and why, because they have a gross concept: of which is, an insensitive feeling and the gross misunderstanding, as to the Divine orchestrated Anointing of their true calling? For many and/or most bishops/pastors know very little about the members of their flock; and even of their relationship with the God they Worship: of which, I (Jesus) am very displeased; and of considering themselves and the Congregation of being lukewarm. And as to many of the other Congregations; that I (Jesus) have already, of for many years been allowing of closing those Churches down: and it is because, I (Jesus) had spued them out of my mouth. For this is what Jesus had to say, as in [Mt. 24:5], **For many shall come in my** (Jesus's) **name** (for because the bishops/pastors; have neglected, as to displaying Jesus' love for the Church,) **saying, I am Christ; and shall deceive many."**

And as to the phase of their ministries of today; of the Churches of mine, I (Jesus) have already removed many beyond my (Jesus') site: for they are offensive to me and my Father. For the time has come to say, as to the bishops/pastors through-out the world that they must begin to repent; and allow, others into the ministries: for as bishops/pastors, they must take charge of not just feeding the flock. But by protecting the flock; of which it means, the pastor will know almost as much about the flock: as each, individual sheep does of themselves. For the Gospel of Jesus Christ, by the Holy Spirit is yet, the most powerful message on earth; but how, can it benefit the Church's Congregation, that are living in sin: yet the bishops/ pastors are not interested in being informed, and or is not interested in knowing anything about it. For many, did not want to offend them, knowing good and well; as they continue, that many will end up in Hell: if the Congregation does not repent. For the Devil is scoffing and laughing at the modern bishops/pastors; for many and/or most bishops/pastors in the whole wide world: that have many of their members leaving. For many have permanently decided to make the world as their dwelling places; and also, are not returning to the Churches: for they lost their Spiritual compassionate calling, and are no longer considered my (Jesus') bishops/pastors. For this is what Jesus had to say, as in [Mt. 24:7], **"For nation** (but the Congregation, will not being prepared Spiritually; to deal, with the struggles that they will be facing) **shall rise against nation, and kingdom against kingdom: and there shall be famines** (of not because of global warming,) **and pestilences** (different viruses,) **and earthquakes** (the earth is of reacting to humanities sins,) **in divers places."**

The Message of Jesus to the Church of the Lord Jesus Christ! * * *
THE FIFTH FIVE-FOLD POSITION, IS A TEACHER

Subject #Six:

And as of **number [05] five, the "teacher;"** of which, do have a pacific role to fulfill: and as of being the teacher, of revealing the Truth of the Gospel. For it is time for the Churches, to place the teacher in their rightful position of authority; as to the calling, the position of bringing the minds of men and women, of boys and girls: to having, their Spiritual sights on the high calling of the Holy Spirit's goals. And again, as of the teachers, which has the most important position; of any and every Church's functional activity ministry: of its position, of making known how to implement; the knowledge of the Scriptures into its Spiritual practical uses. For how can the position be a teacher of totally being ignored, when Jesus placed the teacher; to be a very important calling, of edifying the Body of Christ: for of its greatest priorities? And as to the Church's agenda, the teacher must be placed as the most important assets; as to teaching the Word of God: the teacher, will by the Holy Spirit of revealing the Truth of Jesus' goings. For this is what Jesus had to say, as in [Mt. 24:21], **For then shall be great Tribulation** (for by utilizing the "five-fold" ministries endeavor; the Church, will be the only members of being the ones that will be prepared and established to face the consequences,) **such as was not since the beginning of the world to this day, no, nor ever shall be."**

For as to the ministries of the "five-fold," the ministry of teaching is listed last; but yet, it is the only one that will connect: as to the interaction, of expressing the Truth of the Gospel; to its simplicity of the Gospel of Christ as in part of [II Cor. 11:3-4], "But I (Paul) fear, lest by any means, as the Serpent (of being Lucifer's voice) beguiled Eve through his (of Lucifer, disguising as of the Snake's appearance as being intelligent; of its) subtilty, so your minds should be corrupted (by justifying our own mental thoughts, of obeying, instead of God's Commandments) from the simplicity that is in Christ. For if he (or she and/or others) that cometh preaching another Jesus, whom we have not preached, or if ye receive another spirit (of being another Demonically deceiving person, with false doctrine; which are trying to convince you and all,) which ye have not received, or another Gospel, which ye have not accepted, ye might well bear with him (or her, by convincing them; that even though Paul was not chosen as of the original twelve apostle: Paul wanted them, to understand that what he was preaching; was the Revelation of the Gospel, truly from Jesus Christ Himself.)" And as of Paul's bold statement, as of the Scripture as in [Acts 16:31], "And they (Paul and Silas) said, believe on the Lord Jesus Christ, and thou shalt be saved, and thy house." And Paul also wrote, as in [Rom. 10:13], "For whosoever shall call upon the name of the Lord (for me, I want Jesus; to be my Lord: and there I) <u>shall</u> <u>be</u> <u>saved</u>.)" For this is what Jesus had to say, as in [Mt. 24:24], **"For there shall arise** (of many organized religions of today, as leader speaks of) **false Christs, and false prophets, and shall shew great signs and wonders; insomuch that, if it were possible, they shall deceive the very elect."**

But yet, we cannot ignore of the important ministry of teaching, of "first" being the apostles; of its beginning, is the first of the "five-fold" ministries: but yet, the apostle, supervises and of bringing the Church assembly of being established, with the different apostles. And as of the "second" being the true prophet, which brings the Anointing down from above; of being from Heaven, of by and with the Father's approval. And as of the "third" being the evangelist, seeks all that are lost and brings; by showing them the Way, the Truth, and the Life: that is everlasting, and brings them into the Kingdom of God. And as of the "fourth" being the pastor/bishop. And as of the "fifth" being the teacher, which brings the Truth of having a personal relationship with Jesus; being by the Scriptures, and by word by word, as to the Gospel of Jesus Christ. For many and/or most bishops/pastors and the Church leaders; have ignored the important role of a teacher and they have also, misunderstood the activities that surround: the teacher's ability of presenting the Word of God. For a teacher is also called, by Jesus Himself; and is Anointed, by the Holy Spirit to reveal the Truth: of Jesus, as God in a fleshly human form. And by having teachers, they will prepare our hearts and minds; of which, as to what we are about to face. For this is what Jesus had to say, as in [Mt. 24:27], **For as the lighting cometh** (quickly) **out of the east, and shineth even unto the west; so shall also the coming of the Son** (being Jesus) **of man** (Jesus of humanity) **be** (in a fleshly human form.)"

For the time has come, for the Churches to put into motion; the "five-fold" ministries in its rightful position, so the Holy Spirit will be able to adequately: set in motion the powerful Truth of the God-Head, the Father, the Son and the Holy Spirit. And for of which, then bishops/pastors will understand as to the Churches role, as they are able to connect; to one and another, as to the importance of each members functions: the Lord Jesus will be able to bring, that unity of the saints. And of that oneness, which of being in unity; as Jesus told His disciples, of them being in Jesus and of Jesus being in them. For at the time of Paul the apostle, he was interacting; in the simplicity of the Gospel as in [Col. 3:1], "<u>If ye</u>

then be Risen with Christ, seek those things which are above (by Faith,) where Christ sitteth on the right hand of God (the Father.)" For then we are being truly free, from the spiritual conflict of being connected to this natural world as in [Col. 3:16], "Let the Word of Christ dwell in you richly in all wisdom; teaching (as of being one of the "five-fold" ministries) and admonishing one (of the audience, to) another (the same audience) in psalms and hymns and Spiritual songs (of allowing the gift of tongues to be spoken,) singing with Grace (as of reminding ourselves; that by Grace, Jesus brought the solution: of dying on the Cross, and of His Resurrection) in your hearts to the Lord." For this is what Jesus Christ had to say, as in [Mt. 24:28], **for wheresoever** (of being the ones, that have heard the Gospel; throughout the world, as the "five-fold" ministries: have reached the lost, the unbelieving will be; where) **the carcase is, there will the eagles be gathered together** (as the battles, of the world ravages and devastates.)"

For as to the position of a teacher; of now, by facing the audience: but of then, the teacher is centered in the middle of the gathering; and is being surrounded, by the audience from all four sides. And again, of that setting of the teacher's position; of being surrounded by the audience, and there they will be able to interact: of allowing, all that are in the audience to participate; as to the questions and answers, that are shared by the audience themselves. For which has been proven to be most successful way to present the Scripture, in its entirety. And of which, will enhance the discussions; as to the only Biblical Truths of the Word of God: and therefore, by provoking the thinking mind of the hearer and of the speaker, for the Truth will set us free. And as to each of the "five-fold" members, that are in unity with the triune God; Jesus is able to allow the Holy Spirit to move within all of the "nine-gifts" of the Spirit: which are, intertwined within the "five-fold" ministries. For the "nine-gifts" are beginning with; of wisdom, of knowledge, of faith, of healing, of miracles, of prophecy, of decerning of spirit, of divers kinds of tongues, and of the interpretation of tongues: and there, being involved with the "five-fold" ministries. For as of being the teacher, this will be the beginning, of establishing its proper functions; and there, with the love being expressed openly and freely: the Gospel, will have an impact and will have its mission completed; of reaching the masses. For the Gospel will only come to its fulfillment; when the Word of God is filled with the power of Jesus: of His Resurrection, and then Jesus will bring a climax; as He appears, by bringing His "Remnant" to safety. For this is what Jesus had to say, as in [Mt. 24:38], **For as in the days that were before the flood they were eating and drinking, marrying and giving in marriage** (and again, but how can the (01) one of the (99) "ninety-nine" of being found? For if the "five-fold" ministries are ignored, that including the evangelist; which will shake to the core, the apathy that is in the Church's administrator: of today as in part of [II Th. 2:3], "For that day shall not come, except there come a falling away first (of the Gospel's true message,) **until the day that Noe** (Noah) **entered into the Ark** (the ship.)"

The Message of Jesus to the Church of the Lord Jesus Christ! * * * THE ASSIGNMENT, AS TO THE FIVE-FOLD MINISTRIES

Subject #Seven:

So let the "**five-fold ministries;**" that included, the position of the bishops, now being called pastors, the elders, the deacons: of which supplemented, of when it was first established; in the form of a Church governmental body, of the believers by the apostles. And again, the word "missionary" of its working, is not mentioned in the Scriptures; of which, is because, as the apostle would first establish a group of believers: in their own regions or country. And then the evangelist in every Churches in the world, should have been to activate with each of the body of believers; in their own regions or country, and would not have to send "missionaries:" to preach, by spreading the Gospel of salvation, to a very long distant regions or countries. And as of being about the flock; of which is, the sheep of the Congregation: it is all about the role of the bishop/pastor, being the Shepherd of Jesus' special flock; and again, as Jesus did by Him, picking the young Shepherd boy called David. For as of adding all those three ministries; as of the "first position," again being called the bishop and/or eventually also called a pastor, that compliments and are intertwined into something similar: to what the pastor does, of overseers the elders and the deacons. And the "second position;" of the second one being the older members, but yet called an elder; and the "third position," as of the third one being younger, but yet the third being called the deacon: of both doing similar task, being under the supervisor of the pastors and/or bishops; of enhancing the work of the ministries in the Church Body. For this is what Jesus had to say, as He (Jesus) was walking on the earth as in [Mt. 25:14], **For the Kingdom of Heaven is as a man (or woman) travelling into a far country, who called his (or her) servants, and delivered unto them his** (or her) **goods** (for when it comes to the servants; which is, for also as of us today, as to the "five-fold" ministries: Jesus will reward by our talents; for it is up to us to preform our duties in its fullest.)**"**

And for David, was a true Shepherd that kept the lion and the bear; away from the sheep, and as of today: there are false preachers and false teachers, which will not be noticed. And as to the lions and the bears, that are lurking near the Congregation; for they will not be totally discovered, by any of the bishops/pastors: unless each of the bishops/pastors are aware of their goings. And as also of their moral standard; which is a sinful act, for this will only happen when they, the true bishop/pastor is carry out his (or her) duties as a Shepherd. For of which will only be fulfilled, when a bishop/pastor understand their full duty; that is required by the Scriptures, for Jesus was a true Shepherd to His followers: and there, they were able to see and understand their assignment as a Congregation. For the apostles, by the Holy Spirit did reach the known world; with the Gospel of the Lord Jesus Christ, by what Jesus taught them: for the effect that happened to their mind set, it is because Jesus played the role of the first bishop/pastor of the new formed Church. So, bishops/pastors to consider of the role as a protector; to the sheep of Jesus' fold, being the Shepherd: for as of all must face this issue head on, of as most bishops/pastors are not today. And also, the other "four-fold" ministries; for they are not really being considered a bishops/pastors or leaders: in the eyes of the Lord Jesus Christ. For this is what Jesus had to say, as in [Mt. 25:29], **"For unto every one that hath** (for from a child, of growing up; has the ability to acquire more, if they are willing to search for it: and so when, Jesus gives us more then what we had already acquired originally) **shall be given, and he** (or she) **shall have abundance** (even more:) **but from him** (or her) **that hath not** (of not desiring in times past, then why would Jesus expect us to hold on too and of wanting; of what he wants to give us now) **shall be taken away even that which he** (or she) **hath** (and give it to someone else.)**"**

And as to the role of a leader of the flock; which is, the position to ministates, of its position of authorities: when it comes to direct the activities, for most bishops/pastors thinks that they are the only one; that has and are of the very importance, to its calling. For if the bishops/ pastors, do not really believe in the Scriptures and allow the apostles, the prophets, the evangelists, the teachers; to have their input, as to seeing the maturity of establishing a power movement of the Holy Spirit: then that Church Body, will never be able to fulfill its full callings; of which, the Lord Jesus Christ had placed on that Congregation. And then, Jesus will send the Holy Spirit to another Congregation; for the Anointing will only come when there is a fulfillment of Jesus' calling: which is, the perfecting of the saints, as to their hearts desire; of bringing Jesus' atmosphere of His Presence of the Holy Spirit, from Heaven to the earth. For this is what Jesus had to say, as in [Mt. 25:35], **"For I** (Jesus) **was an hungered, and ye gave me meat: I** (Jesus) **was thirsty, and ye gave me drink: I** (Jesus) **was a stranger, and ye took me in** (as of Jesus' reply as in [Mt. 25:40], "And the King (Jesus) shall answer and say unto them (including the "five-fold" ministers,) verily I (Jesus) say unto you, inasmuch as ye have done it unto one of the least of these my brethren (or sisters,) ye have done it unto me (Jesus.)"

The Message of Jesus to the Church of the Lord Jesus Christ! * * *
THE EFFECT WILL HAPPEN, AS TO THE FIVE-FOLD MINISTRIES

Subject #Eight:

And so, the **five-fold ministries**, of the original mandate of the apostles; of which, Jesus placed into the hearts, and minds of the ones: that were there preaching and establishing Churches all over the Continent of Asia and Europe; especially Paul, for the Scripture is very clear as to Jesus' intention as in [I Cor. 12:4], "Now there are diversities of gifts, but the same (Holy) Spirit (for each of the "nine-gifts," are intertwined and to interact within the Body of Christ; at the time of them assembling together: as they were Worshipping, as of ministering by having a one-on-one interaction; among the members of the Congregation. For as of the preaching and/ or the teaching is scheduled of its happenings; it would be holding by embracing, as one or more of the "nine-gifts" will be functioning by the proportion to what the needs are. For as the Holy Spirit is invited in the midst of the assembly; to bring that full connection, to its completion as to the effect of seeing the "nine-gifts:" of fulfilling the needs of the believers.)" For this is what Jesus had to say, as in [Mt. 25:42], "**For I** (Jesus) **was an hungered** (of food or of a Spiritual satisfaction,) **and ye gave me** (Jesus) **no meat** (no substance of value:) **I** (Jesus) **was thirsty** (of water or of a Spiritual Anointing,) **and ye gave me** (Jesus) **no drink** (no substance of value.)**"**

And then, Paul also said as in [I Cor. 12:5], "And there are differences of administrations, but the same Lord (and as to the "five-fold" ministries are in the process, of administrating its position; of authority by the Holy Spirit, Jesus will set in order as to the apostles and of the other "four-fold" ministries positions: of whoever is monitoring the order of the service. And as to the Presence of the Lord Jesus Christ, He will bring to Light; of what our Father in Heaven is saying, through the messenger: that will of also edify the Body of Believers, which are assembled together in the Church. For Jesus will definitely have the Anointed ones; to speak, by proclaiming the Holy Spirit's demonstration of healing and bringing that wholeness: of that "Born-Again" experience, form into their inner being.)" For this is what Jesus had to say, as in [Mt. 26:11], **"For ye have the poor** (of needing food or of a Spiritual satisfaction and/or of needing water or of a Spiritual Anointing) **always with you; but me** (Jesus) **ye have not always** (in the fleshly appearances.)**"**

And then, Paul also said as in [I Cor. 12:6], "And there are diversities of operations, but it is the same God which worketh all in all (for as Jesus is in the midst of its beginning; as the apostles are in the process, of allowing the diversities of operations: which is of speaking out with power, by calling one or more of the "nine-gifts" to be performed by the Holy Spirit. And also, of allowing one or more of the "nine-gifts" to be able to function properly; as Jesus confronts those in the audiences: of fulfilling, of the needs that are confronting them. For it could as the Holy Spirit moves, be the gift of healing or of wisdom; and there, of acquiring wealth or a transforming in a business transaction: or of other incidences that needed attention. And possibly the prophet or the prophetess, or one of the other anointed "four-fold" ministries; as a presentation, of presenting before the Congregation: of someone facing healing, or as of the gift, to edifying the Body of Christ. And/or of the Holy Spirit revealing; of someone, being faced with a warning: that has to do with, being spoken disciplining words of caution; as the Holy Spirit brings conviction, to those that need to repent.)" For this is what Jesus had to say, as in [Mt. 26:12], **For in that she hath poured this Ointment** (which was a ministry; but yet, it symbolized what Jesus was about to face: the Anointing, as the Holy Spirit walked it through with Jesus; to His burial and His Resurrection) on my (Jesus') **Body, she did it for my** (Jesus') **burial** (the Holy Spirit's Anointing, that raised Jesus from the grave.)"

And then, Paul also said as in part of [I Cor. 12:3], "And that no man (or woman) can say that Jesus is the Lord, but by the Holy Ghost (the Holy Spirit, and as of them truly being "Born-Again;" as of the God's Anointed apostles, that should and are being in charge, of every established Church assembly, throughout the world. For as of the apostle's, the Holy Spirit's Anointing will confront the gates of Hell; the Revival will begin, as the prophets or prophetesses are permitted to speak: of what is on the Father in Heaven's heart. For Jesus will bring and allow those words, from the prophet's or prophetess' sounding the utterances; to proclaim liberty, to all that are willing to hear and of the dire warning to those that refuse to accept the Gospel message: of which possibly, will be coming by the words in the language of tongues first and then also in the interpretation of tongues or by prophesying.)" For as the assembly are searching, many and/or most bishops/pastors are so busy; with the businesses' affairs, that they ignored the sheep's urning for comfort: of which, the Holy Spirit is the only one that can bring the words of comforts and solutions. For this is what Jesus had to say, as in [Mt. 26:28], **"For this is my** (Jesus') **Blood of the New Testament** (the New Covenant, as Jesus brought the solution; by dying and being Risen, for Jesus is bringing the Anointed power: to the Church's, so the "five-fold" ministries can fulfill their calling,) **which is shed for many for the remission of sins** (by bringing hope, as all of us were sinners once.)"

For as of an evangelist, they are spreading the Gospel through-out their territories; as one of the "five-fold" ministries, especially with the bishops/pastors: of which, will be by and near as the keeper of the sheep; that is, of the new converts as the Holy Spirit desires, as for each of them to be found. And as the bishops/pastors, do take their rightful place of protecting and leading; them into the path of Righteousness. For Jesus' sheep needs the bishops/pastors; to keep their eyes, permanently on the sheep: so that, they will find Jesus' pasture; which is, toward a safe environment, for Jesus' pasture is the environment of that Godly lifestyle. And as Jesus sends the teachers out; to teach, which is by showing them the way: of having a flock of believers. For they will not stray from the pasture; that the bishops/pastors, of originally placed them: of which is, of them knowing the borders of their save haven; which is, the Anointed Doctrine of the Lord Jesus Christ. For they will not wander away, for they already are and will be fed with the truly pure and true Word of God; and of which, them being in the narrow path, that will bring them into the promised land: and that is, the territory of being the word; Him being Jesus as the life giver, of eternal life with the Father in Heaven. For this is what Jesus had to say, as in [Lk. 6:32,34-35], **"For if ye love them which love you, what thank have ye? For sinners also love those that love them. And if ye lend to them of whom ye hope to receive, what thank have ye? For sinners also lend to sinners, to receive as much again. But love ye your enemies, and do good, and lend, hoping for nothing again; and your reward shall be great, and ye shall be the Children of the Highest: for he** (or she) **is kind unto the unthankful and to the evil** (for we all will find, our point of connection; with common sense.)"

The Message of Jesus to the Church of the Lord Jesus Christ! * * *
THE REHABILITATION OF THE HOMELESSNESS' LIFESTYLE

Subject #Nine:

For as to **"rehabilitate the homeless,"** is by being expressed as to a person that is being restored; of which, is an in-stabled person, and as to the definition: of which is, as of having the lack of the will to be able to determine, as to the processing of how to begin. And Jesus is not pleased, as to the way we are trying to alleviate the crisis; for as to what is happening, that many are being placed in a small box sized shed: of which, will just remove them from the public view; as though, they do not really exist. For Jesus wants, every minister through-out the lost world; to always, of to reevaluate their mental, and of their psychological abilities: and also, to face the world crisis, as to the "five-fold" ministries and the "nine-gifts;" as to restoring and placing into the Holy Spirit's perspectives, with the principles that are laid out in the Scriptures.

For Jesus wants us to "rehabilitate" them, and the first is the process of having and allowing the Holy Spirit; to heal and restore them, of which has been an issue with the Israelites: even before the birth of Christ as in [II Chr. 7:14], "**If my** (Jesus') **people** (that call themselves believers,) **which are called by my** (Jesus') **name** (that actually prays to Jesus,) **shall humble themselves** (and there repenting, of those that are accepting the sinful lifestyle of those that live around them and us; including our families and friends, that are living a sinful lifestyle: without of showing any regret, or expression of concern and even any remorse,) **and pray** (to form words, as of expressions to communicate,) **and seek my** (Jesus') **face** (the true prayer of repentance, within the Church and within the "homeless;" that are in or near the Church and are on the city streets,) **and turn from their wicked ways** (which might only happen, when the Church is involved in a "rehabilitation" program; so the Lord Jesus Christ, by the Holy Spirit can heal them;) **then will I** (Jesus with the Father, will there) **hear from Heaven, and will forgive** (by all, the Congregations and including the leaders of the Churches, and including the "homeless," of) **their sin, and** (then, the Father, the Son named Jesus, and the Holy Spirit) **will heal** (by establishing with the "five-fold" ministries a Godly principles and prescription of remedies to) **their land."**

For most of the Christians, must first realize that the issues of the "homeless;" did not, just happened over-night, this is formed by the constant rejection of God's Grace: which is, of denying, that Jesus brought the solution to all our dilemmas. And as being them and us sinners, and there Jesus laid down His life to Redeem them and us; therefore now, we are considered being Christians in the Father of Heaven's eyes: and as of re-establishing themselves and us, into a normal lifestyle; as of what, needs and should be happening, with the "homeless" all over the lost world. But yet, the apostle Paul's firm reminder the Church as in [Gal. 2:10], "<u>Only they</u> (of other Churches, that Paul was there preaching at) <u>would that we should remember the poor</u> (of which, possibly do include some or many "homeless;") <u>the same which I</u> (Paul) <u>also was forward</u> (intended) <u>to do."</u>

And of which constitutes, as to the meaning and/or definition of the word "homeless;" of being spiritually, physically, mentally, and emotionally dysfunctional: in dealings, with the thoughts of being themselves the victim; of their own demise, of which is setting the goal toward a solution, of what they are facing and then by rerouting their behavior. For as to the Church's long-range goals, Jesus wants to establish a solid Godly program; that will, totally rearrange of their wandering and/or on a destructive path: that they are, themselves possibly unintentionally inherited. And there focusing themselves on, to another mental thought as to the "homeless;" of which is, to place a Spiritual application, as to the "nine-gifts," of having each of them being restored: by the Holy Spirit's healing process, and of the "fine-fold" ministries there of reexamining themselves: into a major shift of priorities, and there of effecting the future outcome of the "homeless."

So, as we examine, of what the nations of the world; are facing, as to the situation of the "homeless," for by the way it is being dealt with: as of today, it will only increase in numeral size, the amount of "homeless" and not the reduction in numbers. For as to the way it is being handled, this is not a cure, but an extension; of placing a bandage over their wound. And that was caused, by the huge governmental disabilities' funds; as to correct, the lack of funds to feed all the poor: but yet, they ignored the fundamental required efforts to stabilize, the economic issues that all countries are facing. And as of having a goal, the establishing of the efforts, by each Church Ministry; by and through their own ignorance, as of why's and how's, did this all began: of the void, to establishing a system, by looking and finding a solution; that created this giant gap in the social and business structure in the first place?

For the apostle Paul, was travelling all over the known world; for his objective, was to preach the Gospel: though, in his time period he was dealing with many; that had just left an ungodly lifestyle and became a believer. But yet, Paul's objective was to please Jesus as to their good works; and before Jesus, He does want us to do and occupy until He return's as in [Heb. 13:20-21], **"Now the God** (the Father) **of peace, that brought again from the dead our Lord Jesus, that great Shepherd of the sheep** (the saints,) **through the Blood of the everlasting Covenant, make you perfect in every good work** (as of almost every religious leaders, that really do include the "five-fold" ministries; of which, will be affecting the community that they live in) **to do His** (Jesus') **will, working** (as we allow the Holy Spirit, being) **in you** (and us) **that which is well-pleasing in His** (Jesus') **sight, through Jesus Christ; to whom be glory for ever and ever. Amen."**

For most nations of the world must, by allowing the organizing structure, as an organized "homeless" shelter to exist; but yet, it is not the final solution: of which, do have some that are functional as of today; being again, by financial grants and/or a non-profit financial venture; of which, such as the ones that are affiliated with Churches, all over the world. And again, it must have the manifestation, of being the Holy Spirit's remedy as of the driving force; of which, does affect as it constitutes of the "homeless" of being healed spiritually, physically, mentally, and emotionally of their dysfunctional acts: in dealings, with the thoughts of them being themselves the victim of their actions; for otherwise, it will just being a temporary band-aid. And as of what the apostle James wrote, of the ones that were facing the issues of needing help as in [Jas. 5:16], "Confess your faults one to another (to those people, that are involved in ministries,) and pray one for another (not just once, but many times,) that ye may be healed. The effectual fervent prayer of a Righteous man (or woman) availeth (will profit and benefit's) much." For of many of them need a complete miraculous healing, of each "homeless" person and of the restructuring; of their lifestyle, will come as a miracle from the Lord Jesus Christ: and not, from any secular or Church's organized programs; unless, with Jesus being in the center of its activities.

So again, as we approach this monstruous ventures, of tackling these issues as to the "homeless;" with the recourses that they have, for when it comes to them receiving donations and/or grants from outside of their own recourses: for the (30) "thirty percent" of the finances should automatically go to the funds, which is needed to completely "rehabilitate" the "homeless." For it is a crisis, but by having the "five-fold" ministries involved; of which is, through the structural counseling process: and also, of having the "nine-gifts" in operation, of being demonstrated by the power of the Holy Spirit; many lives, will be transformed by alternative's path and healings, as they themselves willingly accept a change in their priorities. And not, to supply the unending process of feeding the "homeless," for the time will come soon, of being in the process of multiplication; of which is, of being into the evolution of increasing the population of the "homeless." For which will, overwhelmingly be much larger; then now, when the whole nation will be completely depending on someone else's food: of most and/or everyone will be "homeless."

And again, as we approach this monstruous ventures; this will only, truly being accomplished when all the Churches: will adopt the principles, that are in the written Scriptures of the Bible. For it includes all and again all the remedies, the first being the "five-fold" Spiritual Ministries; as of an apostle, a prophet, an evangelist, a bishop/pastor, and a teacher: for the Scriptures, consider the "five-fold" ministries of being the complete "five-gifts" to the Church as in [I Cor. 12:27-30], **"Now ye are the Body of Christ, and members in particular. And God** (including the Father) **hath set some** (saints) **in the Church, first** (of having the gifts of an Anointed) **"apostles"** (and not the gifts of the bishops/pastors, as it is of being handled today,) **secondarily** (the gifts of the Anointed) **"prophets,"** (the gifts of an evangelists is never mentioned) **thirdly** (the gifts of the Anointed) **"teachers"** (for pastors, were established later; as the Shepherd to Jesus' flock,) **after that** (gifts of) **miracles, then gifts of healing,** (gifts of) **helps,** (gifts of) **governments,** (the gifts of) **diversities of tongues. Are all** (as an individual, having the gifts of an) **apostles? Are all** (as an individual, having the gifts of the) **prophets? Are all** (as an individual, having the gifts of the Anointed) **teachers? Have all** (as an individual) **the gifts of healing? Do all** (as an individual) **speak with** (the gifts of) **tongues? Do all** (as an individual, having the gifts to) **interpret?**

For the apostle Paul, realized that by working; in the ministry, it was all about the plan of salvation: as Paul seeing many coming, by accepting Jesus and being "Born-Again." For it was the love of Jesus, that of Him portraying; as He literally died for humanity, so Paul was telling the Churches: as for Paul, he went through great and many sufferings, of what really was important; of which, was the reason of the ministries to only succeed as in [I Cor. 12:31, 13:1], **"But covet** (desires) **earnestly the best gifts: and yet shew I** (the apostle Paul) **unto you a more excellent way. And though I** (Paul, a very active apostle) **have the gifts of prophecy, and understand all mysteries, and all knowledge; and though I** (Paul) **have all Faith, so that I** (Paul) **could remove mountains, and have not charity** (of expressing a compassionate love for the Church Body,) **I** (Paul) **am nothing** (a zero in value.)" For the Holy Spirit will only begin to accomplish His goals, as we allow Him to participate; only with the "five-fold" ministries in their rightful position: for Jesus, will come in the power of the Holy Spirit with signs and wonders to perform. And there, to correct and to heal our and all the nations; of being, in each of the solid

Church's organized Righteous establishments, as the "five-fold" ministries are functioning.

For then also, of having the "nine-gifts" fully in operation; by the Holy Spirit, which is the gifts of wisdom, knowledge, faith, healing, working of miracles, prophecy, discerning of spirits, the divers kind of tongues, the interpretation of tongues: and for that to happen, all the ministers of the true Gospel must be equipped; to be able, to introduce the message of salvation to each "homeless" person. And for all that to happen, the "five-fold" ministers, as Paul mentioned; they must be Anointed by the Holy Spirit: to be equipped and to be established, and also being actively involved as in [Rom. 1:11], "For I (Paul) long to see you, that I (Paul) may impart unto you some Spiritual gift (one or all the "nine-gifts,") to the end ye (the Church's ministries) may be established." And so, each "gift" or all "gifts" will bring restoration to many, hopefully to all "homeless" persons; by having, the stabilities to function properly: and again, is of which constitutes by addressing them; as of them being dysfunctional spiritually, physically, mentally, and emotionally. For a "homeless" as of dealing prayerfully with each person's functional duties, of seeing Jesus' healing and restoring them of their abnormalities. And again, as each person have and can function with the proper will, of accepting their own responsibility; that is, of having the required latitudes, for all or most of the "homeless:" do have a will of being free, so they can live healthy, and there being secure economically as to their own lifestyle.

And as to the organized Church's functional standards; that are established, the "first" is to form a committee: and there, appoint a

three or more "Born-Again" board members, with the apostle in charge; remember that bishops/pastors are to be only a Shepherd (the protector) over the flock. For the name as to the title of the committee, possibly could be called the "Starter;" for they, being the ones that will start each "homeless," on their journey: on a new lifestyle, that could last to the end of their life span. So, as the Church board members picks and confirms; the task, then they will begin by laying down the main guidelines: as of how to begin each "homeless" person's activities and then to its completion.

For each individual member of the "homeless," as they are being interviewed; the "Starter," board members for the "homeless," will have a clear understanding: as to why they are "homeless." As for some, the "first," it will be because they are disabled; the "second," it will be because they are handicapped: the "third," it will be because they are on drugs; and possibly their own mind is partially destroyed, and/or of the "fourth," it will be because each of them, is of needing to be "rehabilitated." For as to the "homeless" issues with each of them, of wanting them to having an alternative; as to having a complete restorations and healings, as to their Spiritual walk of Faith; from their chaotic situation. So, as to the "nine-gifts," of having the Holy Spirit moving in among the "homeless," and as to some of the "nine-gifts:" the three gifts being, as of the "divers kind of tongues," and the "interpretation of tongues," and of prophecy.

For Jesus wants to bring a message, to all of the group assemblies and/or the active Church's ministering Congregation; including the "homeless," of listening and hearing, by them openly acknowledging that Jesus really does care for them: of which, including of bringing strength and fatalities. And as, of the other "six-gifts," as those are just as important; as of the Holy Spirit's message, for Jesus wants the Holy Spirit to be moving in power: as much with the others "gifts" and especially including the "gift of healing."

And as to the "homeless" mind-set, that are not on the focusing process; of which is, the lengthy journey of improving: and again, being the advantage of improving in their living standard. For being lazy is an issue for some and/or many "homeless;" as of what Paul discussed with the Churches as in [II Th. 3:10-11], **"For even when we were with you, this we commanded you, that if any would not "work," neither should they eat. For we hear that there are some which walk among you disorderly, "working" not at all,** (no "working") **but are busy-bodies** (moving about, but not working.)**"**

So, as the "homeless" issues are being reevaluated, the "homeless" program that the "Starter" member board has in place; they can begin, their very long-range plans to bring help to most: that will, accept the board members suggestions. And therefore, in about two or three years or even longer, possibly majorities of them; will be reintroduced, into the public-society and/or into the work-forces: and there, the Churches through-out the world. For they all will definitely benefit, as to the "homeless;" of strengthening their own relationship with the Lord Jesus Christ.

But yet, of which by then of the "homelessness's" new-comers, the predicament as of the way the "homeless" are facing; will be into a different environmental established "homeless" shelter: that in, the matter of a few years, many nations that are facing the issues with the "homeless" will definitely be declining. For by then, it will not be a depressing issue, but will be a blessing; for the out-come, will be a positive-effect on society; as it has already been proven that it is working: by the fruit, which is the evidence of the progresses; that of its effect on each community through-out the world. For if the Churches are not being involved, in the "rehabilitation" process; the commandments of the Scriptures will have very little effect on our society as in [I Ti. 5:12-13], "Having damnation (sin deserving of punishment,) because they have cast off their first Faith (of just believing, that Jesus is their Savior.) and withal they learn to be idle, wandering (as the 'homeless' do) about from house to house; and not only idle, but tattlers also and busybodies, speaking things which they ought not."

And so, as we conclude these issues of the "homeless," Jesus is the one that has brought stabilities to us; for as of Jesus' beginning, in His three years of ministering: and of Jesus revealing to Israel, that He is the "I Am;" as He read in the Synagogue, the Scripture from the old Scroll of Isaiah as in [Lk. 4:18], "The Spirit of the Lord (the Father) is upon me, because He (the Father) hath Anointed me to preach the Gospel to the poor (in spirit;) He (the Father) hath sent me to heal the brokenhearted (and as of their very disappointing past life,) to preach deliverance to the captives (including the "homeless,") and recovering of sight (possibly, including the backsliders) to the blind, to set at liberty them that are bruise (of which constitutes of them living and being of spiritually, physically, mentally, and emotionally dysfunctional.)" For the Temple rulers were not happy as of what He said as in [Jn. 8:58], "Jesus said unto them, verily, verily, I say unto you, before Abraham was, I Am." And also, later as in [Jn. 10:30], "I (Jesus) and my Father are one." For at times, the Jews were in the process of casting Him over a cliff; and/or of wanting to stone Him, for as by killing Him. Let us remember what Jesus said, because of the Temple rulers; for He truly, understood what it was like to be a "homeless" person: as He was walking on the earth, in His physical body as they were trying to kill Him as in [Mt. 8:20], "And Jesus saith unto him (a Scribe or the religious rulers,) the foxes have holes,

and the birds of the air have nests; but the Son (named Jesus) **of man hath not where** (possibly because, Jesus knew that the religious leaders; were looking for Him, to kill Him) **to lay His** (Jesus') head."

For Jesus is saying to His Church Body, throughout the world; of being in oneness with the Holy Spirit, the "first" we must do as of what David did: of protecting each of the sheep from the lions and the bears. And of the pastors, that have lost their first love for the flock of Jesus' pasture; of being distracted, for because of the leaders ignoring of their role: the apostles need to replace the pastor. For this must begin, with someone that will care for the sheep; for as of Satan, he is now scattering the flock in my (Jesus') pasture through-out the whole wide world. We must pray, the "five-fold" Ministries will complete the task; of spreading Jesus' Message of the Gospel.

CHAPTER SIX
THE SEVENTH CHURCH NAMED LAODICEA

The Message of Jesus to the Church of the Lord Jesus Christ! * * *
THE MOMENT THE CHURCH OF JESUS CHRIST, WAS BEING
BORN

Subject #One:

As of "**book number [01 – 27] being Matthew – Revelation**," it is all about what God is saying and that is (**He** (Jesus) **has set in motion, by establishing the Truthful Church of the Lord Jesus Christ.**)

For this was the apostle John's territories of Asia, as to the "Seven Churches;" that he wrote about, being on the Island of Patmos: in the Mediterranean Sea: which is, very close to where the Churches are located then, of now being called the Nation of Turkey. And as to the "Seven Churches" that were active; and listed in the Book of Revelation, they are all located on the eastern end of the Nation of Turkey as of today: of which is by the Mediterranean Sea, near where the Island of Patmos is.

For Jesus is there, walking among all the different Churches of Asia, and Europe, and possibly part of Africa; of which, eventually included all the believers; of those living in Rome, and its surrounding areas. For Paul was the one Jesus choose, to spread the Gospel; so, all can hear as the time eventually came: when the entire Roman empire completely destroyed Solomon's Temple and some of the Walls in Jerusalem. And there and then, the Jews of Israel were forced to leave; of the complete surrounding of all the Roman ruled territories, that surrounded all of Jerusalem and its territories. And as of the Romans, which eventually began to round up all the apostle; and had them killed, the apostle John was sent to the Island of Patmos before they killed him: of which he had the time to finish of writing the "seven letters;" to the Churches in Asia. And the "first" being unto Ephesus the Loveless Church, and the "second" being unto Smyrna the Faithful Struggling Church, and the "third" being unto Pergamos the Compromising Church, and the "fourth" being unto Thyatira the Corrupt Church, and the "fifth" being unto Sardis the Dead Church, and the "sixth" being unto Philadelphia the Faithful Enduring Church, and as of the "seventh" being unto Laodicea the Lukewarm Church. For each of the "Seven Churches," of which has a percentage of (14.3 %;) "fourteen-point three percent" affect world-wide: and again, of symbolizing being of their influence of then on the Church's behavior. And of which it is affecting the Churches, until the time, approximately (2,000) "two thousand years" later; being of our present time period, and as of the whole world.

For the Church of the Lord Jesus Christ; was born, as the twelve disciples assembled together with and by Jesus Himself: as they had finished their evening supper meal. And on the beginning, of the "Feast of Passover;" of when Jesus grabbed a basin, which is a pan and filled it with water: which was, the time of the Church being born as in [Jn. 13:4-5,10-11], **"He** (Jesus) **riseth from supper, and laid aside His garments, and took a towel, and girded Himself. After that He** (Jesus) **poureth water into a basin, and began to wash the disciples' feet, and to wipe them with the towel wherewith He** (Jesus) was girded. **Jesus saith to him** (Peter, as the others heard Him,) **he** (he himself and the other eleven) **that is washed needeth not save to wash his** (the other eleven's) feet (again,) **but is clean, but not all. For He** (Jesus) **knew who should betray Him** (Jesus;) **therefore said He** (Jesus,) **ye are not all** (but Judas, of not being) **clean** (yet Judas, did hear what Jesus had said; about him, but he did not repent.)**"**

For after His Resurrection, as Jesus spent many days with His disciples; this is, what He told them before He was ascended into Heaven as in [Acts

1:4-5], "And (Jesus,) <u>being</u> <u>assembled</u> <u>together</u> <u>with</u> <u>them</u> (His disciples,) <u>commanded</u> <u>them</u> <u>that</u> <u>they</u> <u>should</u> <u>not</u> <u>depart</u> <u>from</u> <u>Jerusalem</u>, <u>but</u> <u>wait</u> <u>for</u> <u>the</u> <u>Promise</u> <u>of</u> <u>the</u> <u>Father</u> (in Heaven,) <u>which</u>, <u>saith</u> <u>He</u> (Jesus,) <u>ye</u> <u>have</u> <u>heard</u> <u>of</u> <u>me</u>. <u>For</u> <u>John</u> <u>truly</u> <u>Baptized</u> <u>with</u> <u>water</u>; <u>but</u> <u>ye</u> <u>shall</u> <u>be</u> <u>Baptized</u> <u>with</u> <u>the</u> <u>Holy</u> <u>Ghost</u> (Spirit) <u>not</u> <u>many</u> <u>days</u> <u>hence</u> (which was, of what happened; on the day of the "Feast of Pentecost.)"

The Message of Jesus to the Church of the Lord Jesus Christ! * * *
THE LETTER TO THE CHURCH #SEVEN, NAMED LAODICEA

Subject #Two:

And as to the apostle's seven Churches, of the time when they were established; the different apostles sent letters out, which were possibly distributed: to all the Churches in Asia. For they heard themselves, by their own bishops/pastors, or probably they read on the Scrolls that were distributed through-out the Roman Empire. And as John wrote the Anointed letters to the Seven Churches, for most later including the leaderships; were completely ignoring what was read and/or of what were written out or told them: by the Scriptures and therefore, they were facing the consequences of their actions; which also, of including the bishops/pastors.

And as of what Jesus said as in [Mt. 16:18], **"And I** (Jesus) **say unto thee, that thou art Peter** (an apostle, of an immortal spirit, which being indestructible; that has been "Born-Again,") **and upon this rock** (being Peter) **I** (Jesus) **will build my Church** (the Church, of the Lord Jesus Christ; being believers, the saints;) **and the gates of Hell shall not prevail against it** (the Church, being believers.)"

For the Congregations, heard the Gospel message; through-out the Roman Empire, after Christ's death and Resurrection: and now, as of sometime later: most lost their focusses as in [I Jn. 2:15-17], "<u>Love</u> <u>not</u> <u>the</u> <u>world</u>, <u>neither</u> <u>the</u> <u>things</u> (of ungodly) <u>that</u> <u>are</u> <u>in</u> <u>the</u> <u>world</u>. <u>If</u> <u>any</u> <u>man</u> (or woman) <u>love</u> <u>the</u> <u>world</u> (of ungodly,) <u>the</u> <u>love</u> <u>of</u> <u>the</u> <u>Father</u> (including Jesus) <u>is</u> <u>not</u> <u>in</u> <u>him</u> (or her.) <u>For</u> <u>all</u> <u>that</u> <u>is</u> <u>in</u> <u>the</u> <u>world</u> (of ungodly,) <u>the</u> <u>lust</u> <u>of</u> <u>the</u> <u>flesh</u>, <u>and</u> <u>the</u> <u>lust</u> <u>of</u> <u>the</u> <u>eyes</u>, <u>and</u> <u>the</u> <u>pride</u> <u>of</u> <u>life</u>, <u>is</u> <u>not</u> <u>of</u> <u>the</u> <u>Father</u>, <u>but</u> <u>is</u> <u>of</u> <u>the</u> <u>world</u> (of ungodly.) <u>And</u> <u>the</u> <u>world</u> <u>passeth</u> <u>away</u>, <u>and</u>

the lust thereof: but he (or she) that doeth the will of God (the Father, the Son named Jesus, and including the guiding help of the Holy Spirit; as being of the triune God) abideth for ever."

And as of Church number (#07,) being the ones that assembled in Laodiceans, being described as the lukewarm Church as in [Rev. 3:14-22], **"And unto the Angel** (that brought the message, with the approval of the Father; by the Holy Spirit from Heaven) **of the Church of the Laodiceans** (for John to) **write; these things saith the Amen** (Jesus, that is approved by the Father in Heaven; so be it,) **the faithful** (Jesus being their only Way, the Truth, the Life and the only hope of eternal life; for with Jesus, the solution as to our sins was for Him to die: being the Sacrificial Offering, and now we have a mediator as in [I Jn. 1:8-10], "If we say that we have no sin, we deceiveth ourselves, and the (Savior called Jesus Christ, being the) Truth is not in us. If we confess our sins, He (the Lord Jesus) is faithful and just to forgive us our sins, and to cleanse us from all unrighteousness. If we say that we have not sinned, we make Him (Jesus) a liar, and the Word (being Jesus) is not in us." **And true witness** (of literally, being in the middle of all the activities; from,) **the beginning of the creation** (of being Heaven; where God is, the Heaven's: of which is, the firmaments and/or outer spaces; and the earth) **of God; I** (Jesus) **know thy works** (the efforts, of engaging with the Scriptural Doctrine,) **that thou art neither cold or hot: I** (Jesus) **would thou wert cold or hot. So then because thou art lukewarm, and neither cold nor hot, I** (Jesus) **will spue** (vomit) **thee out of my mouth** (for this is how Jesus' expression of Himself was; as He addressed, the Scribes and the Pharisees as hypocrites as in part of [Mt. 23:1-3,13-15], "Then spake Jesus to the multitude, and to His (Jesus') disciples, saying, the Scribes and the Pharisees sit in Moses' seat (being the role of pastors; as of the Scribes, they are the main interpreters of the Law of Moses, the Commandments that is: for the Israelite people;) all therefore (as Jesus explained) whatsoever they bid you observe, that observe and do (as to the law of Moses, being the correct interpretation of the Scriptures;) but do not ye after their works (which is by their behavior:) for they say, and do not (for they, themselves do not practice of what they all preach; as many of the modern preachers of present.) But woe unto you, Scribes and Pharisees, hypocrites! For you shut up the Kingdom of Heaven against men (and of the women, by a socialistic Gospel; for their own financial gain:) for you neither go in yourselves (as to the true message, of the Gospel of Christ Jesus) <u>neither</u> <u>suffer</u> <u>ye</u> <u>them</u> <u>who</u> <u>are</u> <u>entering</u> (of them accepting Jesus) <u>to go in.</u> <u>Woe</u> <u>unto</u> <u>you,</u> <u>Scribes</u> <u>and</u> <u>Pharisees,</u> <u>hypocrites!</u> <u>For</u> <u>you</u> <u>compass</u> (travelling the) <u>sea</u> <u>and</u> <u>land</u> <u>to</u> <u>make</u> <u>one</u> <u>proselyte</u> (convert,) <u>and</u> <u>when</u> <u>he</u> (or she) <u>is</u> <u>made</u> (converted,) <u>you</u> <u>make</u> <u>him</u> (or her) <u>twofold</u> (two times) <u>more</u> <u>the</u> <u>child</u> <u>of</u> <u>Hell</u> (of believing the doctrines of Demons in Hell, that they had just taught them) <u>than</u> <u>yourselves.</u>) **Because thou sayest, I** (he or she) **am rich** (of having money saved up, and/or knows everything about God; of not having Jesus, by being filled with the Holy Spirit in the Church's Congregation's heart,) **and increased with goods** (as of thinking, having everything they need,) **and have need of nothing** (as the shelves are full:) **and knowest not that thou art wretched** (of spiritually facing bankruptcy and/or degradation,) **and miserable** (of great discomfort,) **and poor** (the state of being very poor, or possibly has a dual consequences; of not having, any spiritual depth as to a Spiritual experience: with Jesus Christ and/or of having very little food, no clothing, and no adequate housing,) **and blind** (of literally not being able to see and/or possibly have a dual consequences; which is, as of not having, of any spiritual depth as to a Spiritual experience of with Jesus and/or the lacking discernment: being unable or unwilling to understand or judge,) **and naked** (of not having any clothing, or possibly has a dual consequences; of not having, any spiritual depth as to a Spiritual experience: with Jesus, and/or of not having any wisdom or knowledge as to confirm or support of any Godly actions:) I (Jesus) **counsel thee to buy of me** (Jesus) **gold** (the precious image of Jesus) **tried in the fire** (is a chosen symbol, of the Holiness of the triune God,) **that thou mayest be rich** (of having Jesus in the Congregation's heart;) **and white raiment** (of having no trace of unfaithfulness,) **that thou mayest be clothed** (with praise and thanksgiving, toward Jesus our God,) **and that the shame of thy nakedness** (of not having, and/or of any spiritual depth as to a Spiritual experience; with Jesus, and/or of not having any wisdom or knowledge as to confirm or support of any as to our Godly actions) **do not appear** (by being forgiven, through repentance;) **and Anoint** (by the Holy Spirit) **thine eyes with eye-salve** (the Anointing Oil, being the Holy Spirit,) **that thou mayest see** (the consequences of our actions.) **As many as I** (Jesus) **love, I** (Jesus) **rebuke** (convict and convince) **and chasten** (to purify and/or refine, by freeing from faults:) **be zealous** (enthusiastic) **therefore, and repent** (by returning, to the True Biblical Doctrine; and as of what happened to the Israelites, at the time of facing the Babylonian Empire: when they did not repent as in part of [Jer. 32:30,32-33], "For the Children of Israel and the Children of Judah have only done evil before me (Jesus) from their youth (one is of worshiping idols.) And including) they, their Kings, their Princes, their Priests, and their (of the false) prophets. And they (many of the population) have turned unto me (Jeremiah) the back (by refusing to hear,) and not the face (by refusing to see, of acknowledging that they heard:) though I (Jeremiah the prophet) taught them, rising up early and teaching them, yet they (as of many of the population) have not hearkened to receive instruction." And also, of them not thinking of repenting; at the time of Jesus' appearance, as He was walking among them: as He was speaking of the judgement that was coming as in [Mt. 24:1-2], "And Jesus went out, and departed from the Temple: and His (Jesus') disciples came (being near) to Him for to shew Him the buildings of the Temple. And Jesus said unto them, see ye not all these things? Verily I (Jesus) say unto you, there shall not be left here one stone upon another, that shall not be thrown down (which happened later by the Romans, of Jesus being rejected, of judgement facing by Israel.) **Behold, I** (Jesus) **stand at the door** (of our heart,) **and knock** (to get our attention:) **if any man** (or woman) **hear my** (Jesus') **voice, and open the door** (as of our heart,) **I** (Jesus) **will come in to him** (or her,) **and will sup** (by allowing the Holy Spirit, to transform our spirit; through the "Born-Again" experience, which will renew our mind as in [Jn. 3:5-6], "Jesus answered, verily, verily, I (Jesus) say unto thee, except a man (or woman) be born of water (first being a natural birth) and of the spirit (by the Holy Spirit, second being a Spiritual Birth) he (or she) cannot enter into the Kingdom of God. That which is born of the flesh is flesh (the natural birth, by the mother;) and that which is Born of Spirit (the Supernatural Birth, by the Holy Spirit) is Spirit (of being the power of the Supernatural Birth, through the human spirit.) Marvel not that I (Jesus) said unto thee, ye must be Born-Again." **with him** (or her,) **and he** (or she) **with me** (Jesus.) To him (or her) **that overcometh** (that has accepted and being a participant of the Gospel of Jesus; of being "Born-Again") **will I** (Jesus) grant (you) **to sit with me** (Jesus) in my (Jesus') **Throne** (of Jesus being the Sovereign Power.) **He** (or she) **that hath an ear, let him** (or her) **hear what the** (Holy) **Spirit saith unto the Churches."**

So, as we review the many Scriptures as to the seven Churches; Jesus is not pleased with the other five Churches, for the two Churches represents the percentage of (28.6%,) "twenty-eight-point six percent:" of the Churches, in the whole wide world as to their conduct of being pleasing to Jesus. For as to the other Five Church's establishments, which represents the (71.5%,) "seventy-one-point five percent;" of the world, that were not pleasing to Jesus: will be the ones, that will allow sinful acts to be openly displayed with very little disapproval; as of what is happening today.

And as of what Jesus is saying, by revealing to John the apostle; as to the Churches of today, that are similar to the "seventh" Church of Laodicea: which is, to the bishops/pastors and possibly also of today, as to the assistant bishops/pastors. For as of observing, of possibly then they were also called elders and deacons; and the other "four-fold" ministries, as of being a "lukewarm" Congregation: of facing "indifferences," of what Paul was also facing as in [I Pet. 4:4-10], **"Wherein they think it strange that ye (saints) run not with them to the same excess of riot** (wild and loose festivity and/or disorderly behavior,) **speaking evil of you** (the saints:) **who shall give account to Him** (referring to Jesus) **that is ready to judge the quick and the dead. For this cause was the Gospel preached also to them that are dead** (as Jesus did, on His way to the Father in Heaven,) that they might be judged according to men (or women) **in the flesh, but live according to God in the Spirit** (of the heart.) **But the end of all things is at hand: be ye therefore sober, and watch** (for Jesus will appear soon) **unto prayer. And above all things have fervent charity** (love) **among yourselves: for charity (of loving) shall cover the multitude of sins. Use hospitality** (caring) **one to another without grudging. As every man** (or woman) **hath received the gift** (one of the "nine gifts," by the Holy Spirit,) **even so minister the same one to another, as good steward of the manifold Grace** (as Jesus brought the solution for us, so bring the solution to others; of revealing, that Jesus is the only Way, the Truth and the Life) **of God."**

And as of what Jesus is saying, by revealing to John; as to the Churches, that are similar to the Church in Laodicea: which is, to the pastors and possibly also to assistant pastors; as of them being a lukewarm Congregation. And as we consider the dilemma; of the Churches, throughout the world that are similar to the one in Laodicea. For Jesus there is saying, for the time has come for Him (Jesus;) to express Himself, to many of the apostles, to many of the prophets, to many of the evangelists, to many of the pastors, and to many of the teachers: that are travelling to many nations. For as of their fancy titles of their sermons, it will not change the landscape of their hearts; for it is only when they will literally stop in their tracks: and confess, that the only way to confront the enemy of their souls; is of them realizing that Jesus is being the only Way as in [I Pet. 4:11-13], "If any man (or any woman) speak, let him (or her audibly) speak as the oracles (as of revealing Jesus' hidden Spiritual knowledge; and then, makes known the Divine purposes) of God; if any man (or woman) minister, let him (or her) do it as of the ability which God giveth: glorified through Jesus Christ, to whom be praise and dominion for ever and ever. Amen. Beloved, think it not strange concerning the fiery trial (of being tried, but by suffering) which is to try you, as though some strange thing happened unto you: but rejoice, in as much as ye are partakers of Christ's sufferings (as in [Acts 26:23], **"That Christ** (Jesus) **should suffer, and that He** (Jesus) **should be the first that should Rise from the dead, and should shew Light** (the Gospel of salvation, of being "Born-Again") **unto the people** (the Jews also,) **and to the Gentiles;)"** that, when His (Jesus') Glory shall be revealed, ye may be glad also with exceeding joy." For many have other ways to approach God; that is, for them to hear a message: which has to do with the only one, that is the helper. And the helper, of being the is the Holy Spirit from God; which will, bring a powerful transformation into multitudes: as they are filled with the Holy Spirit of Pentecost.

For Jesus will guide the pastors and the others; and again, it is when they allow the Holy Spirit to be the double-edged Sword: as how, Jesus sent Him (the Holy Spirit) to those in the upper room. For the Holy Spirit's power did revitalize their concept of who God is. For the triune God is our very living, an active, and a powerful entity, which has the power to move mountains; by changing, the arrangement of their environment of their mind set: as Jesus is then, and now have brought and are bringing multitudes into the Kingdom of the Father as in [I Pet. 4:14-16], "If ye be reproached (rebuked) for the name of Christ (as in [II Ti. 3:12], **"Yea, and all that will live Godly in Christ Jesus shall suffer persecution,)"** happy are ye; for the (Holy) Spirit of glory and of God (the Father) resteth upon you: on their part he (or she) is evil spoken of, but on your part he (or she) is glorified. But let none of you suffer as a murderer, or as a thief, or as an evildoer, or as a busybody in other men's (or women's) matters. Yet if any man (or woman) <u>suffer</u> <u>as</u> <u>a</u> <u>Christian</u>, <u>let</u> <u>him</u> (or her) <u>not</u> <u>be</u> <u>ashamed</u>; <u>but</u> <u>let</u> <u>him</u> (or her) <u>glorify</u> <u>God</u> <u>on</u> <u>this</u> <u>behalf</u> (for judgement will come, to those of whoever harms someone else; in of words or of deeds, unless they repent.)" So, as of the leader's mind set, are reestablished in the right Doctrines of the Scriptures; as of the "five-fold" ministry's rightful activities and also as of the "nine-gifts" of the Holy Spirit: that there will come, of that great powerful awakening; and this must happen soon. For as the dry bones, which is of those dry bones; that symbolizes of being inactive, of the souls of men (and women,) and of the boys (and girls,) which must hear the Truth. For the Truth, will set them free; with the Holy Spirit involved, of which is not the doctrines of the humanities of the world (the ungodly:) that does not, having the approval of the Father, the Son named Jesus, the Spirit, of being the Holy Spirit. For Jesus sent the Holy Spirit to finalize; His (Jesus') position, as the rightful energy that all humanity needs: of the Righteous position, that are required to be in God's Kingdom.

For the issue as with the Church called Laodicea; being really lukewarm, it is just that the Holy Spirit is not being manifested in them: and also, with the pastors and of the others, of that time period; except for Paul and the other apostles. And as to the insight into who God is; Jesus at first, did reveal to them: by the Scriptures, that could and will have affected the regions of their surroundings; which is, also the apparent condition of the world (the ungodly) as of today as in [I Pet. 4:17-19], "<u>For</u> <u>the</u> <u>time</u> <u>is</u> <u>come</u> <u>that</u> <u>judgement</u> (will of pronouncing of a formal opinion and/or decision given and it) <u>must</u> <u>begin</u> <u>at</u> <u>the</u> <u>House</u> <u>of</u> <u>God</u> (in with the Congregation and the pastors, and the other "four-fold" ministries as in [Rom. 11:33], **"Oh the depth of the riches both of the wisdom and knowledge of God** (the Father in Heaven!) **How unsearchable** (be mysterious) **are His** (Jesus') **judgements, and His** (Jesus') **ways past finding out:)"** <u>and</u> <u>if</u> <u>it</u> <u>first</u> <u>begin</u> <u>at</u> <u>us</u>, <u>what</u> <u>shall</u> <u>the</u> <u>end</u> <u>be</u> <u>of</u> <u>them</u> <u>that</u> <u>obey</u> <u>not</u> <u>the</u> <u>Gospel</u> <u>of</u> <u>God</u> (of which, is the Father's Gospel of salvation; of being, "Born-Again" as by being in Jesus' name: by the Holy Spirit?) <u>And</u> <u>if</u> <u>the</u> <u>Righteous</u> <u>scarcely</u> <u>be</u> <u>Saved</u>, <u>where</u> <u>shall</u> <u>the</u> <u>ungodly</u> (the world) <u>and</u> (all the) <u>sinner</u> <u>appear</u>? <u>Wherefore</u> <u>let</u> <u>them</u> <u>that</u> <u>suffer</u> (as in [I Pet. 4:1], **"Forasmuch then as Christ** (Jesus) **hath suffered for us in the flesh, arm yourselves likewise with the same mind: for he** (or she) **that hath suffered** (by denying our desires) **in the flesh hath ceased**

from sin (and again, by denying our desires; but yet, living by the will of Jesus.)" according to the will of God commit the keeping of their souls to Him (Jesus) in well-doing, as unto a faithful creator (to the triune God, of which is the Father, the Son named Jesus, and the Holy Spirit.)" For it is only being the Holy Spirit, of allowing to manifest; as to its true Image of who He is, will we all see the full demonstration: with the "nine gifts," for as the Holy Spirit of Heaven being brought to earth; and us, watching Him actively functioning.

And as of its beginnings, with their prayer language; as they prayed and fasted, for that Heavenly Presence of the triune God: will and did penetrate into their innermost being. And as of what our prayer is also desiring; that will cause, this great Revival of what happened: on the day of the "Feast of Pentecost," which never should have stopped; of which, the prophets of old spoke in their own words as in [Is. 40:28-31], **"Hast thou not known? Hast thou not heard, that the everlasting God, the Lord, the creator of the ends of the earth, fainteth not, neither is weary? There is no searching** (of Him knowing everything, which means, He does not have to do research) **of His** (Jesus') **understanding. He** (Jesus) **giveth power to the faint; and to them that have no might He** (being Jesus) **increaseth strength. Even the youths shall faint and be weary, and the young men** (or women) **shall utterly fall** (be exhausted:) **but they that wait** (by hanging around Jesus, of which is, by all reading and hearing the Scriptures; that is, about and) **upon the Lord** (Jesus) **shall renew their strength; they shall mount up with wings as eagles** (by being in control;) **they shall run** (being busy,) **and not be weary; and they shall walk** (being active,) **and not faint."**

For there are hundreds of millions of people out there; and that I (Jesus) have my eyes on them, so as you and me (being Jesus) are led by my (Jesus') Holy Spirit: there is coming a Revival of the Word of God, so large in magnitude that it will overwhelm most. For the dry bones that Ezekiel prophesied, which is soon about to come to its fulfillment; now all they and you must do, is to trust me (Jesus) by opening your yes, your and their mouth: as listed in some of the "nine-gifts," of interpreting the Anointed tongue language and/or of prophesying. And then, by beginning to speak forth the articles; of what the Holy Spirit is clearly saying to the Church, the true Church of the Lord Jesus Christ: the one that the Father in Heaven has His stamped of approval on.

CHAPTER SEVEN
THE RESURRECTING CHURCH

The Message of Jesus to the Church of the Lord Jesus Christ! * * *
THE RESURRECTION OF JESUS, WAS NOT LEFT IN HELL

Subject #One:

As of "<u>book</u> <u>number</u> [01 – 27] <u>being</u> <u>Matthew</u> – <u>Revelation</u>," it is all about what God is saying and that is (He (Jesus) **has** **set** **in** **motion,** **by** **establishing** **the** **Truthful** **Church** **of** **the** **Lord** **Jesus** **Christ**.)

So, listen America, the world; as of the Alarm, it is sounding, for as we consider Jesus' plan for humanity, of all the nations of the world: of which again, has the same demand from Him (Jesus,) as to our Righteous or unrighteous behavior. So, as our behavior displays the demonstration of ungodliness; as what the Scriptures of the Bible reads: then all must review, the standards that were established by the Holy Spirit; through the writings by the prophets.

For Jesus is concerned as to our wellbeing, for if Jesus considers our life as being displeasing to Him (Jesus;) of which, is of our Spiritual application, and as to our heart's endeavor: to what the Father considers as of Righteousness; then all must repent, as of what was said by Peter as in part of [Acts 2:29-33], **"Men** (and women) **and brethren** (and sisters,) **let me freely speak unto you of the patriarch** (David.) Therefore (David) **being a prophet, and knowing that God had sworn with an oath to him** (David,) **that of the fruit** (of which is, the seed of David's Lineage; being) **of his** (David's) **loins** (the seat of generations,) **according to the flesh, he** (David) **would raise up Christ to sit on his** (David's) **Throne; he** (David) **seeing this before** (hand by Jesus' Revelation) **spake of the Resurrection of Christ, that His** (Jesus') **soul was not left in Hell** (of that constant harassment; as was prophesied by David, as to what Jesus had to face: of His goal to Redeem a sinful humanity as in [Ps. 86:14,139:15,88:6-7,86:13,15], "Oh God (the Father,) the proud (of the ungodly, as of the Jews and the Gentiles) are Risen against me (Jesus,) and the assemblies of violent men (and women) have sought after my (Jesus') soul (to kill me;) and have not set (by not confessing that I, Jesus is your son; and as of importance, as of) thee (Father) before them. My substance (the physical body) was not hid from thee (Father,) when I (Jesus) was made in secret (from being the world,) and curiously (carefully and anxiously) brought in the lowest parts of the earth (of Hell.) Thou (Father) hast (allowed to) laid me (Jesus) in the lowest pit (of Hell,) in darkness (where there are no Righteousness,) in the deeps (being brought to of nothing; as Jesus was being covered, with the sins of humanity.) Thy wrath (of the Father, turning your face away from Jesus, as Himself was carrying the sins) lieth hard (of Him, feeling rejected) upon me Jesus,) and thou (Father) hast afflicted (by allowing Satan, to drag Him into Hell; and also) me (Jesus) with all the waves (of all the Demonic, to harass. Selah (as I, Jesus reflect back.) For great is thy (the Father's) Mercy (of not allowing Satan; to destroy, by coming) toward me (Jesus:) and thou (Father) hast delivered my (Jesus') soul from the lowest Hell (for after three days, as the Blood of Jesus had covered the sins; of those that have Repented, from the time of Adam and Eve. And then my and your Father in Heaven came into Hell; and embraced me (Jesus,) and the Father dressed me (Jesus) in the armor of His Righteousness: and there, with the helmet of salvation, Satan was there stripped of all; that he was created with, for now he is just a loud roaring lion.) But thou (Father,) oh Lord (my precious Father,) art a God (with of no beginnings or of no endings, but) full of compassion (sympathy,) and gracious (cordial,) longsuffering (patient,) and plenteous in Mercy (of being protected) and Truth (the quality as of trust,)" **neither**

His (of being Jesus' own) **flesh did see corruption** (being Raised, on the end of third day.) **Therefore being** (seated) **by the right hand of God** (my and also your Father) **exalted, and having received of the Father** (God) the promise of the Holy Ghost (Spirit,) **He** (Jesus) **hath shed** (by Him bringing) **forth this, which ye now see and hear** (of what just happened, as the Holy Spirit came in and filled each heart in the upper room, being the first day of the "Feast of Pentecost.)**"**

And so, as Jesus is the mediator between humanity and the Father in Heaven; Jesus does demands, that our lifestyle reflects: which is, of us being like-minded as of what is mentioned in the Scriptures. For Jesus will and is being near all of us; which also, to conflict us by the Holy Spirit of our sins. And that is, if we have drifted away from Jesus' only path; as of which, is considered the Righteous, a narrow road toward eternal life with Jesus Christ: and that, has Scriptural demands of our focusing; of being by the Holy Spirit, of reviewing our own lifestyle daily. For Jesus do recognizes our mind set, of which is our thought pattern to consider; the signal of completion, of our walk of Faith: that Jesus is the only Way of being with the Father forever; of which, was written before Christ's birth as in [II Chr. 7:14], **"If my** (Jesus') **people** (that had happened, after Jesus' death and Resurrection; of being "Born-Again" and of,) **which are called by my** (Jesus') **name** (of which has openly acknowledged; that He is my Savior,) **shall humble** (by confessing, by the Holy Spirit; that He is the only way for) **themselves** (of thinking that it is, all about letting Jesus begin with them and us,) **and pray** (to Jesus, with an open expressive conversation of love,) **and seek my** (Jesus) **face** (by focusing, of our attention on the person; by honoring Him,) **and turn** (by stirring our mind toward the Scriptural goals; of Godliness) **from their wicked ways** (of considering, the many thoughts of the past as evil; then by reviewing our thought pattern;) **then will I** (Jesus) **hear from Heaven** (being by the Father,) **and will forgive** (of Jesus, making a prayer intercession before the Father; by the Holy Spirit, of Jesus pleading His Blood for our behave: and the Father, of forgiving) **their** (of all our) **sin** (and therefore, the compassionate Father has forgiven their and our shortcoming; of a sinful lifestyle,) **and will heal** (of restoring all; and therefore, being restored by the Holy Spirit: to the rightful place in Righteousness and) **their** (all of them and all of our hearts; that are sincere, being in the) **Land** (of Jesus, Himself being our Rock.)**"**

The Message of Jesus to the Church of the Lord Jesus Christ! * * * THE REPENTING MUST BE, BEFORE THE GREAT TRIBULATION

Subject #Two:

So, dear America, yes America, "the beautiful United States of America and all the other Nations;" your time has come, and it is now when the Word of the Lord Jesus is being proclaimed. He, that is me, (Jesus) is setting in motion the judgments that are coming; as the Lord Jesus Christ stands and knocks at the door: of every heart, of you American's and that includes the entire world as in [Mt. 24:4-5,21-22], **"And Jesus answered and said unto them, take heed that no man** (or woman) **deceive you. For many shall come in my name** (saying, they are sent by God, as they form their own; formed religion,) **saying, I am Christ** (appearing to be, the Father's Son;) **and shall deceive many. For then shall be great Tribulation, such as was not since the beginning of the world to this day, no, nor ever shall be. And except those days should be shortened, there should no flesh be saved** (alive on the earth:) **but for the elect's sake** (of Jesus, having believers on the earth) **those days shall be shortened** (being brought to an ending.)"

America, the call is or will be loud and very, very; oh, so very clear, the Bible which is the inspired Word of God: that this call will be as someone sounding it from the loud bull horn, as of a warning is in progress. And by being on alert or you will be caught between two opinions; that is, of those being the secular, which is the world: for I (Jesus) am including anyone, that will not accept the fact that I (Jesus;) yes, I (Jesus) is the "I Am," the Lord Jesus Christ of the Bible. I (Jesus) am the God of the Old Testament, which is the Son of God, the promised Messiah and that is me (Jesus;) and with the New Testament, I (Jesus) am called Jesus Christ. And of being the Christ; of which is, the office that has the authority and also the same Son of God and is the only Son of God: and that is me (Jesus Christ,) of a Holy Supreme God (the Father;) for He is the living Father in Heaven.

So, listen carefully, your time to choose as to who is your God will be very; very soon of being abruptly cut off, being the end of your life's journey: and I (Jesus) will hear you calling, but it will be after the appointed time; as the world, is being filled with great upheaval and turmoil. Thereafter if you do, did you hear me, for (Jesus,) is hearing the if; for as you repent, and that is if, before the "Raptured of the Churches of Believers:" but if the repenting is later, you will surely be martyred, because of your confession of Faith and of salvation to me (Jesus;) and yes, your only true God, the Lord Jesus Christ, for you will be in Heaven with me?

You know that the gods of this world, have no life and cannot breathe; for fools will try to prove, that they can and do have life. So let me (Jesus) tell you, that I (Jesus) am the only God, the Lord Jesus Christ that can breathe on this earth; I (Jesus) do have flesh, bones, and sinews on me (Jesus) and Blood in me: and yes again, I (Jesus) do have Blood, and of which does have life in my (Jesus') being. So, as of most of the population of the world that has no Spiritual life; without the Holy Spirit's "Born-Again" experience: for this is the greatest of the lasting call from me (Jesus,) that will culminate with my (Jesus') appearance. And so first, Jesus will take in secret those that are mine (Jesus' sheep, that is in my fold;) as of the removing of the Church of believers happens: from the calamities, that is coming on the earth. And then lastly, as I (Jesus) stand on this earth; with my (Jesus) feet firmly in place, to repossess this world for myself: and therefore, of returning the whole earth into my Father's possession into Heaven's control; of its original intention, when it was first created. For the Holy Spirit of God will definitely call; calling into the ears, of all to take their stand for me (Jesus:) of proclaiming the Righteousness of God.

And as to seeing and believing, yes, our Father in Heaven knows before the foundation of the world was created; and who will be His. And of preparing our heart; for the Revival, of the time spend of Worshipping: is the times of rejoicing of those that truly want and have a heart opened toward God (the Father;) and are truly, not deceived by the false prophets.

The Message of Jesus to the Church of the Lord Jesus Christ! * * *
THE UNBELIEVER WILL NOT REPENT, BEFORE THE FINAL DAY

Subject #Three:

And there, America and the rest of the world you must listen; and there of stopping, stop, yes you must stop and should stop and reevaluate your beliefs and convictions: but just, of repenting as of your sins. But yet, first of not denying me (Jesus,) as your Savior the Lord and God and then of those ungodly deeds; remember Sodom and Gomorrah and all the sins that the Bible forbids. For I (Jesus) will come in, and dwell within you, healing you as I (Jesus) forgive; by restoring you all with the right Spirit, the Holy Spirit: of fellowship, as you pray, then being "Born-Again." And that is, of the facing the perilous times, for the future will not look bleak; but filled with promises, of which is with God the Father forever, forever, and ever: of having, with no time laps in between.

And again, America and the world, of (Jesus') call to you at this, that is now; of the year, of being the "twentieth century:" your and everyone's time is running out, that is something to consider. For since it could be everyone's very last breath, when in the limited distant future; you or anyone probably could or would just forget God totally and absolutely. And yes, me (of being Jesus) the Christ; the only Savior of the whole Americas, and the world of Nations: the clock is about to strike the midnight hour. And again, for yes, the midnight sound, and when that sound comes; you will not have the time to repent, and of asking me (Jesus) into your heart, for I (Jesus) am "Time" and if this sound happens afterwards: as if you do repent, you will definitely not of being prepared, as to the secret's unknown consequences. For many will be facing the surprises of the inevitable as to their decision; of which, and again, if you do repent, of facing the inevitable: it will still be happening, of being martyred for your Faith in me (Jesus;) but yet, for by your Faith in me (Jesus) you will be in Heaven with my Father and me (Jesus.)

And as John the Baptist sounded the alarm and even then, they would not believe in me (Jesus;) of his day, and how about the prophet Jeremiah: as he warned them of the calamity that was just a few years away, which they did not listen either? So as of now, for today is the time, my name is Jesus; I (Jesus) am, the "I Am" is doing that repeated call, for you all only have a few years to go: before the wind, did you hear me (Jesus,) the wind of change is coming, that fills completely and totally the air that you breathe. And as the time for anyone to repent will have ended; for suddenly a total destruction will overtake your and all, the span of time on the earth. And again, the unknown consequences will be inevitable; as of what happened in Israel with the prophet Jerimiah: the issues will appear again in our time period as in part of [Jer. 15:5-7], **"For who shall have pity upon**

thee, oh Jerusalem (as of those that once, believed in God?) **Or who shall bemoan** (deeply grieved) **thee? Or who shall go aside to ask** (by being concerned of) **how thou doest? Thou hast forsaken me** (Jesus,) **saith the Lord, thou art gone backward** (to their ungodly, sinful lifestyle of behavior:) **therefore will I** (Jesus) **stretch out my hand against thee, and destroy thee** (for I (Jesus) **do not consider you a believer in** God;) **I** (Jesus) **am weary with repenting** (of Jesus, again and again of delaying judgement; but not again) **therefore will I** (Jesus) **stretch out my** (Jesus') **hand against thee, and destroy** (the unbelieving Israelites, which are the idol Worshippers; but not of His "Remnant," of being believers: but the ungodly of) **thee; I** (Jesus) **am weary with repenting. Since they** (which is not His "Remnant") **return not** (by repenting) **from their** (evil) **ways.**

For you all can also, read about it in the Book of Jeremiah; as to the Nation of Israel, and of the King named Nebuchadnezzar: as of what happened in the City of Babylon. For as of Jerusalem, many sudden deaths became their demise; and will or can be yours too, it will fall on all and all will be affected by it: for the whole world will not escape any of it, just as of then. And as of you might be thinking, that you will see it coming; no, no, no you and others will not see it coming, and of having the time to repent: for Hell, yes, Hell could or will be your reward. For as your actions prove, of you deliberately avoiding any confrontation with the only God of Heaven; of which is, by your ignorance's to my warning calls: that will affect your destiny, that also includes the whole world.

The Message of Jesus to the Church of the Lord Jesus Christ! * * *
THE SPIRITUALLY BLIND, BY SEEKING HEAVEN ANOTHER WAY

Subject #Four:

So, listen carefully, for all of your hearts can be filled with joy; these indescribable feelings, overflowing with the Father's joy, love and peace: a sense of belonging to someone that has it in control; it is something beyond words to express. For I (Jesus,) the "I Am" will come into your empty heart; and fill it with my Shekinah Glory, that Holy Presence of God the Father: for the Holy Spirit of God will bring that new Life, into each one of you that desires it. As of repenting means, of just stopping as of what you are doing; and change the course of your direction, by turning from the sins and dedicate one's selves: to the Biblical amendments of correcting, by putting it right.

Therefore, by placing your life squarely of being in; into the face of the Lord Jesus Christ, that is me (Jesus:) so that again, the Holy Spirit with that "Born-Again" experience from God. And Jesus can take your heart of stone, that hardness and replace it with a heart of flesh; that tenderness, by the infusion of the Holy Spirit. For Jesus is alive in the flesh, and have that tenderness; so, I (Jesus) can stand and proclaim you before my and your Father in Heaven that you: you, yes and you all are the real deal. For you will be brought into the Heavenly Light realm; for the Father is saying, remember what Jesus said when He was on the earth: as the Scriptures reads as in [Jn. 14:6], **"I** (Jesus) **am the Way, the Truth, and the Life: no man** (or woman) **cometh unto the Father, but by me** (Jesus.)" For Jesus is the only door that you must enter through to receive salvation; of being by the Holy Spirit, of that "Born-Again" experience. And there, as to what Jesus said as they heard as in [Jn. 10:1], **"Verily, verily, I say unto you, he** (or she and all) **that entereth not by the door into the sheepfold** (where Jesus is,) **but climbeth up some other way** (of Jesus, being the only Way, but others have persuaded many; that Jesus is not only way) **the same is a thief and a robber** (have deceived many, by giving them a false hope; that by ignoring their sins, which is the same: as saying to them, of living in their sins is fine.)" For so many and all have their own choices, as to who their God is; and now Jesus has walked away, the Holy Spirit's Presence is outside the door: from many or possibly most of the fellowships through-out the whole wide world; because of their unbelief and their own ungodly lifestyle as in [Jer. 25:36], **"A voice of the cry** (as of an emotional expression) **of the Shepherds** (those in charge,) **and an howling** (the loudness) **of the principal** (the owner's) **of the flock** (as of the Congregation or assembly,) **shall be heard: for the Lord** (Jesus) **hath spoiled their pasture** (for Jesus will or is nowhere to be found.)" So, hear me (Jesus) again, of salvation; by saving the human race, from the power and effects of sins; and saved from the evil to come: yes, the evil that is coming. And so, by repenting of your sins, I (Jesus) will restore your mind, your soul, and your spirit; as for healing, it will be that blessing also: to complete you, in your journey through life; as you meditate on me (Jesus') Word as of those healing Scriptures, of being God the Father's medicine, for (Jesus) is the Word.

The Message of Jesus to the Church of the Lord Jesus Christ! * * *
THE ADMIT OF OUR WEAKNESS, IS RELYING ON HIS STRENGTH

Subject #Five:

For the Scriptures speaks about healing; of God's medicine, and as in [Rom. 10:17], **"So then Faith** (of working out our salvation) **cometh by hearing, and hearing** (of Faith of seriously believing) **by the** (written) **Word of God** (and again, of (Jesus) being the Word.)"

And as of [Prov. 4:20-22], **"My son** (and daughter,) **attend** (by paying attention) **to my** (Jesus') **words** (of what I (Jesus) say;) **incline** (by listening closely with) **thine ear unto my sayings** (Jesus' words.) **Let them not depart from thine eyes** (out of your sight) **keep them in the midst** (within) **of thine heart. For they are life unto those that find them, and health to all their flesh** (of the whole body.)"

And as of [Ps. 107:18-21], **"Their soul abhorreth** (hate) **all manner of meat** (that is not the true Word of God;) **and they draw near unto the gates of death** (for the true Word of God, is life.) **Then they cry unto the Lord in their trouble** (of realizing that they, ignored the Anointed Word of God, **and He** (Jesus) **saveth them out of their distresses** (of stumbling.) **He sent His Word** (the Scriptures, of who God is,) **and healed them** (of sicknesses, pestilences, plagues. and more,) **and delivered them from their destructions** (of the enemies, of trying to destroy their cities or their country.) **Oh that men** (and women) **would praise the Lord for His goodness** (instead of ignoring their blessings,) **and for His** (Jesus') **wonderful works** (of bringing rain, so they can have food) **to the children of men** (and women!)"

And as of [Ex. 23:25], **"And ye shall serve** (Worship) **the Lord your God, and He shall bless thy bread** (of food,) **and thy water** (of rain, for the crops;) **and I** (Jesus) **will take sickness** (the diseases from other nations, will stay) **away from the midst of thee."**

And as of [Ps. 30:2], **"Oh Lord my God, I cried** (by emotional expression) **unto thee** (in prayer and thanksgiving,) **and thou hast healed me."**

And as of [Is. 53:4-5], **"Surely He** (Jesus) **hath borne** (a bearer of) **our griefs, and carried our sorrows: yet we did esteem** (there valued) **Him** (of Jesus being) **stricken, smitten of God** (the Father, by allowing Jesus Christ,) **and** (there also, of being) **afflicted** (being referred too, of what the prophet Isaiah foresees as in [Mt. 8:17], "That it might be fulfilled which was spoken by Esaias (Isaiah) the prophet, saying, Himself (of being Jesus) took our infirmities, and bare our sicknesses.) **But** (because of Jesus' own afflictions) **He** (being Jesus) **was** (definitely) **wounded for our transgressions** (of the sins,) **He was bruised for our iniquities** (including being as our weaknesses:) **and chastisement** (and of being severely punished) **of** (promising) **our peace was upon Him** (Jesus alone;) **and with His** (Jesus') **stripes** (being physically harmed) **we are** (guaranteed, the blessing of being) **healed."**

And as of [Ps. 103:2-4], **"Bless the Lord, oh my soul, and forget not all His** (Jesus') **benefits: who forgiveth all thine iniquities** (including weaknesses;) **who healeth all thy diseases** (as to all of the health issues;) **who Redeemeth thy life from destruction** (as by being destroyed, and/or of the lack of food and/or of the warring enemies;) **who crowneth thee with lovingkindness** (as of there, adding the blessings) **and tender Mercies** (of not allowing anyone to harm us.)**"**

And as of [Ps. 41:2-4], **"The Lord** (Jesus Christ) **will preserve him** (and her,) **and keep him** (and her) **alive; and he** (and she) **shall be blessed upon the earth: and thou wilt not deliver him** (and her) **unto the will of his** (and her) **enemies** (the time of King Saul and others, as when, King David's son Absalom; tried to overthrow and even kill his father, King David.) **The Lord will strengthen him** (and her) **upon the bed of languishing** (as David was getting old:) **thou wilt make** (protect and heal of) **all his** (and her) **bed in his** (and her) **sickness. I** (of being King David) **said, Lord** (Jesus.) **Be Merciful unto me** (David being a ruler, is difficult:) **heal my soul** (he realized his frailties:) **for I** (David) **have sinned** (he knew his weaknesses) **against thee** (you Jesus.)**"**

And as of [Ps. 147:3], **"He healeth the broken in heart** (of being King David, being spared by many disappointments,) **and bindeth up their**

wounds (of his soldiers, facing many victories; and also, recovering from injuries.)"

And as of [Jer. 17:14], **"Heal me** (as a weeping prophet,) **oh Lord** (Jesus,) **and I shall be healed** (and find hope;) **save me** (Jerimiah of sparing him, from being killed, by those that did not want to hear the word "Repent,") **and I** (Jeramiah) **shall be saved** (by Jesus:) **for thou** (Jesus) **art my praise** (the God of Abraham.)"

And again, as of [Mt. 8:17], **"That it might be fulfilled which was spoken by Esaias** (Isaiah, the Prophet did speak it out, by the Holy Spirit; and was of speaking and connecting to the future, of being Jesus as in [Is. 53:4], "Surely He (being Jesus) hath borne (of bear) our griefs (placed pain on Himself) and carried our sorrows (as of His suffering:) yet we did esteem Him (of us accepting the fact, that He being a curse for us, a decision of by Jesus Himself; so we will be completely healed and strong: which is, of being healthy) stricken (wounded,) smitten (disabled by diseases) of God (the Father,) and afflicted (being distressed.)" **The prophet, saying, Himself** (of being Jesus) **took our infirmities** (including weaknesses,) **and bare our sicknesses** (diseased conditions, illness and much more.

For with the formations and movements that are happening with the Body of Christ; through the movement of your and my (Jesus') gentle Holy Spirit: your and my (Jesus') goals are of allowing you and me to be filled and overflowing with the Holy Spirit. For your and my (Jesus') Presence is everywhere and of surrounding you and me; for (Jesus,) sees of what you and me and everyone are really facing, as for you and my (Jesus') desires are: that by your and my (Jesus') desires, of the fulfillment be happening as in [Eph. 4:11-15], **"And He** (Jesus) **gave** (the "five-fold" ministries, to every Church Body of saints; as of believers, as of the individual's gifts receiving) **some, apostles; and some, prophets; and some, evangelists; and some, pastors and** (some) **teachers**; (to whatever the need was) **for the perfecting of the saints** (in the Church Body of saints,) **for the work of the ministry, for the edifying of the Body of Christ** (of which is the Church assembly.) **Till we all come in the unity of the faith, and of the knowledge of the Son of God** (being Jesus,) **unto a perfect man** (or woman,) **unto the measure of the stature of the fulness** (as of mentally and spiritually, to the understanding) **of Christ. That we henceforth be no more children** (of unlearned,) **tossed to and fro, and carried**

about with every (of unbiblical falsified by) **wind of doctrine, by the sleight** (trickery) **of men** (or women,) **and cunning** (clever) **craftiness** (of skill,) **whereby they lie in wait to deceive** (anyone that will listen.) **But speaking the Truth** (of the Biblical Word of God) **in love, may grow up into Him** (Jesus) **in all things, which is the head, even Christ** (Jesus.)"

CHAPTER EIGHT
THE UNDERSTANDIN CHURCH

The Message of Jesus to the Church of the Lord Jesus Christ! * * *
THE STABILITY OF BRINGING LIFE, THE DOCTRINE OF TRUTH

Subject #One:

As of "**book number** [01 – 27] **being Matthew – Revelation**," it is all about what God is saying and that is (**He** (Jesus) **has set in motion, by establishing the Truthful Church of the Lord Jesus Christ.**)

For we all must begin, by thinking of what (Jesus) said; **"thus saith the Lord,"** you and I know that the Lord wants to speak to you and me: and all people in your and/or my own modern language, as being simply plain. And "this says the Lord," is about the issues that are on your and my (Jesus') heart; as (Jesus) truly sees your and my desire in what your and my (Jesus') word says: even though, your and my (Jesus') works among us, seem the ministry to be on a small scale compared to others. For which, are of those that have gone state, national or world-wide in their activities of ministries; as your and my (Jesus') eyes see you and me, for (Jesus) sees where you and my ministries and all are at: but do not forget that (Jesus) has the whole world directly in His site. For many thinks that it seems as though, it is just a routine motion that (Jesus) has you and my activities or ministries of being ignored; that are in place, but it is not.

For with the formations and movements that are happening with the Body of Christ; through the movement of your and my (Jesus') gentle Holy Spirit: your and my (Jesus') goals are of allowing you and me to be filled and overflowing with the Holy Spirit. For your and my (Jesus') Presence is everywhere and of surrounding you and me; for (Jesus,) sees of what you and me and everyone are really facing, as for you and my (Jesus') desires are: that by your and my (Jesus') desires, of the fulfillment be happening as in [Eph. 4:11-15], **"And He** (Jesus) **gave** (all the "five-fold" ministries, to every Church Body of saints; as of believers, as of the individual's gift receiving) **some, apostles; and some, prophets; and some, evangelists; and some, pastors and** (some) **teachers**; (to whatever the need was) **for the perfecting of the saints** (in the Church Body of saints,) **for the work of the ministry, for the edifying of the Body of Christ** (of which is the Church assembly.) **Till we all come in the unity of the faith, and of the knowledge of the Son of God** (being Jesus,) **unto a perfect man** (or woman,) **unto the measure of the stature of the fulness** (as of mentally and Spiritually, to the understanding) **of Christ. That we henceforth be no more children** (of unlearned,) **tossed to and fro, and carried about with every** (of unbiblical falsified by) **wind of doctrine, by the sleight** (trickery) **of men** (or women,) **and cunning** (clever) **craftiness** (of skill,) **whereby they lie in wait to deceive** (anyone that will listen.) **But speaking the Truth** (of the Biblical Word of God) **in love, may grow up into Him** (Jesus) **in all things, which is the head, even Christ** (Jesus.)**"**

For there are hundreds of millions of people out there; that I (Jesus) have my eyes on them, so as you and me (being Jesus) are led by my (Jesus') Holy Spirit: there is coming a Revival of the Word of God, so large in magnitude that it will overwhelm most. For the dry bones that Ezekiel prophesied, which is soon about to come to its fulfillment; now all they and you must do, is to trust me (being Jesus) by opening your, yes, your and their mouth: as listed in some of the "nine-gifts," of interpreting the Anointed tongue language and/or of prophesying. And then, by beginning to speak forth the articles; of what the Holy Spirit is clearly saying to the Church, the true Church of the Lord Jesus Christ: the one that the Father in Heaven has His stamped of approval on it.

And as to seeing and believing, yes, our Father in Heaven knows before the foundation of the world was created; and who will be His, so be exceedingly excited, over the fact that Satan will not be of yelling: "hurrah, hurrah they are mine." Yet, the Father in Heaven will soon be, of looking down and saying; of "today is the day of salvation," for you and me (being Jesus) will be in my (being Jesus') Kingdom: in the soon coming Presence of your and my (being Jesus') Holy God (the Father's soon coming Spiritual Revival, as of the time that happened of the "Feast of Pentecost.") And of preparing our heart; for the Revival, of the time spend of Worshipping: is the times of rejoicing of those that truly want and have a heart opened toward God (the Father;) and are truly, of not being deceived by the false prophets. But yet, those that are bound, they will be set free because of you and me (being Jesus) and all other's efforts of Worshipping; of by laboring and mostly you and us, uniting with me (being Jesus,) of all by prayer and fasting: plus, with many other prayer warriors; so, the works will surely definitely be completed.

So let this be the time to say to all, that the time has come; as you and me (Jesus,) and all are establishing the goal, as for the hope of all my (Jesus') Righteous many promises: for you and me (Jesus) and they are the most valuable asset! As Jesus, of them setting into motion; His will of being accomplished as in [Mt. 6:33], **"But seek ye first the Kingdom of God** (of by being with Jesus Christ, forever and ever,) **and His** (Jesus') **Righteousness** (of where there is no stench of evil;) **and all these things shall be added unto you** (and me, for Jesus' Righteousness, will also being ours.)"

And also, as the Lord Jesus Christ is bringing, this issues of a Godly lifestyle; to the forefront, for everyone to place the effort: as of its greatest importance as in [Jn. 7:38], **"He** (or she) **that believeth** (by openly Worshipping) **on me** (Jesus,) **as the Scripture hath said, out of his** (or her) **belly** (the innermost, of being the heart) **shall flow rivers** (abundant) **of living water** (the Presence of Jesus, that is alive and continually of flowing and satisfying.)" As of most that does not understand, the importance of the definition as to our eternal life; for the Father in Heaven, wants all to be in His Kingdom: which is, of being by and/or near Him as in [Ps. 149:6], **"Let the high praises** (which will definitely, effect the environment of all our surroundings; as) **of God** (the Father) **be in their mouth** (for we all will want to Worship,) **and a two-edged sword** (as the Holy Spirit's Presence be) **in their hand** (of being Jesus' workmanship.)"

CHAPTER NINE
THE REDEEMING CHURCH

The Message of Jesus to the Church of the Lord Jesus Christ! * * *
THE NEW GENERATION OF TEENAGERS, WILL BE REVIVED

Subject #One:

As of "**book** **number** [01 – 27] **being** **Matthew** – **Revelation**," it is all about what God is saying and that is (**He** (Jesus) **has** **set** **in** **motion**, **by** **establishing** **the** **Truthful** **Church** **of** **the** **Lord** **Jesus** **Christ**.)

And so, what are on the minds, of the very restless teenagers; did someone insert into their mind, of them willingly, a thought of our present time period: of them mouthing out those ideals, as though they are the ones that originally formed those thoughts? And as they begin to expressly speaking it out clearly, their feelings express of the passion; as though, they would fight to the death, to pressure society of those dogmas: which is, their behavior of how all of humanity ought to live, that is contrary to the Scriptures. For even though others do agree or disagree, it is all about them carrying the ideals through-out every civilization; of their false perception, until everyone becomes a humanly active robot: as some countries have already displayed. For then everyone of all countries will think and be like other dictatorial regimes; that will be put to death if any disagree, for the Gospel has been facing persecution for (2,000) two thousand years: but yet, the Lord Jesus Christ is and will reach those teenagers. And as for many, they will be the ones that the Holy Spirit will use; of spreading the Anointed Gospel through-out the whole world; as the "five-fold" ministries are actively involved: and of which, the Holy Spirit will be a "Fiery Torch," and as the "nine-gifts" are in operation. For (Jesus) will restore the Church's activities and its effectiveness, by the powerful Presence of the Holy Spirit; and as (Jesus) called the apostle Peter the rock: of which, Peter symbolized the one that was going to fulfill the prophecy as in [Acts 10:42-43], **"And He** (Jesus) **Commanded us** (the ones, that were a witness of Jesus' death and His Resurrection) **to preach unto the people** (of the Jews and the Gentiles,) **and to testify that it is He** (Jesus) **which was ordained of God** (the Father) **to be the judge of quick** (the living) **and dead** (for as of yesterday, of today, and of forever, (Jesus Himself is our Savior; possibly tomorrow, He will be our Judge.) **To Him** (Jesus) **give all the prophets** (and all the prophetesses) **witness** (of Jesus, proving to all that He fulfilled; all the prophecies,) **that through His** (Jesus') **name** (and of His name alone) **whosoever** (anyone that) **believeth in Him** (Jesus) **shall receive remission of sins** (of having freedom, deliverance, and forgiveness.)"

So, as long of the men thinks, that they have the only right to dominate the rulership; without the presence of the women, the Holy Spirit will definitely be sad: and by standing, outside the door of the Church's sanctuary. For at the time of Apostle Paul's activities, of establishing Churches; when they would congregate, it was usually in a small group: of possibly, there being in a home setting, and of having no chairs to sit on; but by, assembling together on the floor of surrounding the main speaker. And probably the wives, were sitting separately from their husband and/or if they were sitting nearby; for this new forum concept of assembling, had to have some kind of a structural ruling: as to its adequate behavior, so that the main speaker is not consistently of being interrupted. For there probably also were the young men there, of asking their father or the other men in the crowd; of asking them, of what Paul or other apostles meant, by what they had just said. For of Paul's desiring, will be by the Holy Spirit; of him, establishing a permanent Church structure for men and women as in [I Cor. 14:20], "Brethren (and also sisters,) be not children in understanding: howbeit in malice (usually implies a deep-seated and often unreasonable expression; of having, a pleasure in seeing others struggling or suffer) be ye children, but in understanding be (believing) men (and women.)"

CHAPTER TEN
THE MATURING CHURCH

The Message of Jesus to the Church of the Lord Jesus Christ! * * *
THE DESIRE OF SEEING, THE FULFILLMENT OF THE
REVIVAL

Subject #One:

As of "**book number [01 – 27] being Matthew – Revelation**," it is all about what God is saying and that is (**He** (Jesus) **has set in motion, by establishing the Truthful Church of the Lord Jesus Christ.**)

The time for the Revival, all over the world as (Jesus) shares to me; from His heart, by these sayings, "I the Lord Jesus Christ have some comments for the Church." What is a Revival, the issue has been asked before; that is the question; and that I (Jesus) am asking, and will also answer: it is something that is being revived? So, with excitement, let this be the time for it to be revived! You know the Holy Spirit, and with the approval of the Father in Heaven; has commissioned it to be on earth, the same Holy Spirit's Presence that came, at the time of the first Presence of the "Feast of Pentecost."

And before I (Jesus) had ascended into Heaven, I (Jesus) said this to all the apostles as in part of [Acts 1:4], **"And, being assembled together with them, commanded them that they should not depart from Jerusalem, but wait for the Promise of the Father."** For as they were in one accord, with the obedience of the command from Jesus; of not leaving Jerusalem, by praying and waiting: as the Scripture reads as in [Acts 2:1], **"And, when the** (first) **day of Pentecost was fully come, they were all with one accord** (of fasting and praying) **in one place."** For they looked and saw the evidence as in [Acts 2:2], **"And there appeared unto them cloven tongues as of fire, and it sat upon each of them."** So, in that upper room, therefore they prayed and waited; until Jesus came, and they were all filled from the Holy Spirit of God: from His Holy City, called Jerusalem as in [Acts 2:3-4]**, "And there appeared unto them cloven tongues like as of fire, and it sat upon each of them. And they were all filled with the Holy Ghost** (Spirit,) **and** (they) **began to speak with other tongues** (a Holy Spirit's, prayer language,) **as the** (Holy) **Spirit gave them utterance** (as the Holy Spirit, allowed them to speak it out."

And now is the time, for I (Jesus) have called you; the Church of the Lord Jesus Christ world-wide of beginning this, a Revival with fasting and praying: to bring a shaking on the earth, as I (Jesus) am walking into every heart; those that are tender and to those that are hard. For I (Jesus) am love, so it will be the greatest factor as they all; the whole wide world has a new confrontation: as the gentle, yes, my gentle/tender Holy Spirit of reaching into the deepest part of their hearts; for the respond of acceptances or a complete denial of the Father's love. For they all will be faced, just before the Father in Heaven nudges my ribs with His elbow; and says to me, "Son, go and bring them all home to me," before those dreadful days and nights as of many more: as of humanity faces the harshest of their decisions, and the consequences that follow. But all must not forget, as I (Jesus) was born by the mother named Mary; for she was a humanly formed being, and therefore I myself was born in the flesh: so, as of humanity, I (Jesus) also have a rib missing. And for so, as the Church is reunited with the Lord Jesus Christ; I (Jesus) will have my rib (the Church) by my side forever and forever.

The Message of Jesus to the Church of the Lord Jesus Christ! * * *
THE PROPHECY OF BRINGING, THE WIND OF CHANGE

Subject #Two:

So, listen, says the Lord Jesus Christ, listen; the earth with all its billions of people, the Father in Heaven is at times standing and pointing His finger: and also, opening His mouth and blowing the wind of change. And at times it is solemn, but yet it is filled with love and compassion; and then at times it is an active whirl-wind: because the Demonic, is wanting to interfere with the move of the Holy Spirit.

And as I (Jesus,) the only Lord Jesus Christ stands with one foot in Heaven and one foot on the earth; blowing and yes wind blow: blow to the east, blow to the west, blow to the north and yes, blow to the south. Yes, yes Holy Spirit, the gentle compassionate Holy Spirit move as though the wind is actually blowing; of moving across, the Continent's Lands of Antarctica, the Continent's Lands of North America, the Islands in Central America, and the Continent's Lands of South America. And as of the Continent's large Lands of Africa, including the Island of Madagascar, the Continent's Lands of Europe which includes of Norway, Finland, Ireland, Scotland, England, and of More, with Part of Russia. And as into the Continent's Lands of Asia, with the Nation of Israel and its Surrounding Neighbor's Lands, which does include of China, of India, and of more, with the other Half of Russia; and yes, all the Countless Smaller Islands and also the Larger Islands of the Whole Wide World as of beginning with Greenland, Iceland, Japan, Philippines, Malaysia, Indonesia, New Guinea, and of More: and last, of the Continent's Land of Australia, and the Islands of New Zealand, and of More. And there, let the Holy Spirit penetrate into the Wildest Regions, of the Open Plains, and of the Deepest Remotes Recesses of the many Jungles. So, all must listen carefully, I (Jesus) am coming with great power; for the Revival will be but for a short time, so look toward the Heavens. For I (Jesus) will bring a powerful conclusion as of the many hearts of my people; so, look for my return, of Praising and Worshiping the great "I Am:" for I (Jesus) am the "I Am," that will fulfill the Father in Heaven's will. Amen.

As I (Jesus) reach into every heart, so the (01) one of the (99) "ninety-nine;" will also be in the sheep fold and being safe: with my (Jesus') care, so that none will be lost. For I (Jesus) am the true and faithful Shepherd. So, rejoice of all those that are truly my (Jesus') sheep; for your name, is written in the Lamb's Book of Life: and rejoice with me (being Jesus,) as the Holy Spirit brings the original Pentecost back; which is, being revived and brought back. And again, this great move of the Holy Spirit, that came at the time of the "Feast of Pentecost;" which did sweep the world, into its greatest Spiritual awakening ever: and it will happen again. Yes, yes, as my (Jesus') Holy spirit will cause a great Spiritual awakening; and again, and again, that will be the climax as of the breaking of a new day. For it will be, yes it will be in the day that humanity's heart will have its last confrontation; but you and all that are mine, those that belong to me, will be in Heaven with me: before your and my Father in His Kingdom; Amen, so be it!

The Message of Jesus to the Church of the Lord Jesus Christ! * * *
THE WORDS WE MOUTH, MUST BE THE FATHER'S THOUGHTS

Subject #Three:

For as of being filled, with the Holy Spirit; which began first, on the day of the "Feast of Pentecost:" as they all began to speak in an unknown tongue, of which is in a different language; than the one, they were normally speaking. And so, as they prayed in that prayer language; the Lord Jesus, He will intervene in our behalf: and there, the Holy Spirit will direct and emphasize; of the desire that is in the Father in Heaven's heart. For there, of directing the solution, by the will of the Father; as Jesus stands in the prayer of intercession to fulfill, of what our prayer language requested or proclaimed: and/or of the completion of the prayer petition, that was inspired by the Holy Spirit. But yet, it is not the same; as one of the "nine-gifts," of speaking in an unknown language: and the interpretation of it fully, of which will of being established by the inspiration of the Holy Spirit.

The Church is not a place, just to assemble; singing a few songs, with a little prayer time: of hearing sermon from the preacher, and then of leaving. For a Church is an organism, the Body of Christ, an arm of Jesus'

Commandment, to bring salvation to the masses; which can only happen, when the Church Body of the believers, begin with prayer: in words and/or songs, as the assembly begin by speaking in their own unknown language; as they are approaching the Gates of Heaven, in boldness of heart, in the Holy Spirit of intercession.

And so, as this procedure begins, the power of intercession; of which is the inspiration of the Holy Spirit, will bring that move of the Holy Spirit's power that happened: of which, did happened with "Pentecost" of being brought from Heaven: by reviving it on earth. For then, this will be called a Revival; of which, as the Father intend of it never ending, in its first move of "Pentecost:" of not ever being interrupted, by the division in the assembly and/or lack of prayer; that happened some (2,000) two thousand years ago.

And as we begin to pray for that Revival; the Holy Spirit, will begin to have an effect on the whole world. For this is the reason, Jesus told them not to leave Jerusalem; of which is the epic center, from the time of King David: then of Solomon, and as of today. For the proof of Jesus' goals, is already in motion; for Jesus, just wants us to continue in the Holy Spirit's declaration: of fulfilling the Father's call, of bringing salvation to the world.

And to bring a Revival to earth, by us not being distracted by our own agenda. For Jesus' plan again, was set in motion; for some two thousand years, as of then when the Holy Spirit appeared as a symbolism of a Dove: when it represented the Holy Spirit as it began, by filling their hearts with power to do signs and wonders. And of that power, of being shelved by almost all the Churches; of being through-out the world, as the triune God is waiting: for us to begin by fasting and praying.

The Message of Jesus to the Church of the Lord Jesus Christ! * * *
THE GIFTS OF OPERATIONS, SO THE CHURCH CAN MATURE

Subject #Four:

For there is that confusion, of the difference; of being classified, by declaring someone as being filled with the Holy Spirit: without the evidence of being filled. And of which is, the demonstration of speaking in a prayer language; that is, of that powerful move by Jesus: to bring a solution to our request. And the more and/or the longer of us praying in the Holy Spirit; of which is, the evidence of us speaking in our prayer language. And of which is not, of having one of the "nine-gifts;" but that is, of us speaking in an unknown praying tongue language: of which is, in the demonstration of the Spirit, of that Spiritual communication by the Holy Spirit.

And then, by of being one of the "nine-gifts," of first by the Holy Spirit, of speaking in tongues; and them interpretating it and/or of someone else interpretating the tongues: into the Congregation's language, for all to understand. And again, or by someone else that is among the Congregation; do the interpretation in words, of language so all can understand: of what Jesus is saying directly to the Church. For as to function of the "nine-gifts" of the Holy Spirit; as mentioned in the Scriptures, for each gift has its own specific position: of fulfilling its function, as to the Body of Christ. And as each Church's Body through-out the whole wide world; is properly demonstrating the Holy Spirit's required functions: for then, will the whole Congregation face the consequences of the leadership's agenda. And that is, to fulfill of the Holy Spirit's requirements; of seeing a Spiritual growth in their Church assembly: of which, is the only reason of it happening. And that is, so the Body of Christ, will be willingly following the leading of the Holy Spirit's distribution of the "nine gifts;" as the needs arises as in [I Cor. 12:4], **"Now there are diversities** (of multiformity and/or of different operation, as it is expressed) **of** (the nine) **gifts, but the same** (Holy) **Spirit."**

And as to each of the "two-gifts," of being the word of wisdom and the word of knowledge; are being engaged, by the Holy Spirit, of bringing it to an open display: of wherever the needs arrives in the Church of believers as mentioned as in [I Cor. 12:5], **"And there are differences of administrations** (by doing the affairs, of executing, and/or of having the authorities by the Holy Spirit; of speaking to themselves or others,) **but the same Lord** (as of the needs as in [I Cor. 12:8], "For to one is given by the (Holy) Spirit the word of wisdom; to another the word of knowledge by the same (Holy) Spirit.)"

And again, as each of the "two-gifts," of being faith and healing are being engaged; as the Holy Spirit, of bringing it to an open display: of wherever the needs arrives as in [I Cor. 12:6], **"And there are diversities operations** (by doing the exertion of displaying the power or influence by the Holy Spirit, by speaking out,) **but it is the same God which worketh all in all** (as of the needs as in [I Cor. 12:9], "To another faith by the same (Holy) Spirit; (and) to another the gifts of healing by the same (Holy) Spirit.)"

And again, as to each of the "five-gifts" of being; the working of miracles, prophecy, discerning of spirits, divers kinds of tongues, and the interpretation of tongues are being engaged: by the Holy Spirit, of bringing it to an opening Church display; which is, of wherever the needs arrives as in [I Cor. 12:7], **"But the manifestation** (a public demonstration of power, by the Holy Spirit; and of revealing Jesus' purpose as) **of the** (Holy) Spirit is given to every man (or woman) **to profit withal** (as of the needs, to the "five-gifts" as in [I Cor. 12:10], To another the working of miracles; to another prophecy; to another discerning of spirits (of being of human or of Jesus;) to another divers kinds of tongues; to another the interpretation of tongues.)"

For we must not ever be confused, by being distracted; as to the functions of each or of the "two-gifts" particularly, as of one being called the "divers kinds of tongues:" and of which, the other being called, the "interpretation of tongues." And as of those "two-gifts," for that were not what happened and/or that were spoken about; and again, it was not of what happened on the "day of Pentecost." And as for the demonstration, of the Holy Spirit's power; as they and those as of today, that are speaking in an unknown tongue (being an unknown Spiritual language:) by the evidence of being filled with the Holy Spirit, of the evidence that the Holy Spirit; of Him, has the freedom to openly expressive Himself through their heart's expression. And again, as to being filled with the Holy Spirit; this is not, considered a gift, but of being the evidence of being filled with the Holy Spirit. For they and as of us today, it is considered as a prayer language; sent to earth, by the Father in Heaven: for us, to be the linked together with the Holy Spirit. For of Jesus' mission of completing the work, as Jesus stands with one foot in Heaven and one foot on earth; as of being between Heaven and earth, by them then and as of us today: to fulfill the calling, of reactivating the saints' ministries in the "nine gifts" on the earth.

And as we come before Jesus, He did send the Holy Spirit; then and as of today, to have it accomplished: that is, the calling to empower us as by spreading the message of the Gospel of Jesus Christ. And of our maturity in Jesus Christ throughout our own life and to the world; in power, of which the Holy Spirit, is the only one that can do it properly. For by them then and of us today, of us being enhanced; of giving us the power of Jesus' Anointing: so that the Anointed Gospel message of salvation will leave an impact on the minds and hearts, to of reaching the lost. So as of then and of us today, the speaking in tongues language; will edify our life, and there allowing the Supernatural empowerment of the Holy Spirit: to affect the masses of the world, to clearly understand and also by receiving the Gospel of Jesus; being the Truth in Righteousness, into their hearts.

The Lord Jesus is interested in the Church's functional aspect as of our time period; so let us, begin with the "five-fold" ministries: of considering what is the most important factor, as to the success of any and all ministry's programs; as of what Jesus said, after He was Resurrected and did as in [Jn. 20:21-22], "Then said Jesus to them again, peace be unto you (the apostles:) as my Father hath sent me, even so send I (Jesus) you (of Jesus' apostles.) And when He (Jesus) had said this, He (Jesus) breathed on them (all of the apostles,) and saith unto them (the apostles,) receive ye (the apostles) the Holy Ghost (Spirit.)" For of many and/or of most Christians leaderships through-out the world; have almost totaling ignored, to the fact that if it was not for the Holy Spirit's Presence in us: which included, (the manifestation of the "nine-gifts" of being involved (24) "twenty-four hours" a day with each individual person. For the saints "the Churches world-wide" would be considered lukewarm; and of being useless to the Father, the Son named Jesus: of finding the (01) one of the (99) "ninety-nine," that must be found at the closing of the ages.

CHAPTER ELEVEN
THE COMMANDING CHURCH

The Message of Jesus to the Church of the Lord Jesus Christ! * * *
THE GOING AS I COMMAND YOU, IN MY NAME

Subject #One:

As of **"book number [01 – 27] being Matthew – Revelation,"** it is all about what God is saying and that is **(He (Jesus) has set in motion, by establishing the Truthful Church of the Lord Jesus Christ.)**

For I (myself) saw a sharp barbed (the shape of a fishhook, on the end of the) spear and a regular size two-edged sword. So, I began to speak very softly in an unknown tongue; of which is, of being my prayer language and I sensed that this was a prophetic message. And I felt even later, that it was prophetic; so, then by the next day: I began to write as in [I Cor. 14;5-6], **"I (Paul) would that ye all spake with tongues** (as of what Paul wrote as in [I Cor. 14:18], "I (Paul) thank my God, I (Paul) speak with tongues more than ye all (he needed too, for Jesus to intervene with the issues Paul faced; as he prayed in his prayer language, for the power of the Holy Spirit, which did disrupt the enemies goal: of not allowing, of fully completing Paul's mandate, of the Jews and of also spreading the Gospel of salvation to the Gentiles,)" **but rather that ye prophesied** (when they all

149

are gathering together:) **for greater is he** (or she) **that prophesieth than he** (or she) **that speaketh with tongues** (as being by Jesus, unless it is a one to one communication between us and the Holy Spirit's power; in our prayer language,) **except he** (or she) **interpret** (hearing from the Father's heart,) **that the Church may receive edifying. Now brethren** (and sisters,) **if I come unto you speaking with tongues, what shall I profit you, except I shall speak** (by the Inspirited "nine-gifts" of the Holy Spirit) **to you either by revelation, or by knowledge, or by prophesying, or by doctrine?)"** And then after I had finished this letter; of which to me, it was a message from the Lord Jesus, I had by then understood that it was not a spear: but a large dart, yet even now to me it seems like it was a spear.

So to me, God is reminding everyone, as we are stepping-out or have stepped-out, to actively doing the work of the ministry; the enemy's intentions, were to do the Church great harm, but God as He speaks out: is saying that the "I Am," will be close by and those of the enemy will not be able to succeed with their fiery darts as in [Eph. 6:14-17], "Stand therefore, having your loins (the major part, being of the spinal column; between the hip bone and the ribs, which holds the major strength: of the body's movement, where the center, being near the heart) girt about with Truth (the Word of God,) and having on the breastplate of Righteousness (being of Faith;) and your feet shod with the preparation of the Gospel of Peace (of actively speaking God's Word;) above all, taking the shield of Faith (by believing in Jesus, the only one we Worship; we are considered Righteous,) wherewith ye shall be able to quench all the fiery darts of the wicked. And take the helmet of salvation (being "Born-Again,") and the Sword of the (Holy) Spirit, which is the Word of God (not just by hearing it, but by living it.)" And there, the Lord Jesus Christ filled my mind with these words!

For as the Lord Jesus Christ lives; you, being the Church will succeed because: the "I Am," and the Holy Spirit will go before all of you. For "I Am" the "I Am," Jesus the Revelator; will be by your side and the "I Am," with the Holy Spirit, and the Father in Heaven: will be the one, the triune God which will speak into existence; of which is not yet the evidence but will be. And as we command those things that were not; that they should be and will be as you stand, for as you review each object of clothing: you will have the confidence of feeling safe and protected and dressed; as you are being dressed in your full Armor on, as I (Jesus) is fighting for humanity as in [Is. 59:16-17], "**And He** (Jesus) **saw that there was no man** (or woman, or others) **and wondered that there was no Intercessor: therefore His** (Jesus') **arm brought salvation unto Him** (Jesus Himself;) **and His** (Jesus' Righteousness, it sustained Him (Jesus.) **For He** (being Jesus has definitely) **put on Righteousness as a breastplate, and an helmet of salvation upon His** (Jesus') **head; and He** (Jesus) **put on the garments of vengeance** (of forcing, as the earth being the Lord's) **for clothing, and was clad** (clothe) **with zeal as a cloak."**

And as the firry darts of the enemy is send out; the "I Am," will with the two-edged sword, symbolizing the Holy Spirit: is stopping them as the "I Am," will by my Holy Spirit swinging the sword either way. And oh yes, for as the Anointed sword is being a two-edged sword; and not giving the Demonic enough time and/or spaces: for them to strike back. For because, I (Jesus) the Lord Jesus Christ; of which will, with the Father in Heaven's help: and the Holy Spirit, of breaking the enemy's hold on humanity, of especially the Churches through-out the whole wide world as in [Is. 49:1-2], "Listen, oh isles (those that are by themselves,) unto me (Jesus;) and hearken, ye people, from far; the Lord (my Father) hath called me (being Jesus) from the womb; from the bowels of my mother hath He (my Father) made mention of my (Jesus') name. And He (my Father) hath made my (being Jesus') mouth like a sharp sword; in the shadow of His (my Father's) hand hath He (of my Father) hid me (being Jesus,) and made me (being Jesus) a polished shaft (shiny and swift to move;) in His (my Father's) quiver hath He (my Father) hid me (being Jesus.)" And as of the assignment that you have been called to do; of breaking the enemies hold, by the power of the Holy Spirit, will be a stunning blow to the Demonic: so, be firm in your stand with the Word of God; from the Holy Scriptures, with prayer and fasting, and more prayer.

See the moment, that I (Jesus) considered this mission; that I (Jesus) was preparing, as I (Jesus) hear the Father speaking: so, do not be intimidated or hesitating as you step into the ministry, the "five-fold" ministries. And of conquering all the territories that is the Father's; so, listen carefully, to the prophetic voices: for I (Jesus) will speak out through them as in [Jer. 1:4-5], **"Then the Word of the Lord** (Jesus Christ) **came unto me, saying, before I** (Jesus myself) **formed thee in the belly, I** (Jesus) **knew thee; and before thou camest forth out of the womb I** (Jesus) **sanctified thee, and I** (Jesus) **ordained thee a prophet unto the nations** (for as of yesterday or today, they have many of their "five-fold" ministries; but yet, not knowing if they have it, or of not being manifested.)" For the power of the Holy Spirit will bring to life; as a flower that blooms, those wonderfully beautiful people that Jesus' Father in Heaven definitely saw: before the foundation of the world, was instituted.

So, go in my name, for I (Jesus) will come with the hosts of Heaven; to stand the ground for you, for you and the "I Am" will be in the enemy's territories: but yet, the earth really is mine. So do not doubt, as to your presence there; it does make a difference, for my Holy Spirit will place His hand around and by your mouth: echoing by the loud shouting, as to the command of being the right time. For as you take your place in the ministry; even if it includes, of just a glass of water to those that need it: for your mission, is ordered by the Lord Jesus Christ as in [Mk. 9:40-41], "For he (or she) that is not against us is on our part. For whosoever shall give you a cup of water to drink (for someone, that has not had any clean water for some-time; this is a big deal) in my (Jesus') name, because ye belong to Christ (Jesus,) verily I (Jesus) say unto you, he (or she) shall not lose his (or her) reward (besides watching their ministry, of maturing.)" And as you move by the leading of the powerful Holy Spirit; the land will be possessed in Righteousness, for many will come into the Kingdom of God: by you and me demonstrating the words which are in the Scriptures. And as to fulfilling the "five-fold" ministries, as to its functions; and of allowing, the "nine-gifts" to being brought out of manifesting, for all saints to observe, which will strengthen the evangelistic outreach of finding the (01,) one, of the (99) "ninety-nine."

For the Lord Jesus Christ Blesses those that pray and fast and of more praying; as they focus on me (being Jesus,) by all stepping out in Faith as in [Jas. 2:25-26], **"Likewise also was not Rahab the harlot** (a prostitute) **justified by works** (when she believed the God of Moses and the Israelites,) **when she** (a Gentile) **had received the messengers** (the two spies,) **and has sent them out another way** (to safety and unharmed?) **For as the body without the spirit is dead** (of physically being alive,) **so is Faith** (of believing in the true God of Abraham) **without works** (but of not doing anything) **is dead also."** And as the "I Am," of being of the Lion of the Tribe of Judah, and when it is necessary for victory; as a "Lion," I (Jesus) will tear down the stronghold and to be clearly understood, the enemy will not succeed.

The Message of Jesus to the Church of the Lord Jesus Christ! * * *
THE DIFFERENT TRANSLATIONS OF THE BIBLE, IN QUESTION

Subject #Five:

For too many Churches and individuals, have accepted the various different Bible translations; as the correct wording, even though it was partly revised of what was originally written by the prophets and/or the scribes, of the Old and the New Testament's time periods: for with just a very slight change in wording of the definition of its original script; might certainly remove the Holy Spirit's Anointing. "The Anointing is, definitely only with the King James Version!" And we must consider, the issues with many of the different wordings; as to its true meaning, which at times seems to be puzzling: by the wording as it was written, for the definitions have allot to do with the Bible Scriptures, of its original content. For evidently, the Holy Spirit was involved, as when the Scriptures came; by being written in different languages, and then being translated into English as they were accumulating all the Scrolls from day one: which was headed by the King's project, at the time when King James of England ruled.

And as time went on, they began to retranslate the Scriptures; for this is what the apostle John wrote, which included and relates to their and our time period of today as in [Rev. 22:13-19], **"I am Alpha and Omega, the beginning and the end, the first and the last. Blessed are they that do His** (Christ's) **Commandment, that they may have right to the "Tree of Life," may enter in through the gates into the City. For without are** (very many evil) **dogs, and sorcerers, and whoremongers, and murderers, and idolaters, and whosoever loveth and maketh a lie. I Jesus have sent mine Angel to testify unto you these things** (that are written) **in the Churches. I am the root and offspring** (the Lineage) **of David, and the bright and morning Star. And the** (Holy) **Spirit and the Bride** (the saints of the Church Body) **say, come. And let him** (and/or herself) **that heareth say, come. And whosoever will, let him** (or herself to) **take the Water of Life freely. For I** (John will) **testify unto every man** (or woman) **that heareth the** (even if it is just one or more) **words of the prophecy of this book, if any man** (or of a woman) **shall add unto these things** (that are written,) **God** (the Father, the Son named Jesus, and the Holy Spirit) **shall add unto him** (or her) **the plagues that are written in this book: and if any man** (or woman) **shall take away from the** (even if it is just one or more) **words of the book of this prophecy, God shall take away his** (or her) **part out of the "Book of Life," and out of the Holy City, and from the things which are written in this book** (and possibly, all (66) "sixty six books" of the whole Bible; does have a binding agreement, for us to leave the wording; of the translation as they are, but by in parenthesis: explaining what possibly or probably those definition meant, of bringing clarities; and again, as of an afterthought: of its real meanings, in our language as of present. For many wording in the Bible, as of today are obsolete and archaic; and are never, a part of our present-day vocabulary.)"

For the "Book of Revelation" was placed at the ending of the Bible's Scriptures, as an inspiration; of which is a warning also, and an admonishment to the saints: as to our concept of what our walk of Faith should be, and as of what is; of living a lifestyle that are Righteous. For by comparing the different translation, they are not even near; to the true meaning as of what the King James Version wrote: for it had to be the Holy Spirit, that inspired the translators. For this was not any easy task, of being the first ones to change the language to English and other languages; as to the samples of what Paul wrote, as of the Scriptures as in [II Cor. 11:1-3], "Would to God ye could bear (by enduring and not loosing of any hope) with me (Paul) a little (of Paul or someone else) in my folly (a crazy idea:) and indeed bear (by enduring and not losing hope) with me (Paul.) For I am jealous (of a serious notion) over you with Godly jealousy (as of a very serious notion, of them even imagining; as of by thinking and/or by conceiving:) for I have espoused you to one Husband, that I (Paul) may present you as a chaste (of pure in thought and action, as a modest and humble) Virgin to Christ. But I (Paul) fear (by being uneasy and anxious,) lest by any means, as the Serpent beguiled Eve through his subtility, so your minds (the mental ability) should be corrupted from the simplicity that is in Christ." And so, as we consider the dilemma, that we are all in today; by the different interpretation of the Bible, for we all must say to them that are doing it: shame, shame on you, shame on you, for God is not very pleased. But yet, these Scriptures might possibly be what the true meaning is; by staying with the original text, being the King James and of doing research with the best known dictionary: which is, the Webster's New Collegiate dictionary; so, as to another translation and again as in [II Cor. 11:1-3], **"Oh, that** (the word "God" is not mentioned, the Father in Heaven is not being acknowledged) **you "would"** (the word "would" is replaced, the expression of desiring; and as of the word "could" is not mentioned, of which is, of the expression of capable of doing) **bear** (by enduring and not losing hope) **with me** (Paul) **in a little (**of Paul or someone else) **folly** (a crazy idea:) **and indeed you do** (by assuming that they do) **bear** (by enduring and not losing hope) **with me (**Paul.) **For I** (Paul) **am jealous** (of a serious notion) **for** (being "over," is not mentioned, for Paul was being responsible for them and) **you with Godly jealousy** (of a serious notion, them imagining or conceiving:) **for I** (Paul) **have "betrothed"** (is as to engage or promise in marriage; to "espoused" is replaced, means to make its own, take them up of the cause of embracing, as a spouse of preparing and then to marry;) **you to one Husband, that I** (Paul) **may present you as a chaste** (of pure in thought and action, as a modest and humble) **Virgin to Christ. But I** (Paul) **fear** (by being uneasy and anxious,) **lest "somehow"** ("by any means," is not being mentioned,) **as the Serpent** (the Snake, with the voice of Lucifer) **"deceived"** (of being misled, but as of the word "beguiled" is not mentioned, of charming and deceiving) **Eve** (Adam's wife) **by his** (Lucifer's, but as of "through," is not mentioned, his (Lucifer's) **"craftiness"** (of being skillful at deceiving, but of "subtility," is not mentioned, of being crafty and skillful at deceiving her and others,) **so your minds** (the mental ability) **may be corrupted** (of them being distracted by perversion, which is misinterpreting, and/ or of falsifying the Truth) **from the simplicity** (as of the Gospel way being made simpler, of showing an easier or shorter process of doing; by having no animal sacrifices, but yet we all must be doing a "work of faith," in believing as in [Rom. 10:9], "That if thou shalt confess (of by acknowledging) with thy mouth the Lord Jesus (Christ,) and shalt believe (by forming an opinion) in thine heart that God (the Father) hath Raised Him (Jesus) from the dead, thou shalt be Saved (of being "Born-Again") **that is in Christ."**

And as to another example, of the different translations; and/or of the first, by the original King James Version: and then, the other translation of changing a word and also, removing some words. For Paul was saying, that hope in the Lord Jesus Christ; is a promise, proven by Jesus' actions, as He proved to all the saints: that it was Jesus' love that brought, the solution of

His Grace by dying for their sins. And then being Resurrected, so Jesus can bring the Way, the Truth, and the Life; by sending, the Holy Spirit's Anointing to earth: and there, the saints will have the power, and not of being ashamed; for the signs and wonders will follow their ministries. For if each of the Anointed ministers of the Gospel, were relying and persuaded by the natural feeling of being disappointed; of having no hope, then they are living in unbelief: as of what was addressed, by the old King James Version as mentioned in [Rom. 5:5], "And hope (in the Lord Jesus Christ, of us desiring with full expectation; and also, of obtaining what is desired and/or believed: that by our Faith, it is obtainable by the promise) maketh not ashamed (maketh not, of being very reluctant and/ or of even struggling against; that is, as of feeling the anticipation of even being ashamed, by the promise;) because the love of God is shed abroad (to other saints, which are beyond our borders; that is) in our hearts by the Holy Spirit which is given unto us."

And also of what is mentioned, by another translation as in [Rom. 5:5], **"Now hope** (in the Lord Jesus Christ, of desiring with full expectation; of obtaining what is desired and/or believed: that by Faith, it is obtainable by the promise) **"does not disappoint"** (does not being defeated by the expectation, of thing obtained and/or of thing not obtained; by failing to come up as to the anticipation of being disappointed, by the promise: the word "ashamed" is being replaced, with "maketh not ashamed," is being replaced; of being very reluctant and/or of even struggling against: that is, as of us feeling the anticipation of even being "ashamed," by the promise;) **because the love of God "has been"** ("has been," should have been written with the words; "is being") **poured out** (poured out, should have added the word "abroad;" which means to other saints, which are beyond our borders: that is) **in our hearts by the Holy Spirit who "was"** (was, should being written with the word "is") **given to us."**

For the Gospel that was preached then and of now, is by the power of the Holy Spirit; that Jesus sent, when it came on the day of the "Feast of Pentecost:" so all, must understand of not being ashamed, because of Jesus' message to the Church. And as of the Churches, being the saints are never disappointed; as it comes to the signs and wonders, as the Holy Spirit demonstrates His power: of which is, the power of the Father in Heaven, of allowing the Holy Spirit to fulfill His assignment. For of having the "nine-gifts" being demonstrated, as the ministers take their position; into one or more of the "five-fold" Anointing: of which will allow the Holy Spirit to bring, the Father's completion to the Church as in [Rom. 1:16], "For I am not ashamed of the Gospel of Christ: for it is the power of God unto salvation to everyone that believeth; to the Jew first, and also to the Greek (Gentiles.)"

CHAPTER TWELVE
THE EXAMINING CHURCH

The Message of Jesus to the Church of the Lord Jesus Christ! * * *
THE TIME WILL COME, BEING EXAMINED BY THE BALANCE

Subject #One:

As of **"<u>book number</u> [01 – 27] <u>being Matthew – Revelation</u>,"** it is all about what God is saying and that is (**<u>He</u>** (Jesus) **<u>has set in motion,</u> by establishing <u>the Truthful Church of the Lord Jesus Christ.</u>**)

And by examining one person or more, for all of humanity has the same issues, of being weak in the flesh; which is, of us not renewing our mind as in [Eph. 4:22-24], "<u>That ye put off concerning the former conversation the old man</u> (our life of carnality,) <u>which is corrupt according to the deceitful lusts; and be renewed in the spirit of your mind</u> (as of being by the human mind, meditating on the Scriptures;) <u>and that ye put on the new man</u> (of us all receiving salvation, by being "Born-Again,") <u>which after God is created in Righteousness and true Holiness</u> (as of what Paul stated as in [Rom. 6:11], **"Likewise reckon ye also yourselves to be dead indeed unto sin** (of us being Crucified with Christ, we are dead unto the worldly sin nature; by the virtue of the Cross and of Jesus' Resurrection,) **but alive unto God** (the Father) **through Jesus Christ our Lord** (and as of what Noah and Abraham believed, as to what was mentioned as in [Gen. 7:1], "And the Lord (Jesus) said unto Noah, come thou and all thy house (of eight people) into the Ark; for thee have I (Jesus) seen Righteous before me (of being Jesus speaking) in this generation." And being also, as in [Gen. 15:6], "And he (Abraham) believed in the Lord (Jesus;) and he (and probably Abraham's family) counted to Him (Jesus) for Righteousness." For just before there were any rivalry, as to the two different forces; of being good and/or evil, of having their confrontation, the Lord Jesus Christ will step into the middle of our activities. And then as Jesus appears, Jesus will hold the "balance" in His hand; of a weighing scale, if we have been "Born-Again."

CHAPTER THIRTEEN
THE CHURCH'S LAST FEW DAYS

The Message of Jesus to the Church of the Lord Jesus Christ! * * *
THE NEW THING WILL I DO, I WILL DO IT?

Subject #One:

As of **"<u>book</u> <u>number</u> [01 – 27] <u>being</u> <u>Matthew</u> – <u>Revelation</u>,"** it is all about what God is saying and that is (**<u>He</u> (Jesus) <u>has</u> <u>set</u> <u>in</u> <u>motion</u>, <u>by</u> <u>establishing</u> <u>the</u> <u>Truthful</u> <u>Church</u> <u>of</u> <u>the</u> <u>Lord</u> <u>Jesus</u> <u>Christ</u>.**)

Let the earth listen and hear, perceiving and/or understanding that this earth; humanity itself, that has an ear to hear, will acknowledge that the Father in Heaven: will cause an echoing sound, for the Lord Jesus Christ will begin. And there with the new breath of the Holy Spirit's refreshing Anointing; with first an echo and then a great call for change. For many from Heaven, yes many, of a great host of my Heavenly Angelic beings; will be blowing the Bugle and the Trumpet's musical sound. To bring to attention, so I (Jesus) myself can give the call, "hear, oh hear, my (being Jesus') called-out ones;" to my (being Jesus') only "Remnant" people, the ones that have truly loved me (being Jesus) and obeying all of my sayings, the Scriptures.

For He, my (being the Father's) Son is moving about and coming with laughter on His face; as forceful as the eagles, when they fly and glide with their wide-open wings on the wind of a breezy day: as though saying with audacity, nothing, not even the storms. And of which will threaten, of the dark clouds of despair; of which, will dampen the gusto that is felt in the Righteous heart, the mind, the soul, and the spirit's overwhelming feeling of expressions: that the expressions have concluded, that the Holy Spirit is in charge. As of the Father in Heaven is saying, "It is time for my people to begin to show; an expression, on their faces: to the Lord Jesus Christ."

For I (the triune God) had placed this earth, from its distance to my Throne; and I (the Father) had said, "Oh earth, let this earth carry on: until the time of its end, that appointed time." For the whole earth hangs as in a fog, a clouded covered monument of my (the triune God's) greatest creation; me being the Father and the Son named Jesus, and the Spirit, being the Holy Spirit: of its handiwork, which is the triune God. And yet at times when I (the Father looked in, it is like seeing a silhouette; with the movements of its busy activities, for it appears as being, a neglected field filled with over-grown weeds: overshadowing and covering the whole earth. It seems as if most, all lay hopelessly corrupted; with the evil activities of every imaginable kind and things that are definitely decaying under the Sun.

But the Father is saying as an expression, "My people, stop and smell the roses; for the sweetness of the move, of my Holy Spirit: is and has begun as a fresh scent of mine Anointing." But yet, as the earth shakes more and more and more, as time slowly to some and swiftly to others; as it comes to its closer, the end of all as it is presently viewed: "smell the flowers, the fragrances, for the smell of my wonderful Presences is fresh to all that senses Him; my Holy Spirit, and even more wonderful as times goes on." Yes, for as time goes on, my people will find that as of the Father in Heaven; He (the triune God) is the only solid Rock, as the earth keeps shaking.

For my Son, the Lord Jesus Christ, being the Rock and with the Holy Spirit; of being moved into action; for as the Father has an agenda, there is an Army of believers: that is, beginning to stand up and flexes their muscles. They are not all really totally understanding and quite in conceptional; of how much, of the muscles to flex. For as the Holy Spirit will inspires them, they will stand with a singleness of heart's motive, with sinews over their dry bones, with flesh over their sinews: which is, their nerves and muscles and skins over their flesh.

And with this, a fresh covering with the Anointing from the Father's Throne; and they will not lay as dead for very soon, in the valley of dry bones. They, my people will be standing up; for they will be in unity, a focus toward a oneness of purpose and goal in their "Born-Again" Spirit: as the Holy Spirit inspires my people. The leadership, as a small group, not very many but enough of the pastors; the Shepherds of the flock will stand with me, that is of hearing and doing. There will be an Army of men and women, and boys, and girls, that are going to stand; and as each stand, it is just the beginning of what I (the triune God) will perform: being as a great Miracle of deliverance by my Son's gentle hands, as the Holy Spirit is by His side.

For as the Scriptures are worded as in [Eph. 6:10-13], "Finally, my brethren (and sisters,) be strong in the Lord and in the power of His might. Put on the whole Armour of God, that ye may be able to stand against the wiles of the Devil. For we wrestle not against (our) flesh and Blood, but against principalities, against powers, against the rulers of the darkness of this world, against spiritual wickedness in high places. Therefore take unto you the whole Armour of God, (the triune God) that ye may be able to withstand in the evil day, and having done all, to stand." For I (the triune God) will put into motion and complete that which each one of my people will have begun. So, this is what it Seems to Remind Me and as to All of the Faithful Believers; of which, as we Face our Final Days on Planet Earth.

DO YOU MISS ME, BUT YOU MUST LET ME GO?

When I come to my last journey, and the day is my ending so to be;
I want you to also reflect on our good times, why cry when I am free.

I know you do miss me, not too long your faces will higher lifted too;
Yet must remember the love we also all had, why be saddened again.

For each must go alone, for this is the route that I and all must be on;
It is also about a step into narrow life's road, why cry when I am free.

For as you be think of those you miss just call a friend, lonely that is;
I know you all will also eyeing Heaven's sky, why be saddened again.

Do I know where my next step will to take me, the Throne room be;
Then will I bow my knee also Worship God, why cry when I am free.

CHAPTER FOURTEEN
THE CHURCH'S ENDING DAYS

The Message of Jesus to the Church of the Lord Jesus Christ! * * *
THE NEWS ABOUT THE HARVEST FIELDS

Subject #One:

As of **"book number** [01 – 27] **being Matthew – Revelation,"** it is all about what God is saying and that is (**He** (Jesus) **has set in motion, by establishing the Truthful Church of the Lord Jesus Christ.**)

And so, what is this all about, where will we be; for the fields are ripe, the crops are ready to be harvested: but yet, where are the workers? For the call must be made soon, or we will lose the harvest crops; someone will have gathered it into their own barns, for Jesus is calling for all to be prepared: for this could be the last call; of which, is before the season of harvesting will be completely and/or of it totally being over. And as the Father, begins to count in the (1) one with all of the other (99) "ninety-nine" of which was wandering; for Jesus will, by the Holy Spirit's count, will let of it be final.

Did Jesus Really Come To Earth Of Being Born As A Baby?

For you know as of two thousand years ago; I (Jesus) first came as a baby, then of growing up on this natural created earth and walked the breadth and length of Israel: the territories of the saints of God, even under of the very, very cruel Roman governmental authorities.

And as of then, I (Jesus) am also doing the same today. I am walking the breadth and length; the direction, from the south to the north, the north to the south and from the west to the east and east to the west: as of all the Nations on the face of this beautiful whole earth.

For as I (Jesus) walk, I am examining and evaluating the crops; to see of what grains are and of what are tares. Do you know that I will, and am about to be ready to complete the harvest? The sickle is in our hands and ready; there completing, the work in the harvest field.

For being persistent, as the rain clouds parted and passes over; and as the Sun appears, and until that full development comes: as the crops are all fully ripe, for which is when the workers; in the fields, will be gathering, as it is just of the beginning to the last harvesting.

Even all the gleaning work will be brought from the fields into the storehouse; then I will begin, with a sharp sickle to complete the harvesting before the next storm. For even as the gleanings were completed, of which is, when of the harvesting, will come to an end!

The Message of Jesus to the Church of the Lord Jesus Christ! * * *
THE CHRISTIANS AND UNBELIEVERS, SO WHERE ARE WE?

Subject #Two:

Well, I the observer a Gentile again say, that we are in the middle of somewhere; somewhere, somewhere, it also looks like we are between all the robbers or criminals: being of their dues, were the penalty of death. And so, where do we fit in? For starter, by reading the stories in all the old ancient books, the Scrolls of the Old and New Testaments' writings; of this guy, as He came, that was doing good deeds to many: of the people, and telling a few others, what was wrong with their secret lifestyle. He even had the gall, to tell many of the listeners that He was and is the "I Am." In another words, He was bluntly telling them, that He was and is God. He even had the audacity, by saying to allot of those that followed Him; including His intimate followers, the hand-picked men: that He was the only way to eternal life, in other words of Jesus is being the only door. That is to be in the right course, was to take the narrow road; but that, the wide would never get anyone there, to Heaven that is.

Oh yes, about the two robbers or criminals, that got sentenced to death; for that Roman's governmental criminal department that gave the orders, was able to express their grievances: by beating Him with whips, for Him being referred to as the King of the Jews. So, He was taken to the same hill that He was going to be hung on, you know Golgotha. Today we call that place, the hill of the skull; it really does look as like a dead face. For the Roman's governmental purposes were intentional, they hand-picked a couple of the bad guys; to be near Jesus, so then by executing the two robbers or criminals: they were, able to make a statement to Him and His followers. "Yes, you, you Jesus have robbed or criminalized us; because of you Jesus, and your many prophets and prophetesses that came along. And you Jesus, as of others and I, we could steal, murder, tell lies, commit adultery and commit fornication, and all other fleshly desires, telling off colored jesting's, and jokes, and even covet other's house and/or their wife. And not even being accountable to anyone; of which, was a very refreshing experiences, and we could be ourselves: and not feeling like we belong to someone else, and of their rule of conduct. For maybe of obeying, the Ten Commandments; of which, some seems to be the constructional ethics of today: the rules never did seem to be for us Gentiles, but I know one day we must be judged."

The Message of Jesus to the Church of the Lord Jesus Christ! * * * THE WHYS, WHY AM I (JESUS) SHEDDING TEARS?

Subject #Three:

For as I (Jesus) consider the life span of my journey; from the day of creation, and then from the time spent of travelling: of eyeing the adventure of humanities to the time, of our present day. So why am I still shedding allot of tears, or am I crying, I will tell you; remember as of the Old Testament, when I went before Moses: I Anointed him, with the Holy Spirit; so, he would be able, to speak and write of those things that were necessary? And of how the Israelites were not able to hear, of what was said by me (being Jesus) through him and how they built; yes, they ended up, building a golden calf instead: you know that their hearts were still as hard then, as they were in Egypt. And of there, they eventually rejected my (being Jesus') plan as to walking into the Promise Land. So, are you standing on those same kinds of principles of doubt and debauchery; but yet, many calling themselves Christians: that is, being led away from the virtue and the excellence; but they, must all rise above their fleshly desires? This issue of unity is my greatest, greatest desire; for yours and all fellowships, which is not happening: so, I (Jesus) am shedding tears.

Then and now, I (Jesus) am looking at them, which is you and others; that is, we which are you and me (Jesus), of now are walking toward the Promise Land: I (Jesus) was literally with them of old, and now, which is the Church of today; I (Jesus) am literally walking, walking, and walking toward the River of Life. And so, they will be washed and of being clean; for the Church will be a spotless Church: of having no stains of sin. For all must, must cross, so there will not be that opportunity to look back; also, with all of them, which is the Church Body: was wandered from thought too thought. For as of the last part of the (19th) "nineteenth Century;" and into the (20th) "twentieth Century:" there are always that hesitation of moving. And just think of how long Joshua and all the Israelites were there; on the east-side of the Jordon River, waiting, waiting, and waiting: so, this is what is happening as of now, the hesitation of moving.

Do not be surprised as you see and watch yourselves of this episode, that is of being revealed; the journey that must not be delayed or I (Jesus) will call on others to step-out and become the leading force: for I (Jesus) have waited and watched, watched and waited, and waited and watched. For we must all be crossing the River; of that Anointing, just as like of the way the Israelites were doing. For Joshua was their leader, so what are the issues here; I (Jesus) am now your leader today, for I (Jesus) must say to you: as Joshua waited, waited, and waited; it is exactly what I (Jesus) am doing today? For they seemed ready, but the Israel's secrets of their hearts were there; of contemplating on the journey instead on the Father's plan:

but yet, as their hearts were then thinking of the plan. For as my Father and I (Jesus) were ready to move then, we also are ready to move now. But with you all, and there with the Presence of the Holy Spirit in you; of what the Church of the Lord Jesus Christ is thinking: for you are feeling, that there are so much to be known, of the knowledge of learning, so you can be equipped to finish the race.

Do you think, when I (Jesus) told the (12) twelve or more of waiting, that they had the same thought in mind; that is of the (12,) twelve that eventually filled the upper room: of which, adding to be the (120,) "one hundred and twenty." For as they also were thinking of what really, were ahead of them of possibly being? But yet knew very little of what coming was; for they were eager and willing, so they obeyed me and waited: but prayed, and waited by praying, and waited by praying; their mind-set, was to commune with me. For I will and did come, and did send my power, by the Holy Spirit; and there they were filled. And now I am about to do it again; but yet, there I am crying, crying, and crying: that is, I am shedding allot of tears, for as it is of now; there are no implications that anyone, has been listing, hearing or reading to what I have said in the past. For my very real fire will be moved to another area of the world; for the locations of the world, have desired it: but maybe, they have not truly believed that this is the place. And therefore, all must listen, and listen carefully; for I have the fire in my hand, and I am waiting.

For as over (2,000) "two thousand years," and because of all the apostle's writings; the Scriptures that is, the men and women, and the young boys and girls: over the ages of time, have and are trying to perfect their walk of Faith. For as they all rely on my Presence, to engrave the words into their inter-most being; so as, to the Father in Heaven's approval and the Anointing Presence of the Holy Spirit: this is, a task that will always be an issue and is always the driving force. And it is, of being accomplished, as of what all the Scriptures, the Word of God proclaims; and again, of which will always be the driving force as all walk in Faith.

For we all as the God-Head, the three-in-one, the triune God; have endeavored to do, the plan is that of the "simplicity of the Gospel:" of which, humanity has always and are still grappling with. And yet are trying to make it harder to obtain and as to the completion of the Scriptures; so that the walk of Faith will be impossible to acquire, the Church of the Lord Jesus Christ: will not be side-tracked by any of the enemies of your soul.

And as of one example by Paul as in [Gal 4:9-11], "But now, after that ye have known God (by understanding the Grace of Jesus, His solution; of realizing that Jesus willingly: offered Himself, and therefore you have known God,) or rather are known of God (that the Father, acknowledged that He did send Jesus, to Redeem us,) how turn ye again to the weak and beggarly elements (for as Christians, you must not go back; to the rudiments, of which is the symbolic of your heritage: such as, the "Feasts and Sacraments," and also of all the other symbolism. For of acquiring a Spiritual transformation of the heart; of which, that can only be attained by you being "Born-Again,") whereunto ye desire again to be in bondage (and that, of not just accepting, the plan of salvation; of Jesus shedding His Blood on the Cross and of His Resurrection?) you observe days, and months, and times, and years (for you all were considering, by attempting to reindorse the concept the Judaizers' Law-keeping; and also, of many not accepting Christ's fundamental implication; by believing, of living by Faith. I am afraid of you (of your Spiritual objective,) lest I have bestowed upon you labour in vain (of you definitely setting your goals; away from Christ, by placing your approval on what you have accomplished: as to your efforts, by the works of believing on your own end results; of which, is by the works of the flesh.)"

Therefore, as I (Jesus) watch, and watch, and watch, for my steps are ordered by my Father in Heaven. For as the Churches are side-tracked, this fire will go out; and then, I will walk-out of your territories, the course of all its demises: for I will and am looking for a people, just a small handful; that is, if two or three that will agree, in my name, I will. But as of my observation, of that I see, the fire is about to go out; so those, that have eyes to see the vision, by Faith grab the "Candle Stand:" for the fire is still lid on the Candle, and hold on to it, but do not let go of it. For today probably, I will turn and pause and/or pause once more; for the only way, this will be accomplished, is that the Holy Spirit blows on the very small fire!

And as I (Jesus) stand and watch, my next step is to walk toward, and by crossing the Jordon River; from the many earthly carnality that will separate the world from my Promise Land, which is the territory where my Holy Spirit is in residence. And of which is moving in its glory and power, for there I will fulfill the "Call;" that was laid down in its promises: before the foundation of the world. So, saints, let the true Light of the

Gospel, the gentle Holy Ghost's (Spirit's) fire penetrate your inter-most being, so the fulfillment of crossing the River will be its time; that is, of the season for the harvest: so all, that are willing may come into the Kingdom of God.

The Message of Jesus to the Church of the Lord Jesus Christ! * * *
THE ALTAR, DEFINITELY BECAME THE IMAGE OF THE CROSS!

Subject #Four:

And as to many of the songs which will be written, at the time when the harvest; is about to begin, this will be the greatest blessings, for the saints will be looking up toward Heaven: as of those Words that the Scriptures are reminding us. And as of what Jesus said; when He had just become the Lamb, before He was Sacrificed, of what is coming on earth as in [Mt. 26:41], "Watch and pray, that ye enter not into temptation: the spirit (of us human's) indeed is willing, but the flesh is weak." And as of what Jesus said to the Churches, by the writings of the apostle John as in [Rev. 3:3], **"Remember therefore how thou hast received and heard, and hold fast, and repent. If therefore thou shalt not watch, I (Jesus) will come on thee as a thief, and thou shalt not know what hour I will come upon thee."**

The Song, in a Chorus style Arrangement
THE ALTAR'S CENTER, WHERE JESUS WAS HUNG!

Oh, what a stor-y, that needs to be told to all,
How Je - sus was re - veal - ed to the pro - phet John
and if this was told ov - er and ov - er: then what
will this be, if the whole world would hear of Je - sus?

Arthur J. Besler

Then as the Word, that Je - sus   said,   did   all   come soon,
so   let us em - brace each other, Ho - ly Spir - it's Truth
of   Je - sus being the   Way, the   Truth, and the Life's fruit,
as   we en - coun - ter   the   im   pos - sible, as He   move.

For   life's jour - ney, will on   -   ly fin - ish the long race
When Je - sus is   the sea   son; for the rea - son's sins
and   there, the Lamb is   brought to be Sac - ri - ficed in
the   Al - tar's Cen - ter: where Je - sus was hung to   face.

The   Blood stain - ed Cross, as Je - sus   brings the solu - tion
and   then the sins to   all that comes are for giv - en;
for   the Ho - ly Spir - it will bring the   A - noint - ing,
then Je - sus will say   to all: it   is   fin - ish - ed.

For   as   of Je - sus' death, then be - ing Res - ur - rected
as   this was His, His great - est time of vic - tor - ies,
there Je - sus strip - ped Sa - tan, of   all au - tho - ities
and   now, the De - vil is   be - ing a   roar - ing - Lion.

For   the Hea - ven's, Ho - ly Spir - it   has ful - filled all
With Je - sus' glo - ry, by   hu - man - ity's ex - pres - sion
of   praise, for Je - sus is   our   hope for Re - demp - tion
and   now we all   can come before the Fa - ther of - Light.

We   praise the God of   Hea - ven and   earth with no limits
Je - sus, Ho - ly Spir - it, the ones pro - tect - ing us,
What a   joy you are, as   we Wor - ship, you Je - sus,
we   praise you, we praise you, we praise you, our true God.

I   praise the God, that cre - ated us in   your Im - age,
Oh   what an ho - nor, us   be - ing in   your Like - ness,

171

that we   are one with the   tri - une God of   cre - ation,

I   praise the God, that form - ed   me, so   we   are yours.

The Song, in a Hymn style Arrangement
THE ALTAR'S CENTER, WHERE JESUS WAS HUNG!

The Message of Jesus to the Church of the Lord Jesus Christ! * * *

1. Oh,   what a   stor - y,   that needs to   be told to   all,

2. Then as   the   word, that Je - sus   said, did all   come soon,

3. For life's jour - ney, will   on - ly   fin - ish the long race,

4. The Blood stain - ed   Cross, as   Je - sus brings the solu - tion

5. For as   of   Je - sus' death, then be - ing   Res - ur - rected

6. For the   Hea - ven's Ho - ly   Spir - it   has ful – filled all

7. We praise the God   of   Hea - ven   and earth with no limits,

8. I   praise the God, that cre - ated us, in   your Im – age,

How Je - sus was re - veal - ed   to   the pro - phet John,

so   let   us em - brace each other, Ho - ly   Spir - it's Truth

When Je - sus is   the   sea - son;   for   the rea - son's sins

And   then the sins to   all   that   comes are for - giv - en;

as   this was His, His   great - est   time   of   vic - tor - ies,

With Je - sus' glo - ry,   by   hu - man - ity's ex - pres - sion

Je - sus, Ho - ly Spir - it,   the   ones pro - tect - ing   us,

oh   what an ho - nor, us   be - ing   in   your Like - ness,

And if   this was told ov - er   and   ov - er: then what

of   Je - sus being the Way,   the Truth, and the Life's fruit

and   there, the Lamb is   brought to be   Sac - ri - ficed in

for   the   Ho - ly   Spir - it   will bring the A - noint - ing,

there Je - sus strip ped Sa - tan, of   all   au - thor - ities

of   praise, for Je   sus is   our hope for Re - demp - tion
What a   joy you are, as   we Wor - ship, you Je - sus
That   we   are one, with the   tri - une God of cre - ation,

Will this   be, if   the   whole world would hear of   Je - sus?
as   we   en - coun - ter   the   im - pos - sible, as   He move.
the   Al - tar's Cen - ter: where Je - sus   was   hung to face.
Then Je - sus   will say   to   all: it   is   fin - ish - ed.
and now,   the De - vil   is   be - ing   a   roar - ing Lion.
and now   we   all   can   come before the   Fa - ther of Light.
we   praise you, we   praise you,   we   praise you, our true God.
I   praise the   God, that   form - ed   me,   so   we   are yours.

The Message of Jesus to the Church of the Lord Jesus Christ! * * *
THE THOUGHT OF BEING A WOLF IN SHEEP'S CLOTHING.

Subject #Five:

Who said we were not a sheep, just because we do not act like a sheep; does not mean we are something else? For the nerve some have of trying to say that by watching a sheep, they are not very pushy. And what a thought, for some sheep can be a little bossy at times; knowing that there is a place for good behavior, when it comes to being a sheep. One day we will all realize that we are a sheep, for even the wool on our back is for real. There are allot to say about imitating the wolf, first you have to know that you are not a sheep. Then there are expressions, they can give it away in a minute, see, the movements are always deceiving. And do not forget the smile, those are the things that make a wolf uniquely different. Remember when the sheep would ask us some of the stupidest questions about God and stuff like that. We always had an answer, for they always listen to what we have to say about the good things. We can say the weirdest things about God and the Bible, and they will never question or say, what was that again? Sometimes it would be better for us to say everything but one thought that is true, and it will be the Truth that seem to get the sheep all messed up. Now a goat will follow about anything that moves, it is not always what sounds good. For many will think that the best is right up ahead, they are always sniffing around for the prize. Never underestimate a goat, because they will spot a wolf faster than a sheep. So do not get too comfortable in the presence of a goat, for they will even outsmart a wolf even if they know you are dressed in sheep's clothing. The last being a wolf, you want to do is; let a sheep know you are not one of them too soon, other-wise they will stampede. Best is to move in slow and easy so they only see the wool, and not the smell of a predator. Therefore, not to alarm the Shepherd, of some unknown creature is in the area, ready for the kill. And last, and this is the Gospel Truth about what is false, moving the herd by allowing them to follow you; if not then use a whip, which is the Anti-Christ's spirit, of being the real wolf.

The Message of Jesus to the Church of the Lord Jesus Christ! * * *
THE TIME FOR A HOLY SPIRIT REVIVAL!

Subject #Six:

As I consider the assignments of becoming a writer, that was confirmed by Jesus Himself; of which, has been also my desire for some-time, of me writing this book: and another, that is almost completed called; "The Journey of Jesus Through the Bible." For which began with creation, which included Adam and Eve; and with information as of the time span of the (400) "four hundred years:" before Christ, that are not mentioned in the Scriptures; and then, as the birth of Christ Jesus (A.D.) "after death," to our time period; of which, ended and included beyond the (20th) "Twentieth Century."

For I knew that Jesus wanted me, to write a book; and now, it is more than one, for actually I did write a page earlier: but was distracted by other activities, and then several months later; a prophet saw me in the Church's audience, and there he had a vision. For in the vision, it showed him a real book, that had no letters written yet in it; and then as he looked again, he saw a book filled with letters written therein. And there he made a statement to me, which I still did not take it seriously; that Jesus, wanted me to write a book: of which, I did write two more hand-written pages.

And then about month later, the time of December (1st) first; the year (2,019) "two thousand nineteen;" I had a very loud knock at my bedroom door around midnight: the first time He knocked, I awoke of hearing the knock: but no one was by the door, so I went back to sleep. But as of the second knock, it caused me to wonder and to listen, if there would be another noise; or something, which was when the Lord Jesus Christ spoke to me: it was just enough of a sound, so I could hear Him clearly; Jesus said, I want you to start, by writing the book today!

So, as I began to write that day, of those three pages that were written and accumulated earlier; for it was enough information, to begin: to its completion, of being (two and one/half) years of time; and of which, has brought me it to the second book, which has just been published. For this book is about Jesus's wishes, admonishes every Church assembly; as to the "five-fold" ministries and the "nine-gifts" as of its functions, as to establish a basic understanding, of how to lay down the Scriptural foundational principles: by what the Scriptures, are emphasizing. And of which, will bring the Holy Spirit's importance of revitalizing the energy; as of being applicable to the cause of bringing unity into the Church Body: and there, the Holy Spirit will be able to fulfill the Father's call; of bringing the last day Revival of the Holy Spirit's Presence of the "Feast of Pentecost" to its closer, as Jesus gathers His saints throughout the world.

This is a reminder of our greatest, is yet to come! And as Jesus walks this journey of ours, for at times it could be good; and/or better, yet at times there will be, of the trials and turbulations: of which, can bring some stress as to our walk of Faith. But yet, of not doubting, by the circumstances around us; for Jesus' promises are true, that He will not forsake us as we stumble and fall in our times of worries, fears, and doubts as in [Prov. 25:25-28], **"As cold waters** (the satisfaction that is coming) **to a thirsty soul** (that is facing, the heat of despair,) **so is good news** (to someone being blessed) **from a far country. A Righteous man** (or woman) **falling down** (because of their Spiritual degradation) **before the wicked is as a troubled fountain** (which is unpredictable, as when will there be any stability; or of any common-sense be; and/or as another, is but yet of any water to drink,) **and a corrupt** (of bring clarity to their expression of behavior be; and/or as another, is but yet of being clean or unclean) **spring. It is not good to eat much Honey (could make body system, being imbalanced:) so for men** (or women) **to search their own glory is**

not glory (for humanity, cannot produce celestial bliss of Heaven; but yet, our produced glory will not satisfy us.) **He** (or she) **that hath no rule over his** (or her) **own spirit** (which is the heart) **is like a city that is broken down, and without walls** (and there is no way, to defend themselves.)"

So, as believers, and as we call on Jesus; He has promised, that He will not forsake us: as of what the apostle Paul stated as of his journey, of spreading the Gospel of Jesus as in [II Cor. 4:8-11], "<u>We</u> <u>are</u> <u>troubled</u> <u>on</u> <u>every</u> <u>side</u>, <u>yet</u> <u>not</u> <u>distressed</u>; <u>we</u> <u>are</u> <u>perplexed</u>, <u>but</u> <u>not</u> <u>in</u> <u>despair</u>; <u>persecuted</u>, <u>but</u> <u>not</u> <u>forsaken</u>; <u>cast</u> <u>down</u>, <u>but</u> <u>not</u> <u>destroyed</u>; <u>always</u> <u>bearing</u> <u>about</u> <u>in</u> <u>the</u> <u>body</u> <u>the</u> <u>dying</u> <u>of</u> <u>the</u> <u>Lord</u> <u>Jesus</u>, <u>that</u> <u>the</u> <u>life</u> <u>also</u> <u>of</u> <u>Jesus</u> <u>might</u> <u>be</u> <u>made</u> <u>manifest</u> <u>in</u> <u>our</u> <u>body</u>. <u>For</u> <u>we</u> <u>which</u> <u>live</u> <u>are</u> <u>always</u> <u>delivered</u> <u>unto</u> <u>death</u> <u>for</u> <u>Jesus</u>' <u>sake</u>, <u>that</u> <u>the</u> <u>life</u> <u>also</u> <u>of</u> <u>Jesus</u> <u>might</u> <u>be</u> <u>made</u> <u>manifest</u> <u>in</u> <u>our</u> <u>mortal</u> <u>vw</u>." For the blessings that comes with our continual endurance; will one day, of us receiving our greatest reward, of seeing Jesus' face to face in our Father's Kingdom.

For the writing of this book is exciting to me, of us being able to prepare for Jesus's return. And as the Scriptures, which as originally being the old ancient Scrolls say, to watch and pray means that; the Son of God, which is Jesus, really would like to have us come with Him on His return to the Father's house in Heaven, at the end of time.

I was born from the parents, that were born in Russia, they came to America in (1907) nineteen zero seven; and got married, in South Dakota and became a part of the Home-Stead Act, with total of fifteen: of sons and daughters. By the time I left home at the age of (17,) seventeen years old; the homestead cows and sheep ranch were approximately (5,000) five thousand acres or more. And as I was growing up, my father read the Bible almost every morning; for Jesus became very real to me. For at being nine years old, I began to experience the Holy Spirit's Presence and then at eleven years old; the Lord Jesus Christ, filled me with His Holy Spirit: that changed my life, as I realized that God is a real person.

Arthur Jacob Besler